Filet Crochet from Yesterday

Crocheter's Historical Pattern Series Volume One

ISBN 1-929169-00-0

Pastime Publications
P. O. Box 710057
Oak Hill, VA 20171
www.pastimepubs.com
1-888-275-2020

◆ ◆ ◆

Dear Crocheter,

For years I have looked in bookstores, local craft stores and yarn shops for new books related to crochet, and I have been very disappointed.

What few books I found, I already owned. High quality crochet books were never seen in the stores where I purchased my supplies.

Then someone suggested that I should do something about the crochet pattern book shortage. Why not publish older, uncommon patterns and make them available for others to enjoy.

So that is exactly what I have done with this "Filet Crochet from Yesterday," Volume One of the Crocheter's Historical Pattern Series. Patterns, which heretofore have been lost, can now be crocheted again.

Within the pages of "Filet Crochet from Yesterday," Volume One of the Crocheter's Historical Pattern Series, the crocheter will find two completely unabridged books:

1. Priscilla Filet Crochet Book, published by Priscilla Publishing Company in 1911.
2. Priscilla Filet Crochet Book 2, published by Priscilla Publishing Company in 1914.

I hope these patterns give you as much enjoyment as they have brought me.

Sincerely,
Melissa Johnson

◆ ◆ ◆

Filet Crochet

The definition frequently given of Filet Crochet is, "crocheting in imitation of Filet." While that is true, yet it is, in a way, misleading. The word "imitation" may be objected to because it usually carries with it a meaning of inferiority. Always, a substitute, a pretence, a sham comes to mind when an imitation of the "real" is mentioned.

Rather let us define it as "Crocheting in the style of Filet," for if Filet Crochet is rightly done it is no less a "real" piece of work than the Filet which it is like. It requires no less skill, no less care, and perhaps no less time to crochet a good piece of Filet than it does to net the fabric and darn or weave or embroider through it the pattern. Those who have done both can testify to the truth of this.

Our grandmothers did more or less crocheting, using this principle, so that it is nothing new; and yet, possibly, it has remained for this twentieth century to bring forward and perfect the work, adapting it to more uses and larger designs, and carrying out the designs in finer threads.

It is, like Irish Crochet, at its very best when done with fine thread and the very finest needle. And yet it may be done with coarse thread and a suitable needle and produce a very handsome piece of work, always providing that the crocheting is firm and evenly done.

MATERIALS

The materials used may be any spool thread that is at hand, or one may select any good crochet cotton.

Of the pieces shown in this book, the most of the work was done with "D. M. C." Crochet Cotton (Cordonnet Special), Nos. 10, 30, 50, and 100.

For No. 10 crochet cotton, the crochet hook should be about No. 10, not coarser. For No. 30, a No. 12 hook, and anything finer can best be done with No. 14.

Patterns readily suggest themselves for simple bits of work, after one has started the crocheting, but for larger pieces and more elaborate designs, any block pattern is easily followed.

The collection of patterns given in this book is culled from a variety of sources, and is equally adapted to Filet Crochet, Filet Brodé, Cross-stitch, and various sorts of Canvas-work.

Having procured the needle and thread and pattern (a simple equipment!), one is ready for the lesson.

EXPLANATION OF TERMS

D c — double crochet; having a stitch on the needle, one loop over the needle, one loop through the chain or top of stitch below, one loop through two on the needle, one loop through the remaining two.

S c — single crochet, a stitch on the needle, a loop under the chain below, a loop through the two on the needle. This is used only in finishing edges, not in the designs.

T c — treble crochet, a stitch on the needle, two loops over the needle, one loop through the work, then crochet off two and two.

The first thing to do, is to find out whether one crochets "square." Many people do this naturally; more, we are inclined to believe, do not. Much time is saved if this is one's habit.

Find out in this way; copy Working Model, Fig. 1. Notice there are ten meshes, then the foundation chain will be ten times 3, plus 1, plus 5 to turn, altogether 36 chain.

Turn, join with a d c in the 9th stitch from the needle, which completes the first open mesh. The following nine meshes are each made with 2 chain, 1 d c in the 3d chain-stitch.

Take up two threads of the chain when crocheting the first row. Crochet 5 chain-stitches to turn, join with a d c in the top of the next d c below, taking up two threads.

Proceed in this way until ten rows are finished, and if the piece is square, one may be sure of crocheting easily. If the piece is longer from right to left, then either the chain-stitches and top of d c are too loose, or the d c is drawn up too short. In making the d c pull the top tightly, but do not pull the whole d c too short.

It is easier to apply the remedy in a little piece than in a large one, where a very little difference in the tension makes a big difference in the outcome. If, however, the greater length is in the other direction, the probability is that the d c is drawn out too long.

Then try Working Model, Fig. 2, with the same number of stitches. The first row is ten open meshes, like Fig. 1. The second row is made with 5 chain to turn, 1 d c in d c below, eight solid meshes and one open mesh.

A solid mesh is formed by a d c over the d c, 2 d c over the chain, 1 d c over the next d c, making 4 d c if it is a single solid mesh. If other solid meshes follow then there is added 2 d c for each chain and 1 d c over d c.

The number of d c in any number of solid meshes is equal to 3 times the number of meshes with 1 d c in addition.

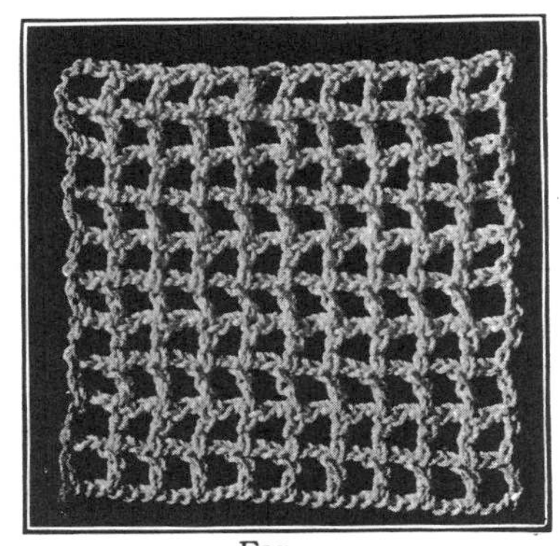

FIG. 1.
Working Model of Filet Crochet, 10 meshes square.

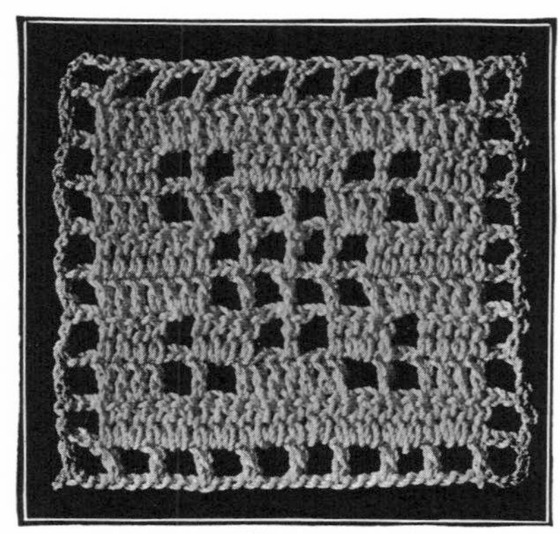

FIG. 2
Working Model of Pattern Fig. 3

It will always be one more than a multiple of 3, as 4, 7, 10, 13, 16, 19, etc.

In the 3d row (following Working Model, Fig. 2, and Block Pattern, Fig. 3) there is, 1 open, 1 solid, 2 open, 2 solid, 2 open, 1 solid, 1 open.

4th row — One open, 1 solid, 1 open, 1 solid, 2 open, 1 solid, 1 open, 1 solid, 1 open.

5th row — One open, 2 solid, 4 open, 2 solid, 1 open.

6th row — Like 5th. 7th row — Like 4th. 8th row — Like 3d. 9th row — Like 2d. 10th row — Like 1st.

Always remembering to make 5 chain for the turn in the square work. This makes an open mesh, and it is always much better to have any design with at least one row of open meshes on all four sides.

It is really quite worth while to make a block like this Fig. 2 and find out if it is square.

When doing a long strip or band, it may not be so essential, although the work is prettier; but when making a square block, it should be square.

Working Model, Fig. 4, is a triangular block, made after the pattern, Fig. 5.

After making nine open meshes, use the t c (with two loops), and join to make the last mesh a triangle. To turn for the 2d row, make 3 rather loose or 4 quite tight chain-stitches and join with d c to make another triangular mesh. This is the first of 4 d c that form a solid mesh. Following the pattern — 1 open, 1 solid, 1 open, 1 solid, 1 open, 1 solid, 1 open. (Turn with 5 chain at this end.)

3d row — Seven open meshes, 1 triangular mesh.

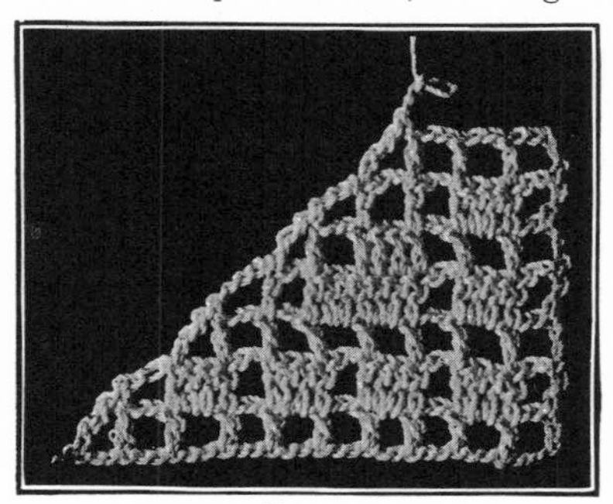

FIG 4
Working Model of Pattern Fig. 5

4th row — Turn with triangle, 1 open, 2 solid, 1 open, 1 solid, 1 open. Turn with 5 chain.

5th row — Three open, 1 solid, 1 open, 1 triangle.

6th row — Turn with triangle, 2 open, 1 solid, 1 open.

7th row — Turn with 5, 3 open, 1 triangle, etc.

FIG. 3
Pattern of Fig. 2

In Filet, it is a rare exception that has not one row, or more, of open meshes outside the design, and we should follow the same rule in Filet Crochet.

The edge of a medallion or insert is usually covered with single crochet, three stitches over each chain of two and four stitches over each triangular mesh. This corresponds nicely with the buttonhole-stitch with which the netted medallion is invariably finished.

Figure 6 is a model of the border of Doily, Fig. 22, showing how to mitre the corner in a way similar to Fig. 4. The two outer rows give the method used to finish the Centrepiece, No. 1452.

Figure 7 is the model showing the heart of flower in the corner of Luncheon Cloth, No. 1454.

A chain of five is made to cover the space of two open meshes.

In estimating the size a pattern will fill, with the various threads, it may be helpful to know that No. 100 D. M. C. Crochet Cotton makes very good fabric, ten meshes to the inch; No. 50, eight meshes to the inch; No. 30, six meshes; and No. 10, between four and five meshes to the inch.

Individual workers vary some, but this is a good average, and represents the work here illustrated.

When crocheting for any length of time, and working as tightly as possible, the fingers may become chafed with the thread or needle. To avoid this, a good plan is to use chamois-skin glove fingers wherever they are needed. Bits of chamois skin may be sewed to fit whichever thumb or finger suffers most. The right-hand thumb, which holds the needle, and the first and second fingers of the left hand, which carry the thread and stop the point of the needle, were all so protected in doing much of the finished work in this book.

Although the crocheting, when in process, can be kept immaculate, by powdering the hands, and keeping the work in a tightly covered box when not in process, yet it is very much improved by laundering.

This should be done by careful squeezing, rather than rubbing, in good soap-suds, and rinsing well without twisting the work. When it is soiled, dampen and lay it on a flat surface and rub soap well into it with a small bristle brush.

Washing shrinks the thread until it is considerably smaller than the original measure. Ironing, face downward, between two pieces of cheese-cloth, on a thickly padded board (when not quite dry), will restore it to the exact size first measured. Careful finishing with the iron next the wrong side, flattens the work and brings out the design beautifully.

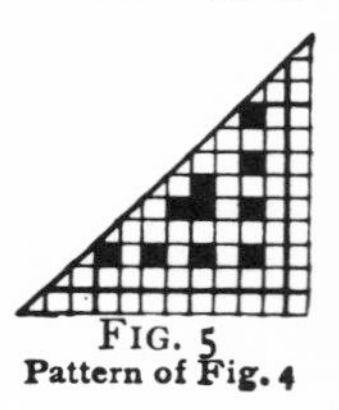

FIG. 5
Pattern of Fig. 4

Filet Crochet is so simple, so easily understood, there is nothing intricate about it; but the fact cannot be overemphasized that great care must be taken to do the work evenly and rather tightly. When one can be sure of the right proportion between the chain-stitch and the double crochet, that one is tight and the other just loose enough, then the worker who can crochet rapidly will make the best work. It becomes almost automatic, and

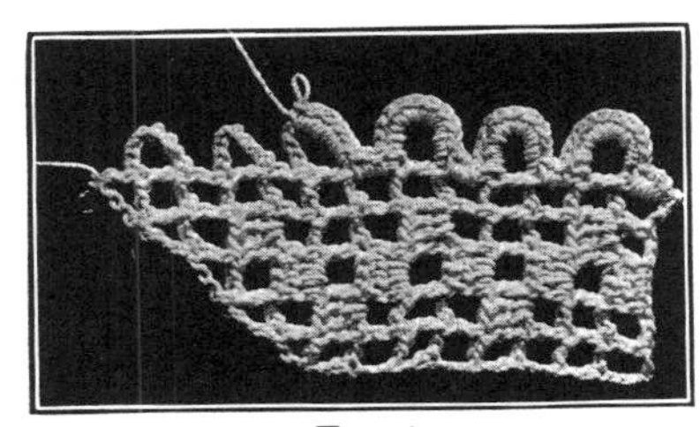

FIG. 6
Working Model, Border, Fig. 22

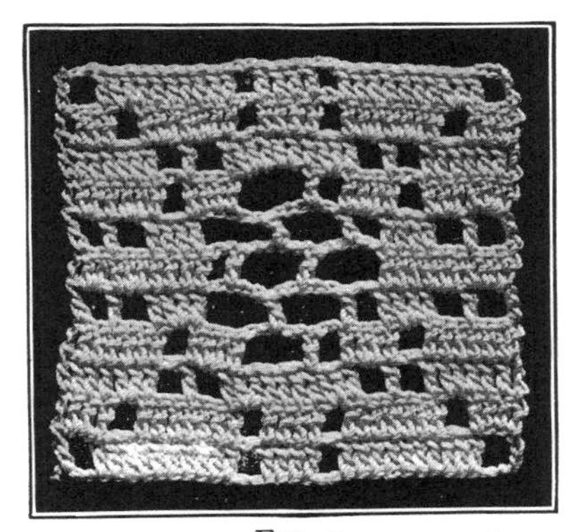

FIG. 7
Working Model, Heart of Flower, Fig. 27

the result is a beautiful uniformity throughout the whole piece, whereas if one must, in a labored way, pull each stitch with a distinct effort, the work is very likely to look pinched and drawn.

No. 1450. Pillow in Filet Crochet and Cross Stitch

This pillow, shown on page 2, is composed of twenty-five blocks, each four inches square. Twelve blocks are of Hardanger cloth, embroidered with cross-stitch, in D. M. C. Stranded Cotton. Two threads of the cotton are used. For the designs see Fig. 12 and Fig. 13 on page 7.

Thirteen blocks are in Filet Crochet of D. M. C. Crochet Cotton No. 50. Three different designs are used, "The Swan," "The Dragon," and a conventional figure, see Fig. 15, Fig. 16, and Fig. 18, on page 7. These blocks are 33 meshes, requiring 105 chain stitches for the foundation chain, this includes 5 chain to turn. Join in the 9th stitch from the needle with a d c. Two chain-stitches separate the d c, making an open mesh. Always at the turn 5 chain are made for the first open mesh.

Two rows of open meshes are made (in the "Swan" block 3 rows are made) before beginning the design. In the 3d row of the "Dragon" make 2 open, 2 solid, 1 open, 1 solid, 6 open, 3 solid, the remainder of the row open. Turn, make 18 open, 1 solid, 1 open, 2 solid, 6 open, 3 solid, 2 open, etc. The designs can be followed back and forth in this way until the squares are completed. Finish

FIG. 8 23 x 35 meshes

FIG. 9 [illegible]5 meshes

the edge around each square with s c, 3 stitches over each chain of 2.

The cross-stitched blocks are cut a big seam larger than the crocheted blocks, machine-stitched just outside the turn, and are overcast in addition to keep them from fraying, as a seam in Hardanger cloth is always treacherous. Then the blocks are overcast together tightly, cross-stitched blocks and crocheted blocks alternating. The pillow-top is ready for the back, which must be overcast to the top. No other seam is possible along the edges of the crocheting. The color used for cross-stitch was old rose. The effect of this "patchwork" determined its selection as Frontispiece.

Fig. 10. Conventional Flower Doily

This doily presents a problem not unlike the proverbial "fitting of a round peg in a square hole," and there is added the puzzling task of crocheting to a foundation where there is no chain. 'Tis true one might break the thread and add a chain, but it can be accomplished with one thread, as was done in this case. Number 100 D. M. C. Crochet Cotton was used, and the doily measured 6¾ inches in diameter. The crochet needle required is No. 14.

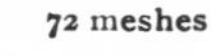

FIG. 10. FLOWER DOILY. See Fig. 43 — 72 meshes

To make the doily, start with 12 meshes, that is, chain 36 plus 1 plus 5 stitches equals 42, d c in 9th stitch and make 12 open meshes in the 1st row.

2d row — Chain 12, plus 5 to turn, d c in 9th st and make 4 open meshes (it is easy to carry out chain at the last end of a row, to widen at the first of the succeeding row), 12 solid meshes, then make 4 open meshes as follows:

Two chain, 1 double treble (d t) (3 loops) and join this d t at the top of the 1st row. Three times more, make this square mesh and join each time on a line with the top of the 1st row, forming 4 open meshes. At the end of each added mesh, the needle is left at the top of the mesh, ready to make another or to turn.

This peculiar method is necessary in widening at the end of a row where there is nothing to crochet to, and three sides of a mesh must be made as one proceeds. To narrow, simply omit one or more meshes at the last end of the row. At the first end, draw the stitch on the needle the length of a mesh and slip in the top of d c. Repeat this for each mesh that is to be omitted, then make 5 chain for an open mesh and proceed according to the design, Fig. 43 on page 22. The loose threads left in this way are nicely covered when the edge is finished with s c.

When the last row of twelve open meshes is finished, make one chain-stitch and cover the edge with 3 s c over each single side of a mesh, and 5 s c where two sides of a mesh form the edge. The final caution is to make the crocheting square.

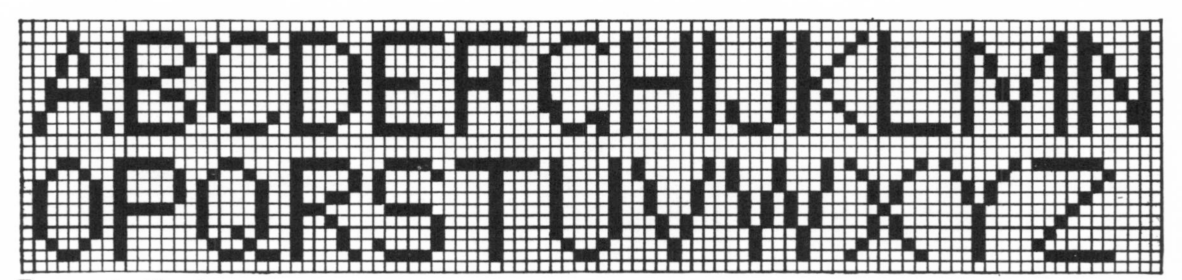

FIG. 11. See Fig. 36 — 9 meshes

FIG. 12. See No. 1450 45 meshes

FIG. 13. See No. 1450 45 meshes

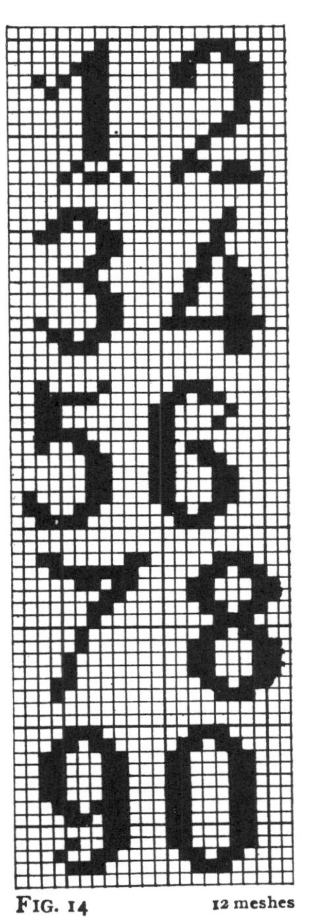

FIG. 14 12 meshes

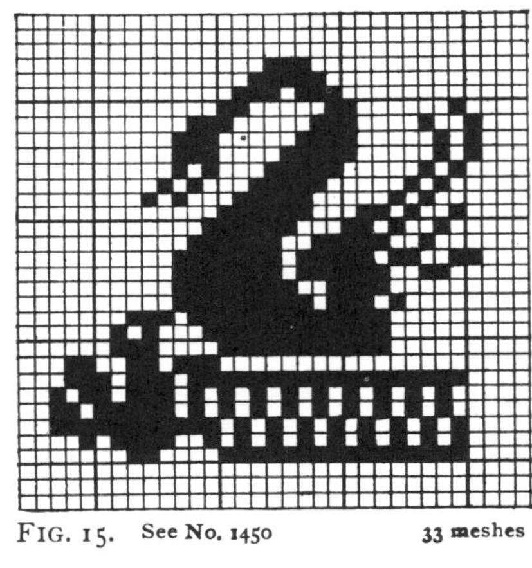

FIG. 15. See No. 1450 33 meshes

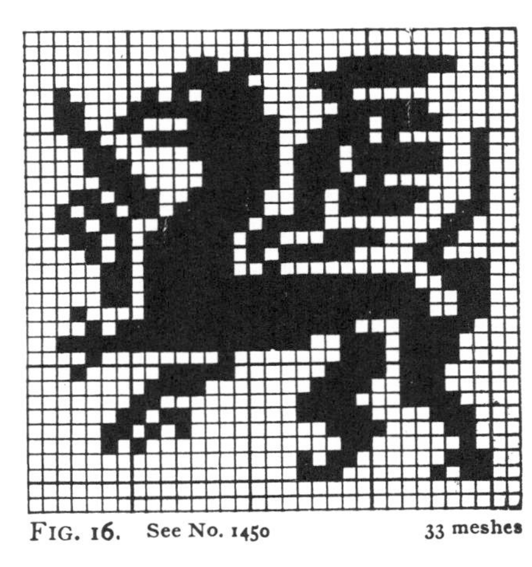

FIG. 16. See No. 1450 33 meshes

FIG. 17 31 meshes

FIG. 18. See No. 1450 33 meshes

Figs. 16, 17, 18. Guest Towels

These guest towels are of 16-inch huckaback, and 30 inches long. The thread used is No. 30 D. M. C. Crochet Cotton. One ball is sufficient for each towel.

Figure 19 — Insertion, at one end, 16 meshes wide, with letters 14 meshes high (see Figs. 114 and 126), and a 5-mesh insertion (see Working Model, Fig. 6) at the other.

Figure 20 — A band, 11 meshes wide, with letters 7 meshes high (Fig. 128), finishes this guest towel at one end, and at the other a band 5 meshes wide. (See Insertion for Baby's Pillow, No. 1451.)

Figure 21 — This insertion is commenced with 9 meshes (for pattern see border, Fig. 59), then widened to 18 meshes through the centre where the initials, 14 meshes wide (Fig. 114), are made. Then the band is continued 9 meshes wide to the end, reversing the pattern at the beginning. The other end of the towel is finished with a band 4 meshes wide and readily followed from the cut.

Fig. 22. Doily

Two medallions of 23 meshes (Fig. 98) and two of 25 meshes (Fig. 105) are inset in this 11-inch doily.

The edge is shown at Fig. 6, page 5. This requires one ball of No. 100 D. M. C. Crochet Cotton, and one-third yard of fine huckaback, 24 inches wide, will make two doilies, useful and pretty.

FIG. 19. GUEST TOWEL. See Figs. 114 and 126

FIG. 20. GUEST TOWEL. See Fig. 128

FIG. 21. GUEST TOWEL. See Fig. 101

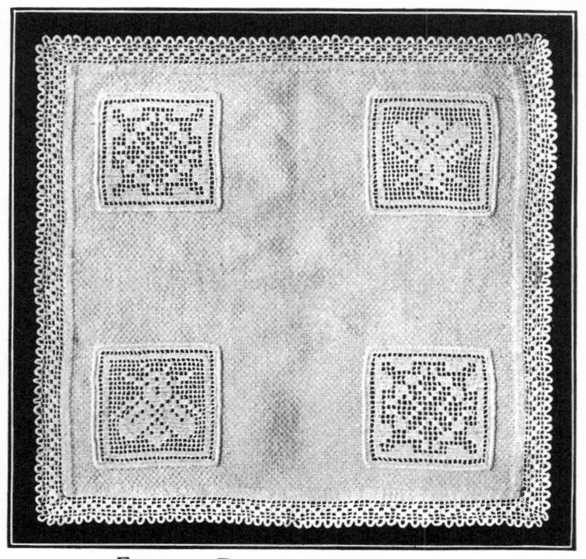

FIG. 22. DOILY. See Figs. 6, 98, 105

No. 1451. Baby Pillow

This daintily embroidered pillow of linen supports a hollow square of Filet Crochet insertion to frame "the baby's face." The centre of the pillow is reserved for that decoration or use.

The insertion is made of No. 100 D. M. C. Crochet Cotton. For the design, see Fig. 32, page 17. It is 100 meshes square and 20 meshes wide, measuring 10 inches each way and 2 inches wide. A little more than one-quarter of the design is given, the rest being reversed. It is started at the lower left-hand corner with 306 stitches (including the turn). One row of open meshes, turn, 1 open, 98 solid, 1 open. Turn, 1 open, 1 solid, 96 open, 1 solid, 1 open, etc. When 20 rows are finished, turn, and follow the design up the right-hand side, 20 meshes wide, until 79 rows are done. Break the thread and begin at the inside of the frame, 20 meshes from the left edge and carry up the left side 80 rows. The 80th row will end at the inside corner of upper left-hand. Do not break the thread, but chain 179 and make 1 d c in the 1st stitch of the right-hand side. Finish this 80th row across according to the pattern and make 20 rows entirely across, reversing the first 20 rows.

Four yards of insertion are required for the ruffle. This insertion is 5 meshes wide. In the 1st and 2d rows the centre mesh is solid. The 3d, 4th, and 5th rows are all open. Repeat these 5 rows for the length required. The pillow appears larger, but is only 16 inches square.

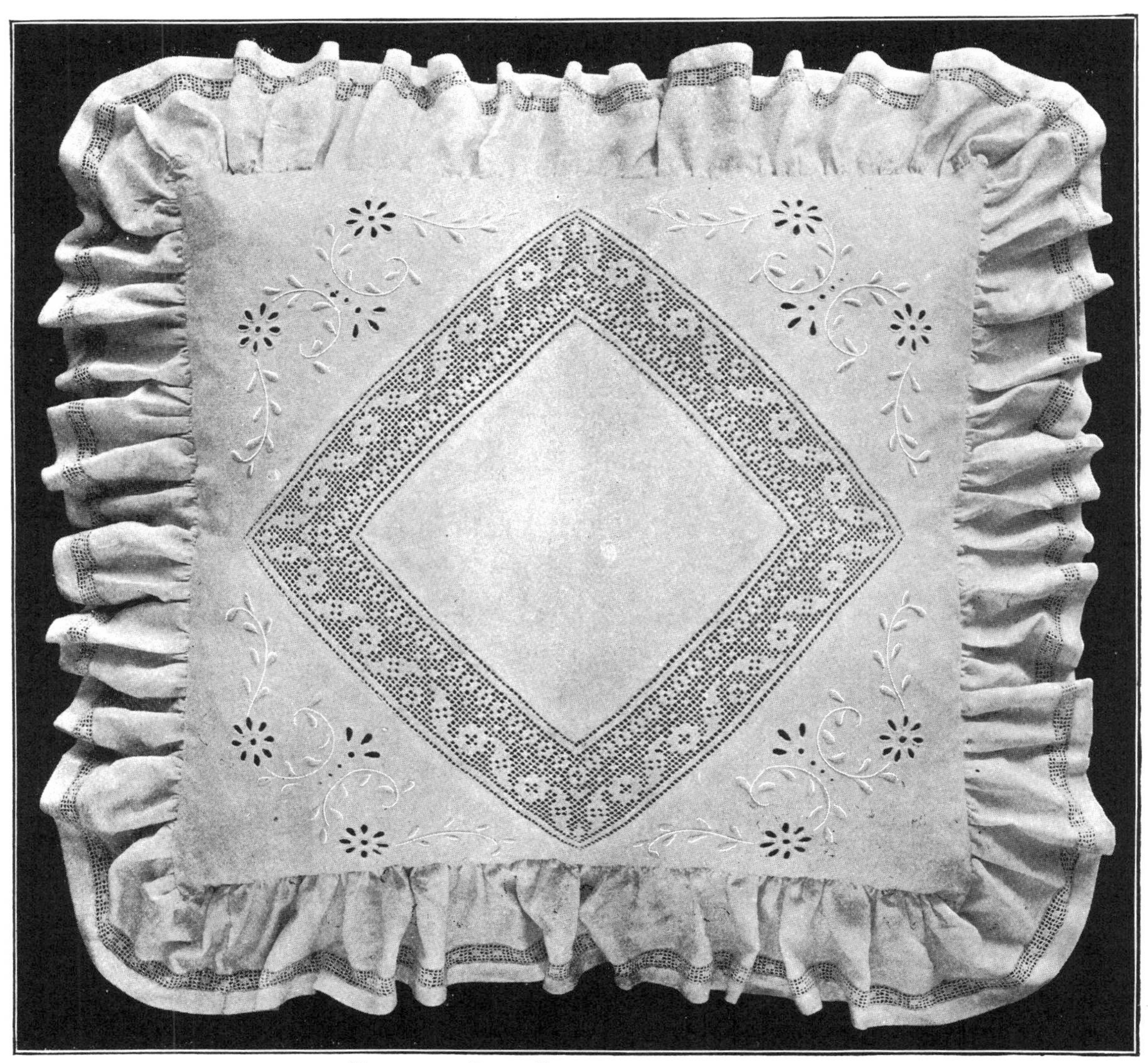

No. 1451. Baby Pillow. See Fig. 32, page 17

No. 1452. Centrepiece in Filet Crochet and Cross Stitch

This novel centrepiece, of No. 10 D. M. C. Crochet Cotton, is made somewhat after the fashion of the crocheted frame in the Baby Pillow, No. 1451. The hollow square is partly filled with a figure in the form of a Greek cross, leaving four openings about 4 inches square. These are filled with cross stitched, hemstitched blocks of Hardanger cloth. The crocheting (see Fig. 23) is started at "A" with a chain of 276 stitches, making 90 meshes.

It may be difficult, in turning the work back and forth, to distinguish right and left, but if a short thread is left at the beginning of the foundation chain, that is to be considered the left side.

When 16 rows of the pattern are completed, at "B," the work is carried on 16 meshes wide until 21 rows of the right-hand side are finished. Leaving the ball of thread at that point, start another thread at "C," and carry this band up until 20 rows are finished. Cut and fasten the thread.

Start at "D" and finish 20 rows of this band, cut and fasten the thread. Then take up the thread left at "E," chain 62 stitches, follow the pattern across the middle band, chain 62, follow the pattern across the left band. This completes the 21st row of the central band and left side.

Make 16 rows entirely across the work.

Starting from "F," make 21 rows, 16 meshes

No. 1452. Centrepiece in Filet Crochet and Cross Stitch Embroidery

See Figs. 23 and 52

wide, leaving the thread at "H" as at "E." Start another thread at "X," make 20 rows of the upper central band, cut and fasten the thread. At "XX" start another thread, make 20 rows of right-hand side, cut and fasten the thread.

Take up the thread left at "H," chain 62, make 1 row across centre band, chain 62, make 1 row across right-hand side. Sixteen rows of the pattern will complete the frame. Make the two outer rows of Fig. 6, page 5, for the edge.

The cross stitch design is Fig. 52, page 23, and when the blocks are overcast in their places, the centrepiece is finished. The cross stitch is done with stranded cotton, and the undivided cotton is used because the crocheting is quite heavy.

Upon comparing the centrepiece and the design, at first glance it may appear that the design has only one row of open meshes for outside margin, while the centrepiece has two rows. But the second of these is part of the border. 1st row — Fasten the thread at the top of a d c, make an open mesh (5 chain, 1 d c), * 8 chain, 1 d c on last d c, 1 d c in next d c of centrepiece, 2 chain, 1 d c in next d c of centrepiece *. Repeat from * to * 2d row — Cover with s c, 7 or 8 over each scallop and 2 or 3 along the meshes.

Different ways in which this handsome square may be used will suggest themselves, and one may also use the border and the cross independently. Omitting the fancy purl edge shown in the illustration, a number of the squares might be joined together to form a counterpane, or the border alone could be set diamond fashion in the centre and enclose an initial or monogram.

FIG. 23. CENTREPIECE DESIGN. See No. 1452, page 10 90 meshes

No. 1453. Peacock Pillow

One large insert of Filet Crochet, ninety-eight meshes square, forms the centre of this very handsome pillow.

The material of the pillow is Hardanger cloth, which lends itself so nicely to cross stitch. The border or frame surrounding the crochet being of that old, lately revived, much prized style of work. This is so fine and so well worked that it appears to be woven in the cloth. For the cross stitch design see Fig. 25 and Fig. 40. It is done with stranded cotton. The square of Filet Crochet, made of No. 100 D. M. C. Crochet Cotton, requires a foundation chain of 300, that includes 5 to turn. Two rows of open meshes, then the design.

3d row — Fifty-two open, 1 solid, 45 open. Turn.

4th row — Forty open, 1 solid, 4 open, 2 solid, 4 open, 1 solid, 46 open. Turn.

5th row — Thirty-one open, 1 solid, 5 open, 1 solid, 8 open, 2 solid, 3 open, 2 solid, 3 open, 2 solid, 40 open, etc.

Both feet being started, the design (Fig. 24) can be easily followed. When the square is finished cover the edge with s c, 3 over each chain. Overcast it to the cloth, a generous seam of which is machine-stitched, overcast, and turned back. B, Fig. 25, is the centre of the cross stitch design.

No. 1453. Pillow in Filet Crochet and Cross Stitch Embroidery
See Figs. 24, 25 and 40

FIG. 24. DESIGN OF FILET CROCHET FOR PILLOW No. 1453. 98 meshes

FIG. 25. BORDER DESIGN OF PILLOW No. 1453. See corner, Fig. 40 27 meshes

No. 1454. Luncheon Cloth

The combination of a corner of Filet Crochet with Venetian cut-work makes a very pretty result in this luncheon cloth.

The corner is crocheted of No. 100 D. M. C. Crochet Cotton; one ball will make a corner. The design is Fig. 27, page 15. In this triangle, the principle, seen at Fig. 4, Working Model, page 4, is used.

One hundred and two meshes is the size, requiring a foundation chain of 312, including turn. Make 101 open meshes, one triangular mesh with treble (two loops over the needle). In turning at the diagonal make 3 loose or 4 tight chain-stitches, and join with a d c — 17 open, 1 solid, 23 open, 1 solid, 36 open, 6 solid, 7 open, 3 solid, 6 open. Turn with 5 chain, etc., following the design. Where the long meshes are shown, in the heart of the flower, make 5 chain (see Fig. 7, Working Model, page 5). Where so long a bias is to be cut in the linen, it is best to mark outside the insert and machine-stitch 1-32 of an inch outside that line. A running line, the same distance outside the stitching, will give a good body for the buttonhole, to which the insert is to be overcast. The cloth is 48 inches square, the hemstitched hem 1¼ inches wide, and it requires one-half dozen D. M. C. Coton Floche No. 8 to do the embroidery. The Venetian cut-work scrolls are very easily and quickly made.

No. 1454. LUNCHEON CLOTH IN FILET CROCHET AND VENETIAN CUT WORK

See page 15, Fig. 27

Fig. 27. Design for Luncheon Cloth, No. 1454, page 14. See Fig. 7, page 5 102 meshes

No. 1455. Pillow in Filet Crochet and Eyelet Work

This pillow of linen is beautifully embroidered, and inset with one large and eight small medallions of Filet Crochet.

The larger medallion is 5½ inches square, 54 meshes. For design, see Fig. 28, page 17.

The smaller medallions are 3 inches square, 31 meshes. For designs, see Fig. 29 and Fig. 30, page 17.

One ball of D. M. C. Crochet Cotton, No. 100, will make the nine medallions.

The embroidery should be finished first and the linen laundered, after which the medallions (laundered) are to be overcast to the buttonholed edge.

Lay the medallions in place, mark lightly (with a hard pencil) outside each one. Make one line of closely run stitches about 1-32 of an inch outside the pencil mark, a second line the same distance outside the first. Buttonhole over these two lines with the edge of the buttonhole on the inner side. Cut close to the work and overcast the medallion in this little frame. The buttonhole should be done with the thread used in the embroidery. D. M. C. Coton Floche, No. 12, is good for that, or any other embroidery cotton that one prefers.

No. 1455. Pillow in Filet Crochet and Eyelet Work. See page 17, Figs. 28, 29 and 30

FIG. 28. See No. 1455, page 16 — 54 meshes

FIG. 31
13 meshes

FIG. 29. See page 16 — 31 meshes

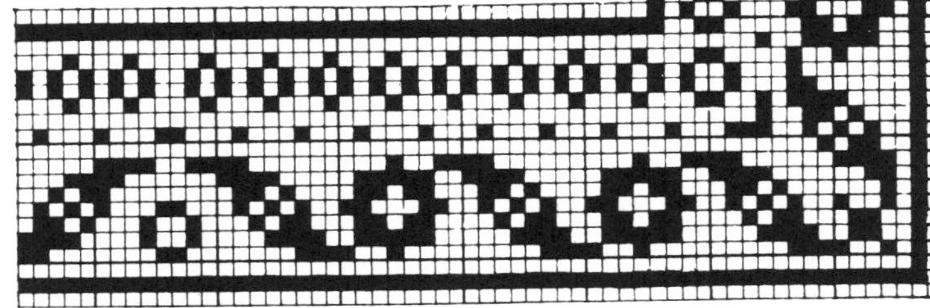

FIG. 32. See Baby Pillow, No. 1451, page 9 — 20 meshes

FIG. 33. See top of Bag, page 19 — 10 meshes

FIG. 30. See page 16 — 31 meshes

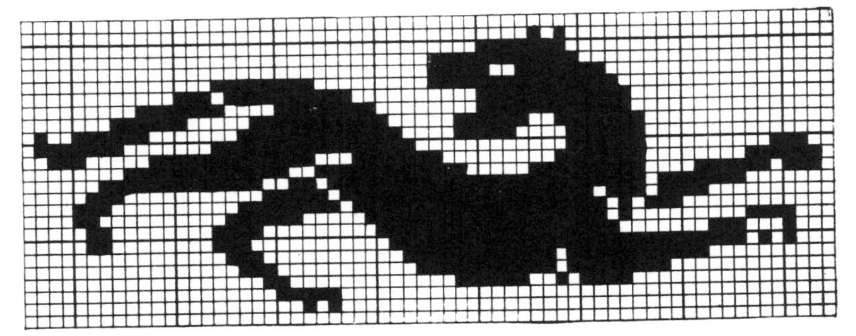

FIG. 34 — 25 x 64 meshes

Figs. 35, 36. Towel with Filet Crochet

This towel, or scarf, of 24-inch huckaback is trimmed at one end with three initialed medallions, 31 meshes square, connected by a band of 3 open meshes, the width of the towel.

The initials are 25 meshes high, from alphabet, Fig. 111, page 42.

An insertion, 13 meshes wide, with name (9 meshes high), repeated, forms the trimming of the other end; see page 6, Fig. 11.

One ball of No. 50 D. M. C. Crochet Cotton and 1¼ yards 24-inch huckaback are the materials.

Fig. 41. Baby's Bonnet

This charming bonnet was made of No. 100 D. M. C. Crochet Cotton, with a No. 14 crochet needle. The directions are as follows:

Chain 6, join in a ring.

1st round — Twelve s c in the ring.

2d round — Two s c in each stitch (making 24).

3d round — * Two s c in 1st, 1 s c in each of next 2 *. Repeat from * to * (making 32).

4th round — * Two s c in 1st, 1 s c in 2d *. Repeat from * to * (making 48).

5th round — * Two s c in 1st, 1 s c in 2d *. Repeat from * to * (making 72).

6th round — Five chain, 1 d c in 2d stitch below, * 2 chain, 1 d c in 2d stitch below *. Repeat from * to * (making 36 open meshes).

7th round — One solid mesh (made by 3 chain, 3 d c), 2 open meshes. Repeat all around.

8th round — One open, 1 solid, * 2 open, 1 solid, *. Repeat from * to *.

9th round — One d c over each d c, 3 d c over each chain.

10th, 11th, 12th, 13th, 14th, 15th, 16th, 17th, 18th, rounds — Like 7th, 8th, and 9th.

19th, 20th, 21st rounds — Open meshes all around.

This completes the crown.

22d row — Turn, with 5 chain, make 19 open, 1 solid, 5 open, 1 solid, 15 open, 1 solid, 5 open, 1 solid, 15 open, 1 solid, 5 open, 1 solid, 15 open, 1 solid, 5 open, 1 solid, 7 open (making 99 meshes).

23d row — Turn, make 7 open, 2 solid, 3 open, 2 solid, 15 open, 2 solid, 3 open, 2 solid, 15 open, 2 solid, 3 open, 2 solid, 15 open, 2 solid, 3 open, 2 solid, 19 open.

24th row — Turn, and since two points of each

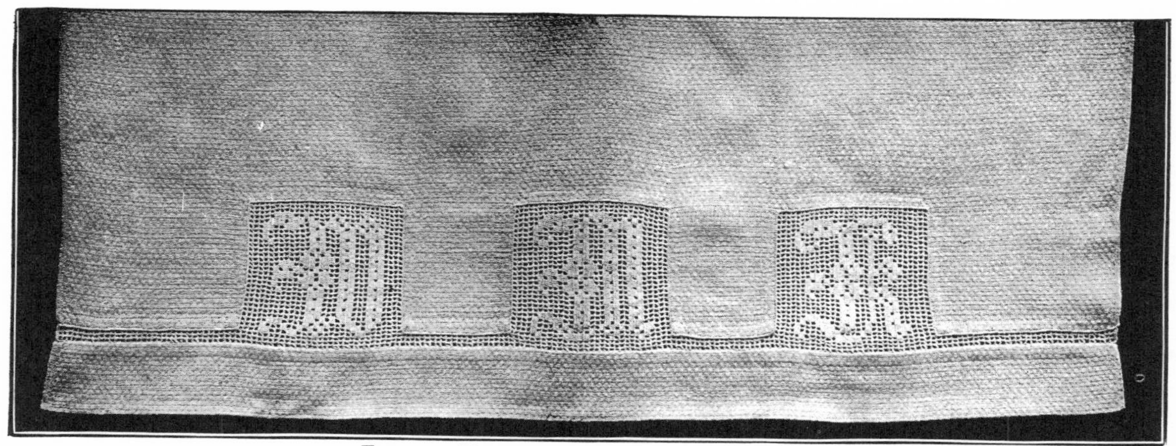

FIG. 35. TOWEL. See Alphabet, page 42, Fig. 111

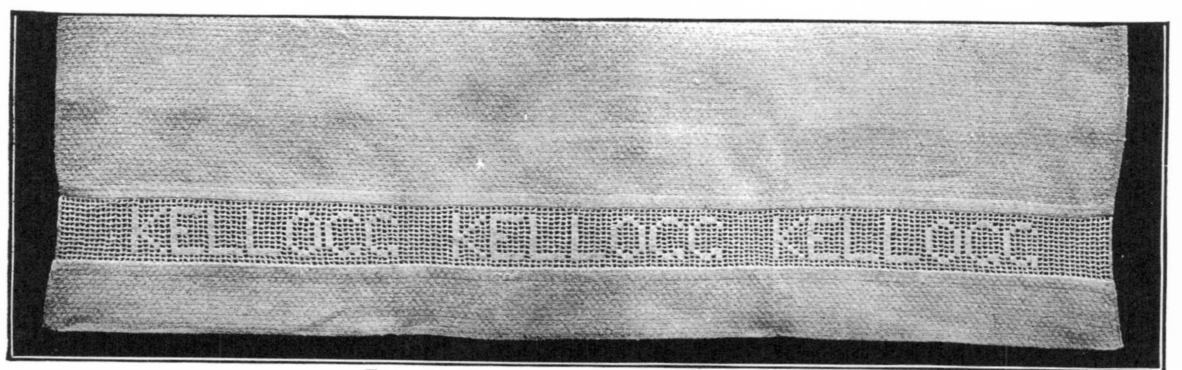

FIG. 36. TOWEL. See Alphabet, page 6, Fig. 11

of four stars are started, they may easily be finished from the illustration, being sure to start the front row of alternating stars in the 36th row, the same row that finishes the first four stars. The 36th row follows — Turn, make 8 open meshes, 1 solid, 5 open, 1 solid, 4 open, 1 solid, 5 open, 1 solid, 4 open, 1 solid, 5 open, 1 solid, 4 open, 1 solid, 5 open, 1 solid, 4 open, 1 solid, 5 open, 1 solid, 4 open, 1 solid, 5 open, 1 solid, 4 open, 1 solid, 5 open, 1 solid, 4 open, 1 solid, 5 open, 1 solid, 7 open.
Finish around the edge with 3 s c over each chain, making a picot of 4 chain after every 6th stitch.

Fig. 42. Hand Bag

This little bag measures 5 inches by 6½ inches, and is made of No. 50 D. M. C. Crochet Cotton. The design used was Fig. 73 for the body and Fig. 33 for the top of 8 rows above the beading.
Each side was crocheted separately, and the edges were held together and covered with s c. Figure 73 is 43 meshes, one more was added to each side, and the size could be varied at one's pleasure. Make 45 meshes, 141 chain, d c in 9th stitch from needle, etc.
The beading is made of double trebles (3 loops) separated by 2 chain. Around the top it is finished with 6 s c, picot of 5, repeated. The cords are chains of No. 2 D. M. C. Crochet Cotton, 30 inches long, about 300 stitches. And balls of No. 2 are crocheted on the ends.

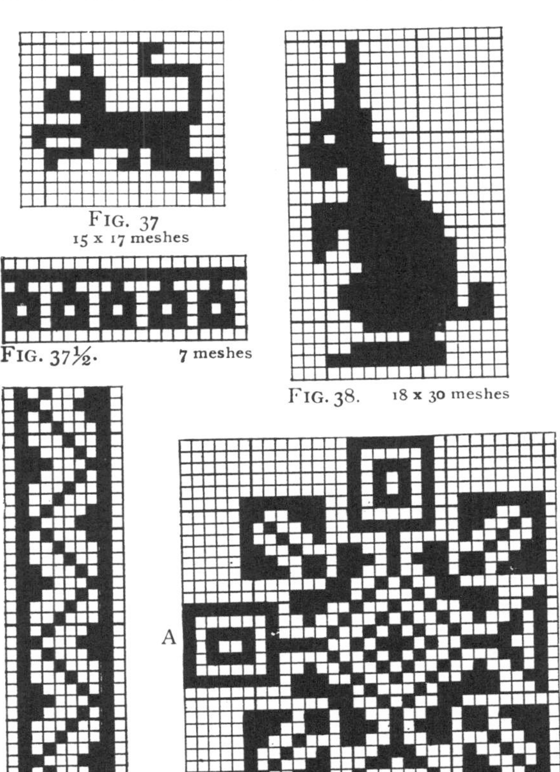

FIG. 37
15 x 17 meshes

FIG. 37½. 7 meshes

FIG. 38. 18 x 30 meshes

FIG. 39
10 meshes

FIG. 40 27 meshes
Corner of Fig. 25

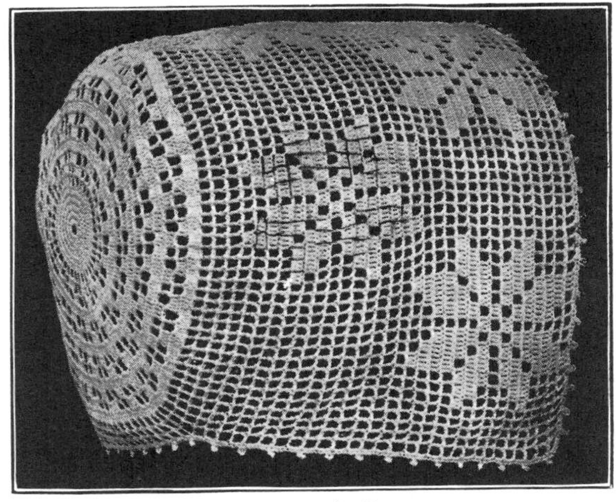

FIG. 41. BABY'S BONNET
See page 18

FIG. 42. SMALL HAND BAG
See Figs. 33 and 73

No. 1456. Bedspread in Filet Crochet

Use 8½ lbs. of carpet chain and a steel hook to suit the thread. One-quarter of the spread is given, half the width and half the length, in the pattern, No. 1456, offered at 10 cents. Begin the work in the lower right-hand corner with a chain of 784, and 5 to turn, to make 261 meshes. The pattern has 259 meshes, but one more on each side must be allowed to make a perfect copy of the spread. Two rows of open meshes are made before the design is started. Follow the first row of the design to the centre mesh, which is the last in the pattern. Reverse this half row, but do not double the centre mesh, and this will complete the 3d row of work. Begin the 4th row at the right and work to the centre, then reverse for the last half of the row. Make each row in this way.

No. 1456. Bedspread in Filet Crochet

No. 1457. Bedspread in Filet Crochet and Relief Crochet

Fourteen pounds of white carpet chain and a steel crochet needle are required to make this very handsome bedspread.

The width is 243 meshes, which takes 729 chain and 5 to turn. Part of the design is in Relief Crochet.

The Relief block is represented by a dot in the pattern, No. 1457, which is offered by the Priscilla Publishing Co., for 10 cents. This block or knob is made of 5 d c worked in the space of one mesh, the needle is taken out and put in the first of the five, and the last loop taken through, make 1 chain and 1 d c over d c.

Bend the 5 d c either toward or away from you, according to which side, the right or wrong side, is uppermost. The raised work is very effective.

No. 1457. Bedspread in Filet Crochet and Relief Crochet

FIG. 43. See Flower Doily, page 6, Fig. 10 — 72 meshes

FIG. 44. 5 meshes

FIG. 45 — 9 meshes

FIG. 45A — 9 meshes

FIG. 45B — 9 meshes

FIG. 46 — 12 x 23 meshes

FIG. 47 — 45 meshes

FIG. 48 — 45 meshes

FIG. 49 — 61 meshes

FIG. 51 — 31 meshes

FIG. 52 — 31 meshes

FIG. 50 — 61 meshes

FIG. 53 — 31 meshes

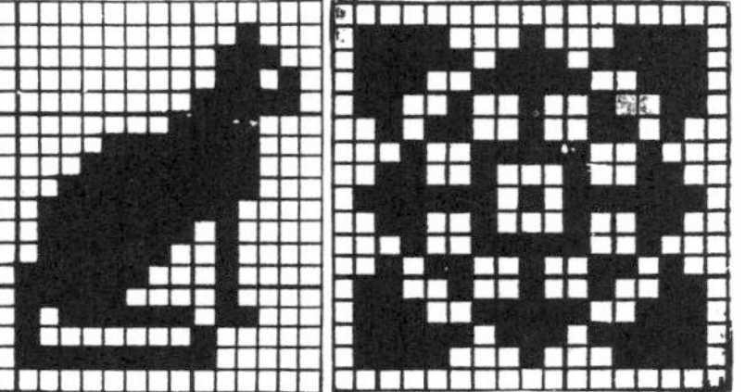

FIG. 54 — 15 x 18 meshes

FIG. 55 — 17 meshes

FIG. 56. BOAR HUNT

116 x 198 meshes. See page 29 for patterns of Border for this design. Fig. 60, A, B, E, is one-half of Top Border. Fig. 62, C, D, F, is one-half of Lower Border. Fig. 61, B, D, is Side Border.

A
B
C
D

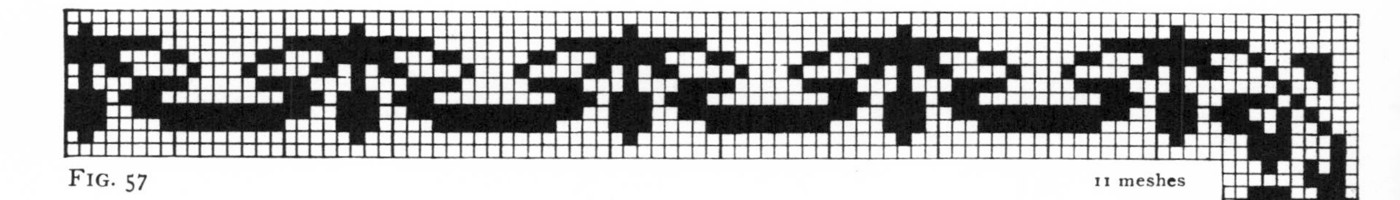

FIG. 57 11 meshes

FIG. 58 DEER HUNT 104 x 186 meshes

Fig. 58. Deer Hunt

The "Deer Hunt," Fig. 58, is completed by joining pages 26 and 27 at X and XX.

The border of the "Boar Hunt," on pages 24 and 25, may be applied to this, using only the narrow design, which is 4 meshes wide, and 2 meshes margin outside.

And there may be added to this the whole border on page 29, which is the right size for either design.

This border is given in three parts, the half of upper border, the half of lower border, and side border which fits exactly between the two.

They are lettered to join together.

The 6-mesh border should be placed directly outside the 104 by 186 meshes on this and the previous page, then the broader border just outside that, which is 116 by 198 meshes.

The measure outside the whole is 176 by 258 meshes. There should be no difficulty in adding either border to either design.

X

XX

FIG. 58. — Continued. For Border see page 24 and page 29.

B

B

A

Fig. 59. 78 x 144 meshes

The size of the page makes it necessary to give this design in two parts. When crocheting this panel of "Neptune," commence at A with a chain of 240 stitches, d c in 9th, etc. Make one row of open meshes, then follow the pattern. When B is reached continue at B of the larger design. The panel would be very pretty for use on a

FIG. 60. 129 x 30 meshes
Half Top Border, Fig. 56

FIG. 61. 116 x 30 meshes
Side Border, Fig. 56

FIG. 62. 129 x 30 meshes
Half Lower Border, Fig. 56

Fig. 63

99 x 133 mesh

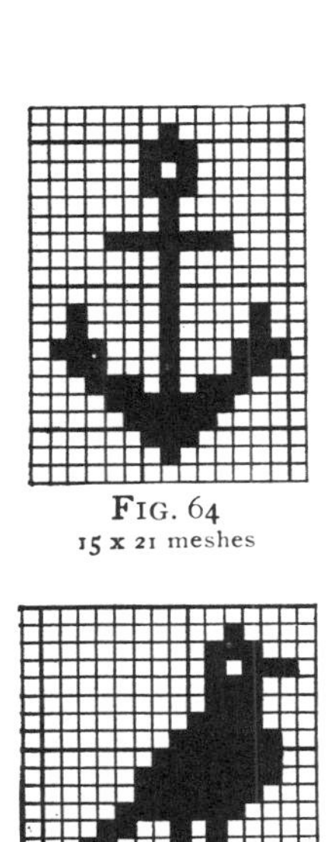

FIG. 64
15 x 21 meshes

FIG. 65
16 x 17 meshes

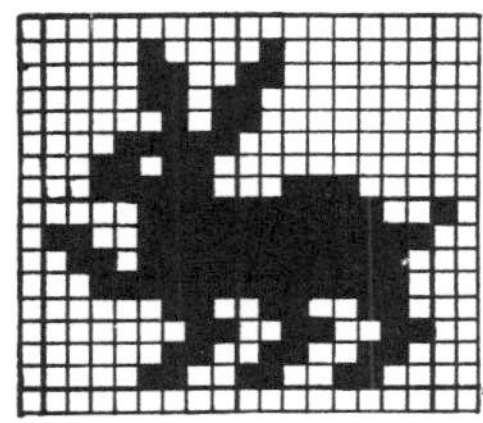

FIG. 66 16 x 19 meshes

FIG. 67 68 meshes

FIG. 68 19 meshes

FIG. 69 20 meshes

FIG. 70 7 meshes

FIG. 71 43 meshes

FIG. 72 43 meshes

FIG. 73 See Fig. 42, page 19 43 meshes

FIG. 74 43 meshes

FIG. 75 31 meshes

FIG. 76 31 meshes

FIG. 77 31 meshes

G. 78 — 61 meshes

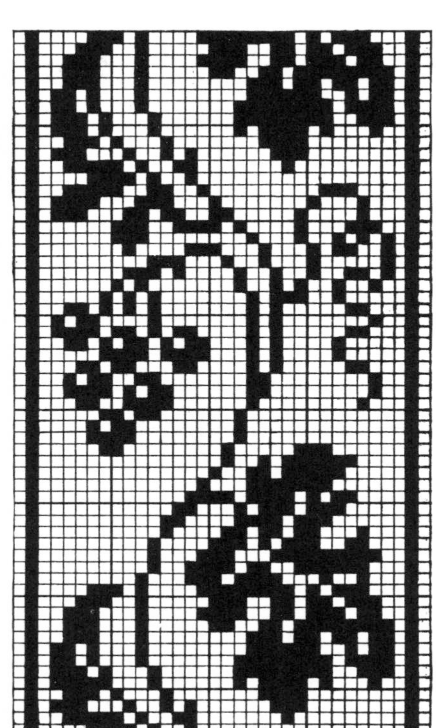

FIG. 79 — 34 meshes

IG. 80 — 25 meshes

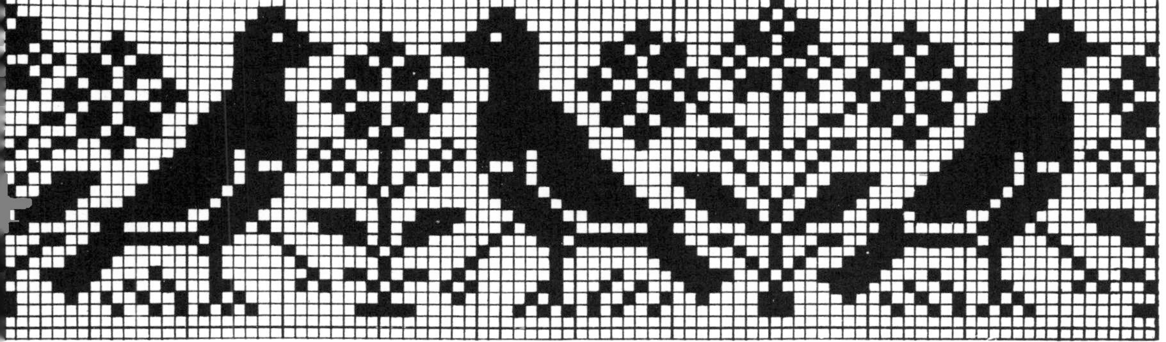

IG. 81 — 29 meshes

FIG. 82

83 meshes

FIG. 83

34 x 103 meshes

FIG. 84 83 meshes

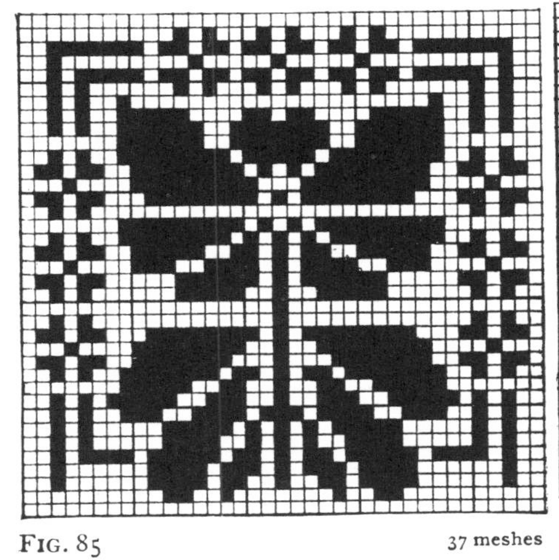

FIG. 85 37 meshes

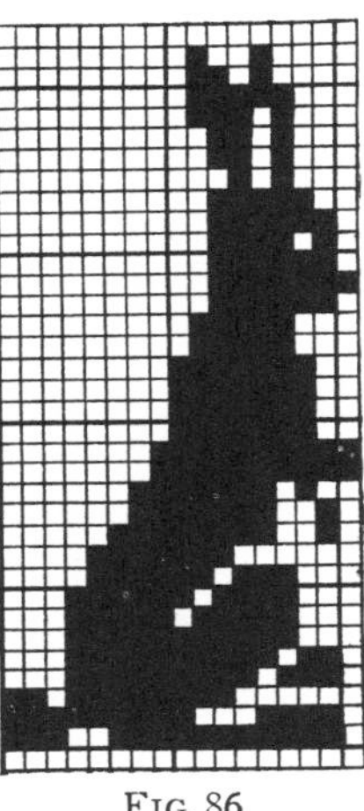

FIG. 86
19 x 36 meshes

FIG. 87 37 meshes

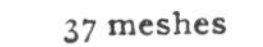

FIG. 88 91 meshes

FIG. 89 28 meshes

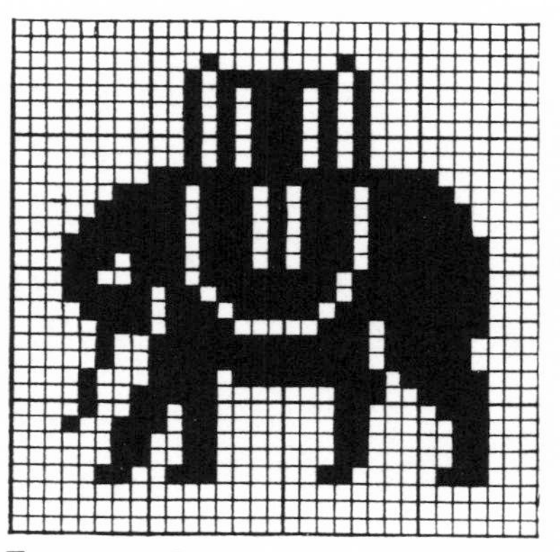

FIG. 90 31 meshes

FIG. 91 29 meshes

FIG. 92 91 meshes

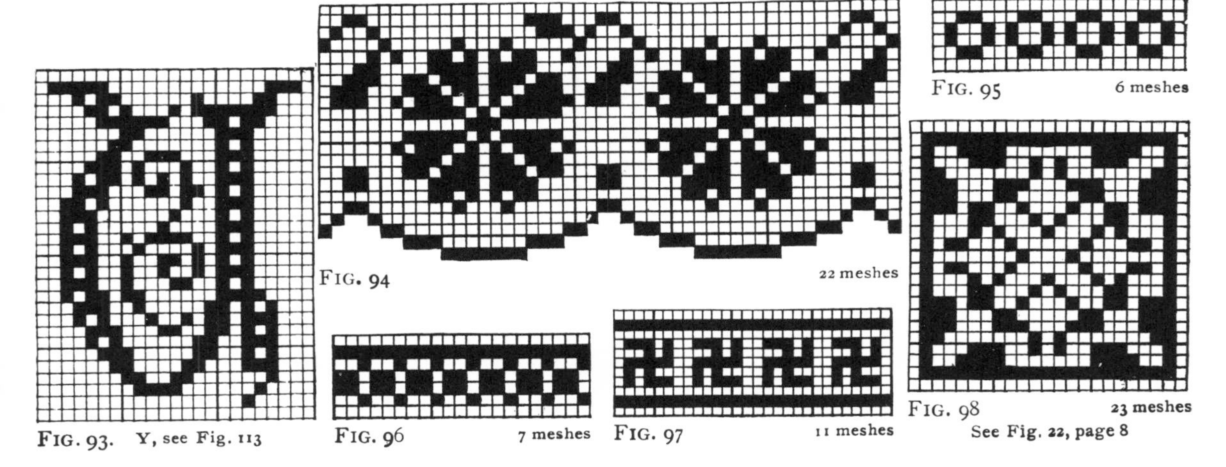

FIG. 93. Y, see Fig. 113

FIG. 94 22 meshes

FIG. 95 6 meshes

FIG. 96 7 meshes

FIG. 97 11 meshes

FIG. 98 23 meshes

See Fig. 22, page 8

FIG. 100 54 meshes

FIG. 101 25 meshes

FIG. 102 25 meshes

FIG. 99 35 meshes

FIG. 103 54 meshes

FIG. 104 25 meshes

FIG. 105 25 meshes
See Fig. 22, page 8

FIG. 106 35 meshes

FIG. 107 95 meshes

FIG. 108 29 meshes

FIG. 109

61 x 84 meshes

FIG. 110

61 x 85 meshes

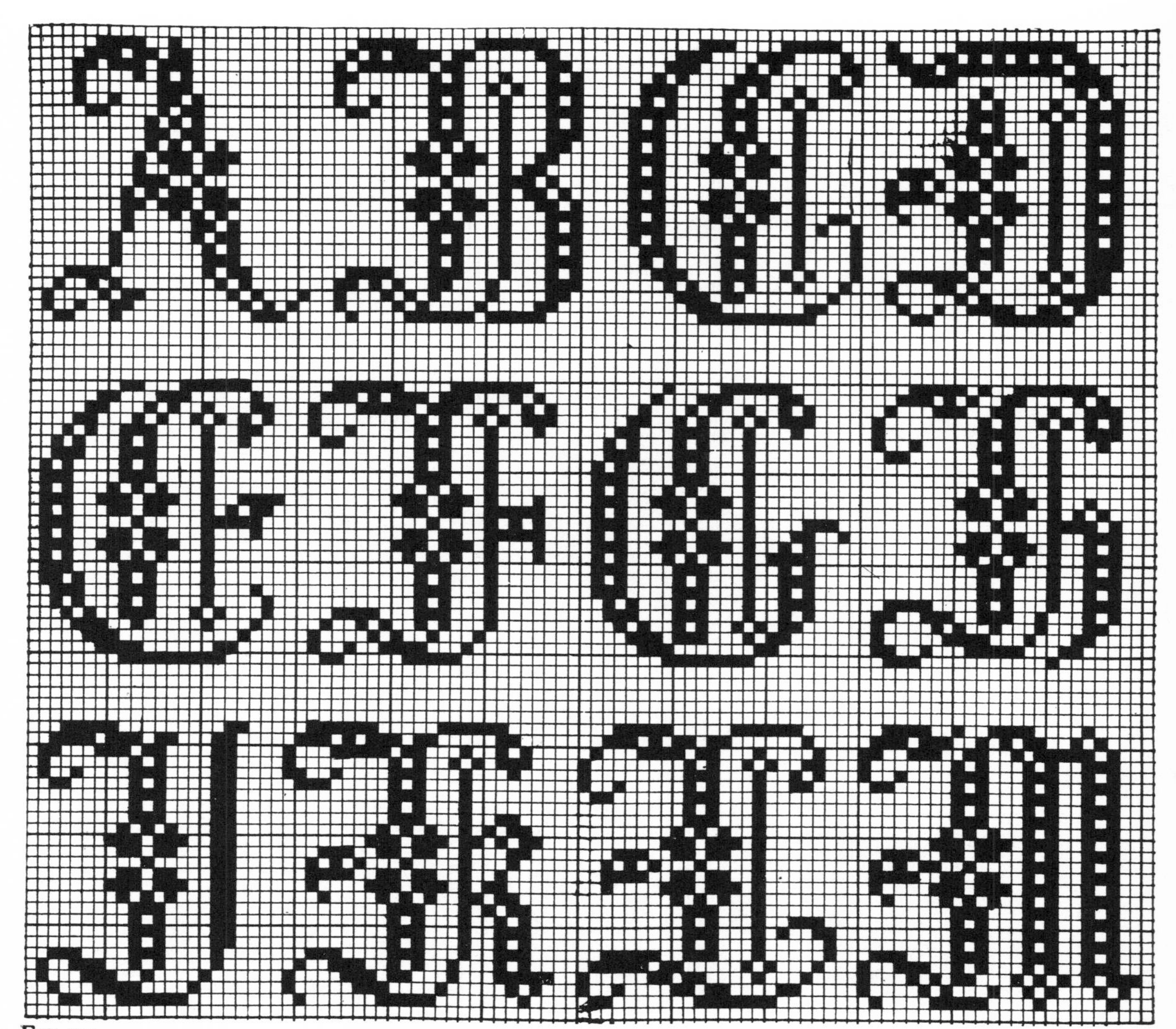

FIG. 111

25 meshes high

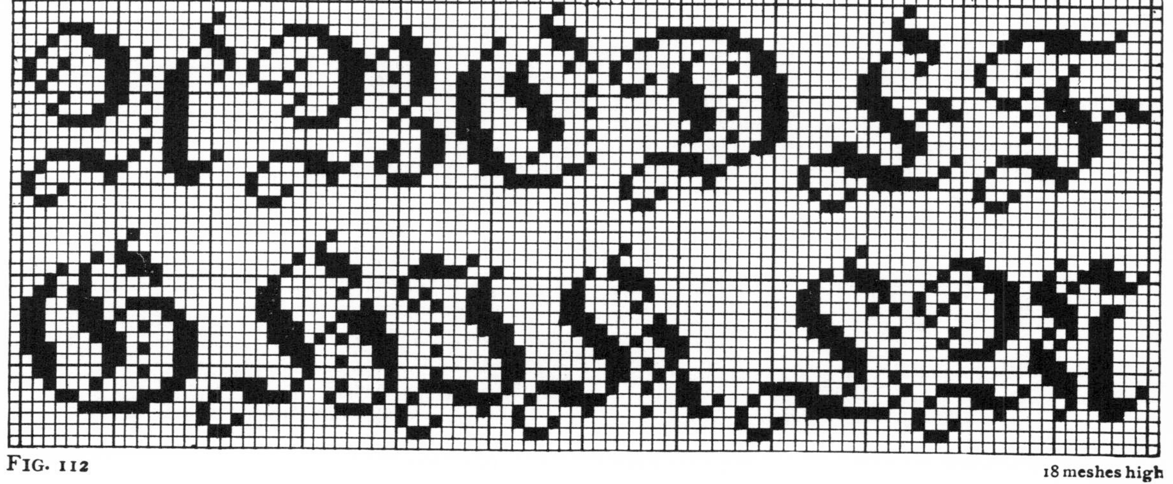

FIG. 112

18 meshes high

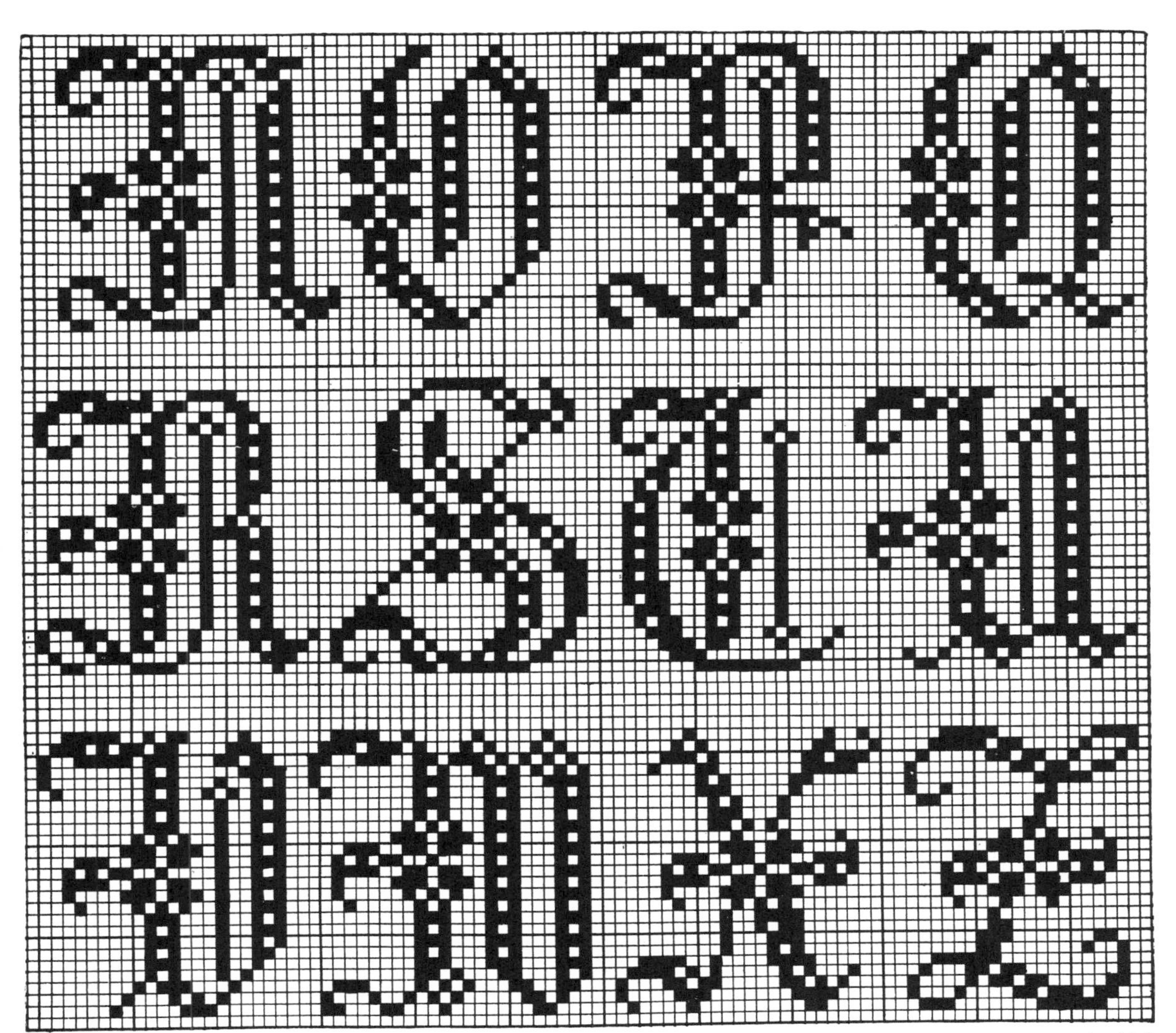

FIG. 111. (*Continued from page 42.*) For Y of this alphabet, see page 47, Fig. 125 25 meshes high

FIG. 112. (*Continued from page 42.*) For X of this alphabet, see page 47, Fig. 122 18 meshes high

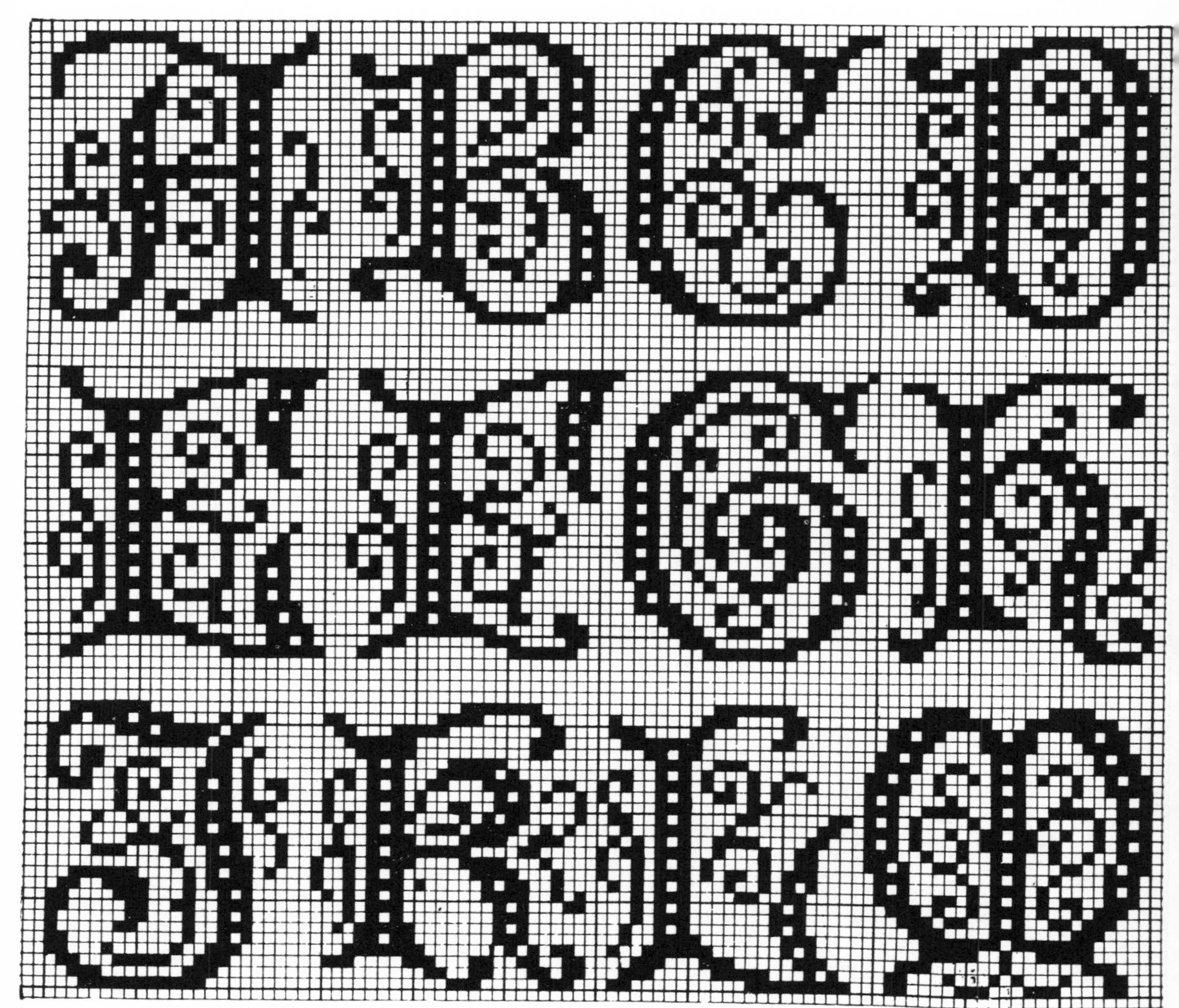

FIG 113. (*Continued on page 45.*)

26 meshes high

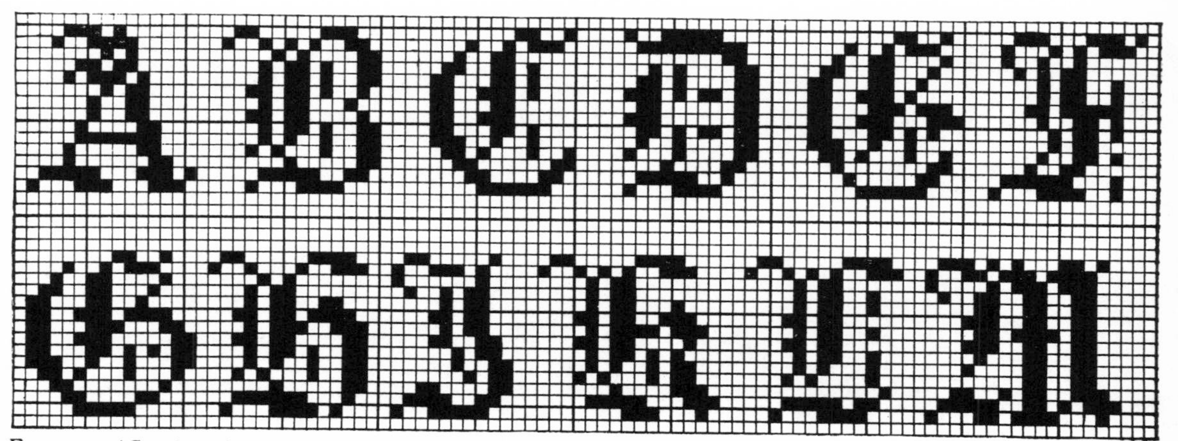

FIG. 114. (*Continued on page 45.*)

14 meshes high

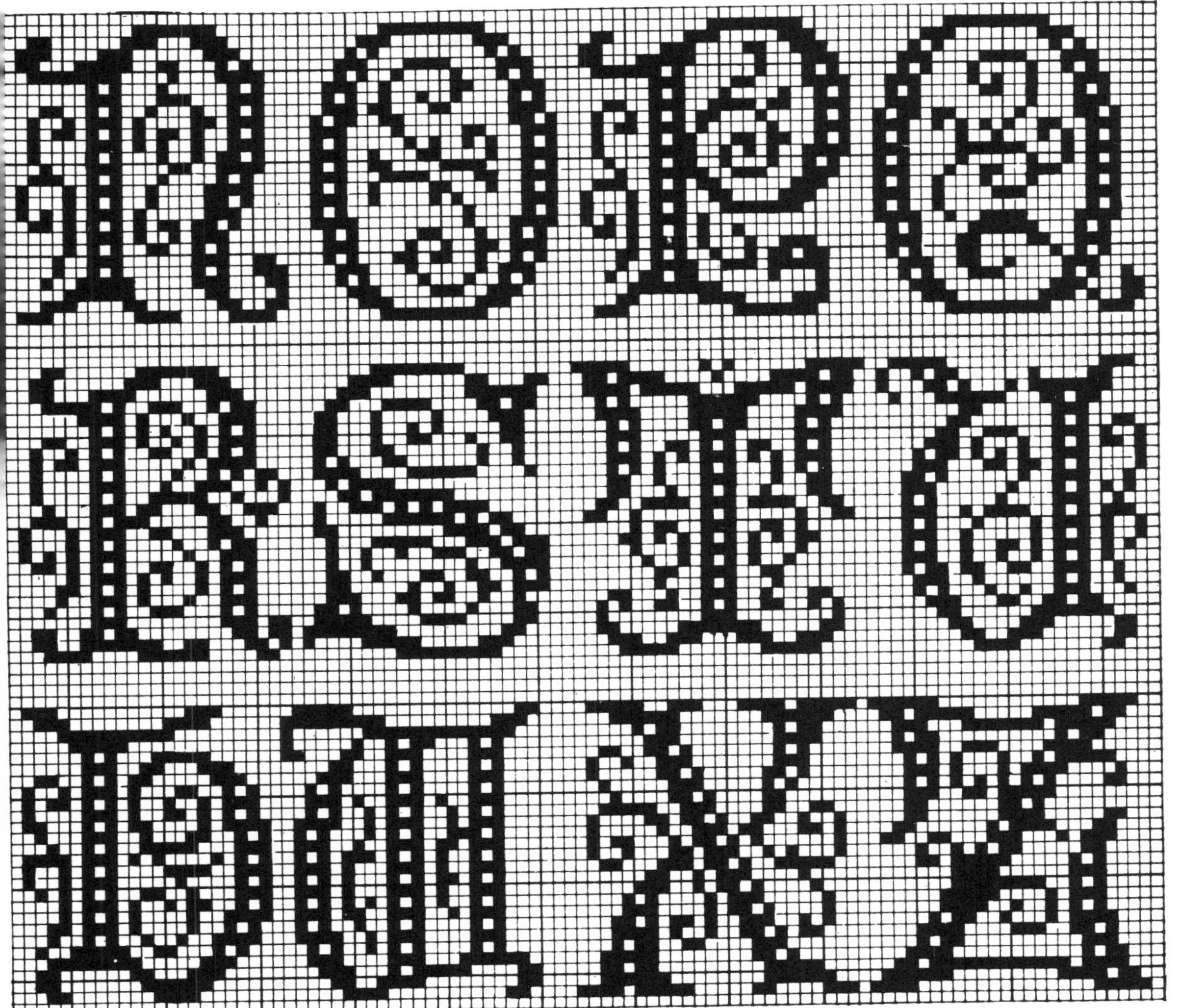

FIG. 113. *(Continued from page 44)* For Y of this alphabet, see page 37, Fig. 93 26 meshes high

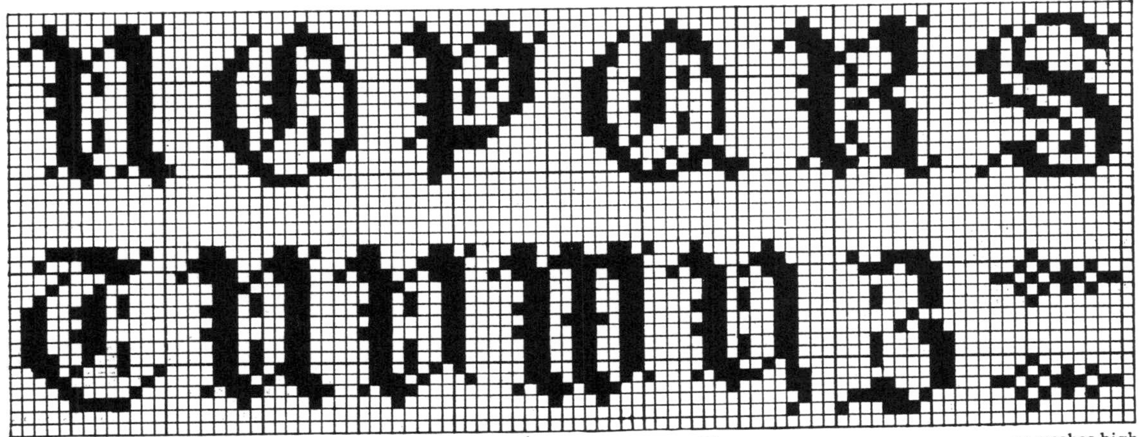

FIG. 114. *(Continued from page 44.)* For X of this alphabet, see page 47, Fig. 123 14 meshes high

FIG. 115 — 29 meshes

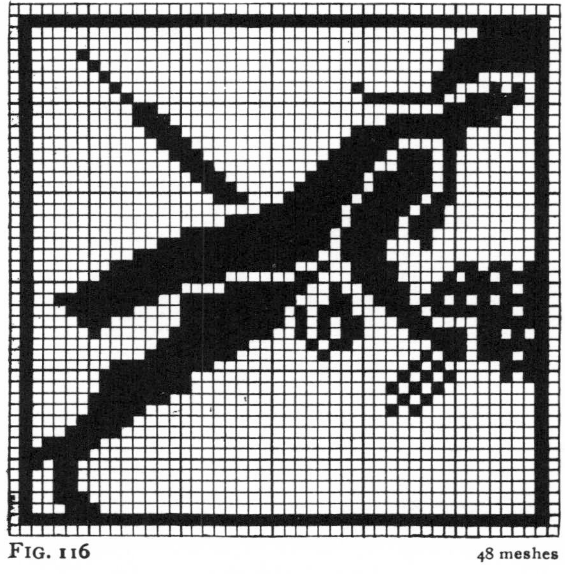

FIG. 116 — 48 meshes

FIG. 117 — 48 meshes

FIG. 118 — 50 meshes

FIG. 119 — 45 meshes

FIG. 120 — 91 meshes

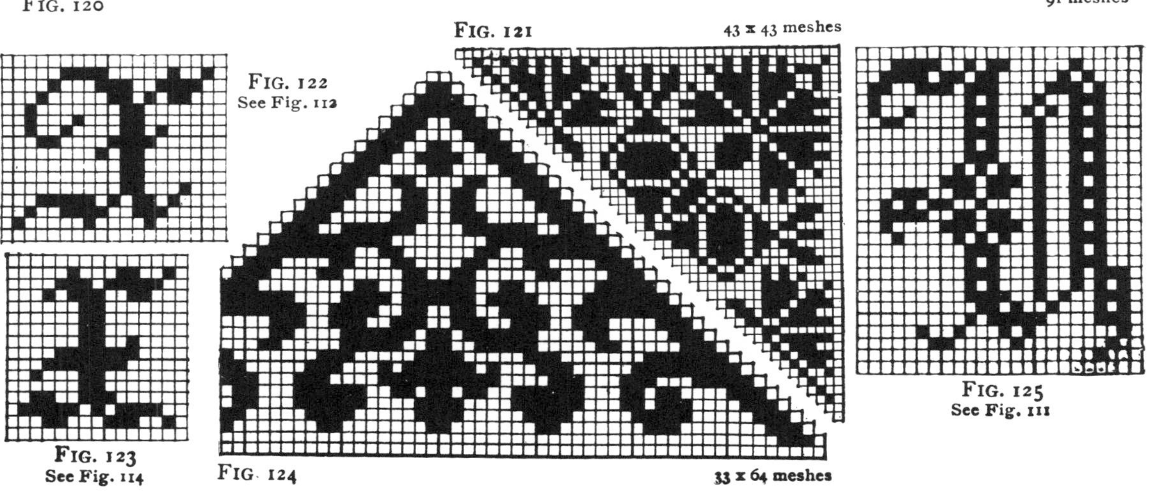

FIG. 121 — 43 x 43 meshes

FIG. 122 — See Fig. 112

FIG. 123 — See Fig. 114

FIG. 124 — 33 x 64 meshes

FIG. 125 — See Fig. 111

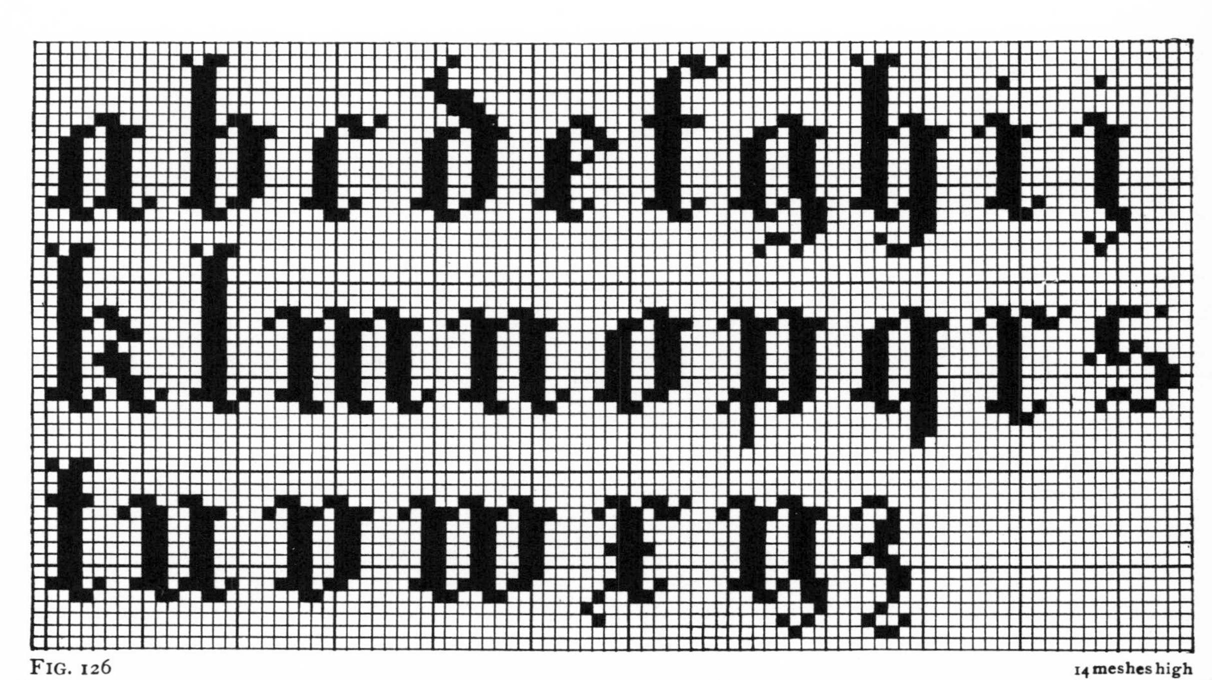

FIG. 126 — 14 meshes high

FIG. 127 — 9 meshes high

FIG. 128 — 7 meshes high

FIG. 129 — 7 meshes

FIG. 130 — 6 meshes high

Filet Crochet from Yesterday

Book 2

FIG. 1. TEA CLOTH IN FANCY FILET CROCHET. (See pages 44 and 45)

FILET CROCHET

MATERIALS. — Where the words "Crochet Cotton" are used in the text of this book, the cotton referred to is the hard-twisted cotton known by such names as Cordonnet, Cordonnet Special, Cordichet, Kord-net, etc., which can be purchased wherever needlework supplies are sold.

The table below should be consulted before beginning work. In this list the size of crochet cotton is given with the size of hook and the number of meshes in an inch of the work. As the size of crochet varies with the worker, the number of spaces given is only approximate.

No. of Cotton	No. of Hook	Meshes to Inch	No. of Cotton	No. of Hook	Meshes to Inch
1	4	3	40	11	7
2	9	4	50	12	7½
3	9	4	60	12	8
5	9	4½	70	14	8½
10	9	5	80	14	8½
20	11	6	100	14	9
30	11	6½	150	14	10

EXPLANATION OF TERMS.—Chain (ch). With a slip knot on the needle, pull a loop through, then a loop through that, etc.

Slip stitch (sl). A loop on the hook, hook through work, pull loop through both.

Single crochet (s c). A loop on the hook, pull loop through work, pull loop through the two loops.

Double crochet (d). A loop on the hook, thread over hook once, pull a loop through work, loop through two loops, loop through remaining two.

Treble crochet (t). A loop on the hook, thread over hook twice, pull a loop through work, crochet off in twos.

Double treble (d t). A loop on the hook, thread over hook three times, pull a loop through work, crochet off in twos.

Space or mesh (s or sp). Chain 2, miss 2 sts of foundation, 1 d in next.

To add meshes at the beginning of a row work the required number of ch, plus 5 for turning, and proceed as usual.

The method of adding open meshes at the end of a row is as follows: Chain 2, a d t, joining where the last d was joined. Each succeeding d t is fastened under 2 threads in the middle of the preceding d t.

Puff stitch (see Figs. 31 and 32). A d in top of d below, 6 d in space below, join top of seventh d to top of second d with a sl st on wrong side of work, a d in top of next d below. Care must be taken to have all puffs on same side of work.

Picot (p). Chain 6, sl in first of chain.

EXPLANATION OF TABLES.—Tabulated directions are used for some of the designs, as they save space, and many workers find them easier to follow than the usual directions.

Each horizontal row of figures stands for one entire row of crochet. Every row is to be read from left to right. When you come to the end of a row of figures, turn your crochet. The letters at the top of each column tell what the numbers in that column represent. "S" means "spaces." "D" means "double crochet." The foundation chain is always three times the number of spaces in the first row, plus six. For example, in the pattern, Fig. 4, the first row has 35 spaces or meshes: therefore, chain 111, turn. The first four rows read as follows:

1st row—Make 1 d in the ninth chain from hook, * ch 2, miss 2 stitches of foundation, 1 d in next. Repeat from * until 35 spaces are made. Chain 5, turn.

2d row—Same as 1st row.

3d row—Two sp, 4 d, 7 sp, 19 d, 10 sp, 4 d, 8 sp, turn.

4th row—Five sp, 4 d, 1 sp, 4 d, 1 sp, 4 d, 1 sp, 4 d, 6 sp, 7 d, 4 sp, 10 d, 2 sp, 13 d, 2 sp.

From this, it will be seen that no attention is paid to blocks (solid mesh), although you can prove up your work in this way. Each single block consists of 4 d. Two or more blocks consist of three times the number of blocks plus 1. Always make 5 chain in turning. This makes the first space. When the row begins with d, use three chain for turning.

REFERENCE LETTERS USED IN TABLES. — Special reference letters are sometimes used in tabulated directions, and their meanings are as follows:

E.—Slip stitch over one space or four d.

W.—Chain 8, turn, 1 d in fourth ch from hook.

X.—Used to fill squares that would otherwise be left blank; the use of the letter prevents confusion.

F.—This means a "festoon" which is made as follows: Chain 3, miss 2 stitches of foundation, s c in next stitch, ch 3, miss 2 stitches of foundation, d in next stitch.

B.—Block. Chain 5, miss 5 stitches of foundation, d in next stitch; blocks are usually combined with festoons.

A neat way of finishing a triangular piece of Filet Crochet is with triangular meshes on the oblique edge. On the end of a row this may be done by joining with a t instead of 2 ch and d. For the beginning of a row, 3 chain are made for turning instead of the ordinary 5 chain. See also the directions for Fig. 55, page 20.

We are aware that some workers in Filet Crochet do not depend on directions, but prefer to follow an illustration of the finished work. It will be found that a number of the designs in this book have been arranged to meet the preference of such workers.

Unless the edge is of d, it is a good plan to reinforce the edge with a row of s c, put [CONCLUDED ON PAGE 40]

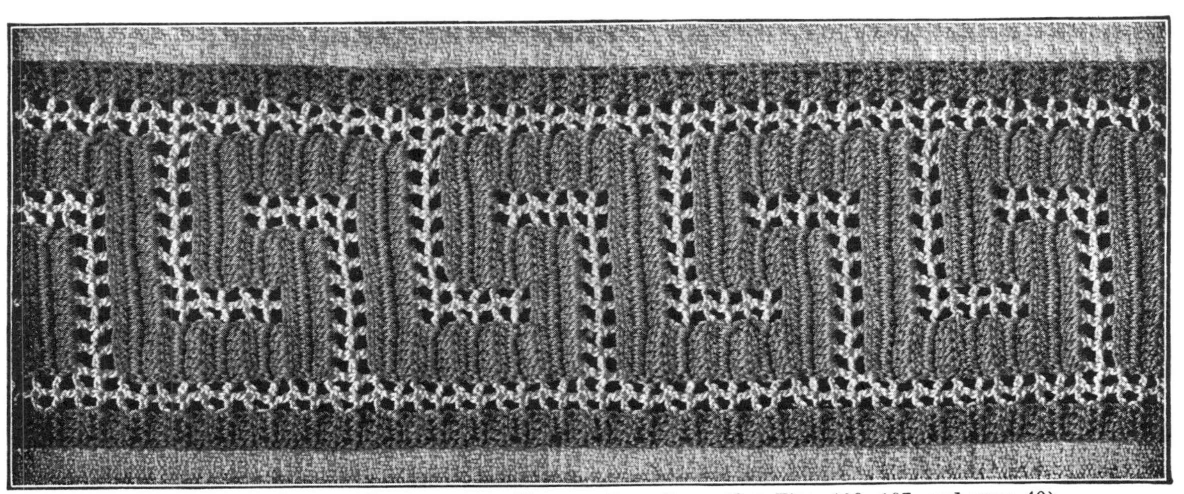

FIG. 2. CAMEO CROCHET INSERTION FOR TOWEL. FULL SIZE. (See Figs. 106, 107, and page 40)

FIG. 3. CENTREPIECE. (See Table, Fig. 4.) 35 meshes

Figure 3. CENTREPIECE. — Use No. 40 linen thread and No. 11 hook. Take a piece of linen 18 inches square and pin on the completed corners. Mark the outline of the crochet with a basting thread, and cut out the corners, allowing ¼ inch for a hem. After the corners are sewn in, work a row of spaces around the piece; finish the edge with a row of single crochet, a picot at every fifth space. These corners may be used for a table-runner or bureau-scarf, by using a strip of linen of the desired length. In a runner, the crochet should be inserted so that the rows of work are parallel to the ends of the piece. Four tassels at each end make a pretty finish for a piece of this description.

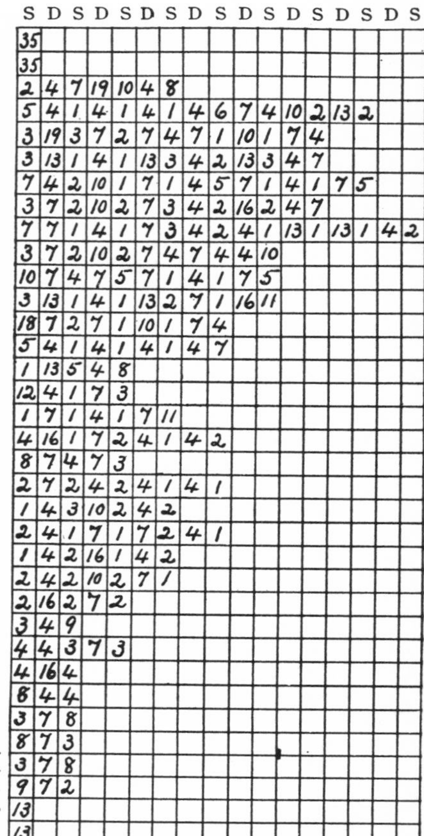

S	D	S	D	S	D	S	D	S	D	S	D	S	D	S	D	S
35																
35																
2	4	7	19	10	4	8										
5	4	1	4	1	4	1	4	6	7	4	10	2	13	2		
3	19	3	7	2	7	4	7	1	10	1	7	4				
3	13	1	4	1	13	3	4	2	13	3	4	7				
7	4	2	10	1	7	1	4	5	7	1	4	1	7	5		
3	7	2	10	2	7	3	4	2	16	2	4	7				
7	7	1	4	1	7	3	4	2	4	1	13	1	13	1	4	2
3	7	2	10	2	7	4	7	4	4	10						
10	7	4	7	5	7	1	4	1	7	5						
3	13	1	4	1	13	2	7	1	16	11						
18	7	2	7	1	10	1	7	4								
5	4	1	4	1	4	1	4	7								
1	13	5	4	8												
12	4	1	7	3												
1	7	1	4	1	7	11										
4	16	1	7	2	4	1	4	2								
8	7	4	7	3												
2	7	2	4	2	4	1	4	1								
1	4	3	10	2	4	2										
2	4	1	7	1	7	2	4	1								
1	4	2	16	1	4	2										
2	4	2	10	2	7	1										
2	16	2	7	2												
3	4	9														
4	4	3	7	3												
4	16	4														
8	4	4														
3	7	8														
8	7	3														
3	7	8														
9	7	2														
13																
13																

FIG. 4. TABULATED DIRECTIONS FOR CENTREPIECE, FIG. 3

FIG. 5. (No. 30 linen thread and No. 11 hook) 157 x 113 meshes

FIG. 6. PILLOW. (See block pattern, pages 6 and 7, Fig. 11)

In this pillow the crochet is done with No. 30 hard-twist crochet cotton and No. 11 hook, and is inserted in a narrow frame of linen. The edge may be finished with bobbin lace or an edging of filet crochet. Attention is called to the two beautiful panels, Fig. 63, "Spring," page 24, and Fig. 69, "Autumn," page 26. These designs would make attractive pillows, and could be made up in the same way as the Peacock design.

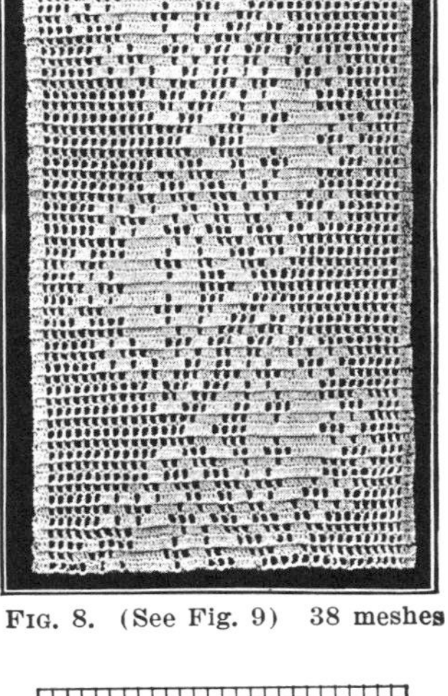

FIG. 8. (See Fig. 9) 38 meshes

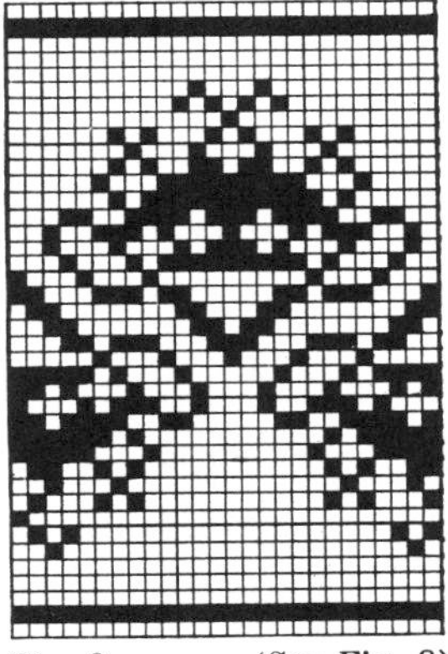

Fig. 9 (See Fig. 8)

FIG. 7. CHURCH LACE 64 meshes

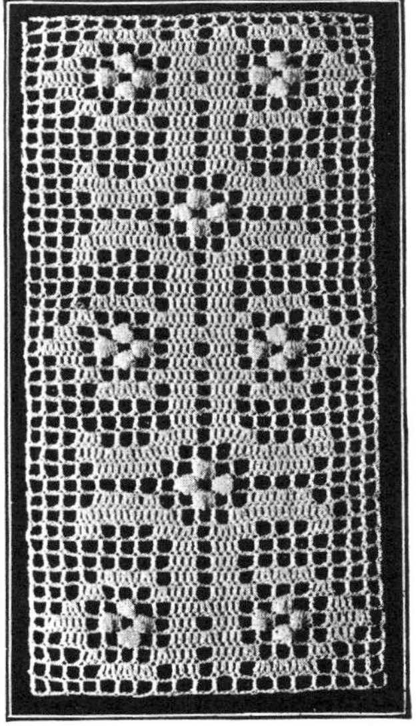

FIG. 10. 19 meshes

FIG. 11. (See Fig. 6)

127 x 178 meshes

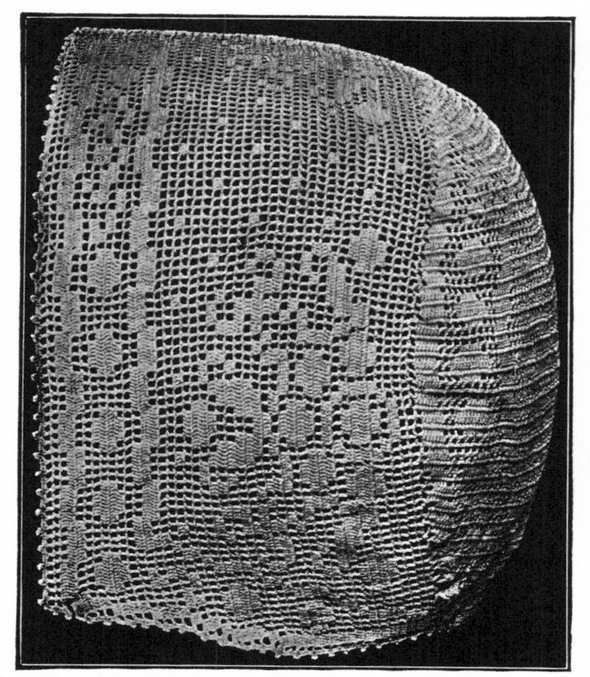

FIG. 12. BABY'S CAP, SIDE VIEW. (See Fig. 15)

FIG. 13. BABY'S CAP, BACK VIEW. (See Fig. 14)

FIG. 14. HALF OF CROWN OF BABY'S CAP. (See Fig. 13.) Commence crown at X; chain 36, double in ninth chain, etc. When B is reached, make the last half like the first half. Materials.—One ball hard-twist crochet cotton No. 150, hook No. 14.

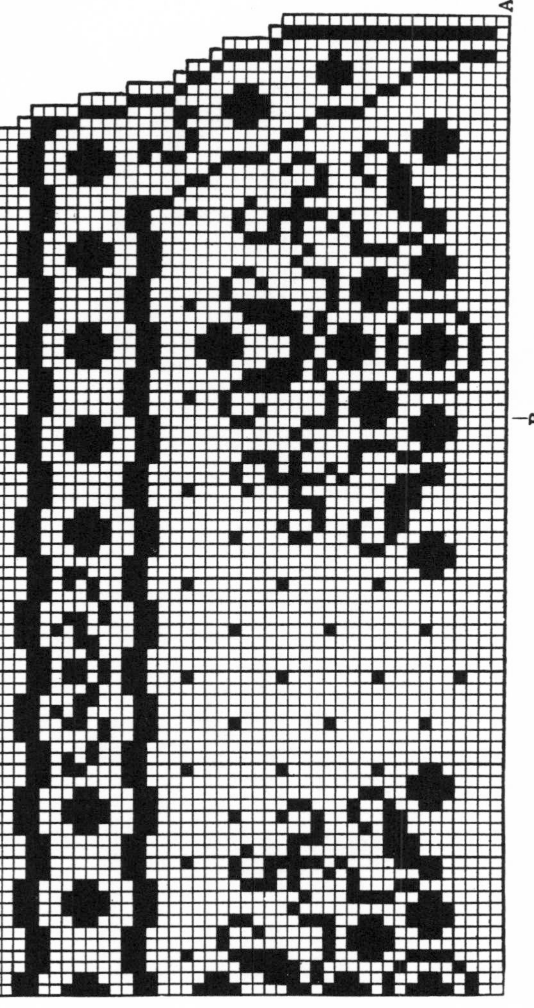

FIG. 15. HALF OF FRONT OF BABY'S CAP. (See Fig. 12.) Start the front at A on the crown.

Figure 16. **CANDLE-SHADE.** — The four block patterns for this shade are given on this page (see Fig. 17). Use No. 60 hard-twist crochet cotton and No. 12 hook. The four sides are sewed together by the slanting edges, leaving all the short sides together at the top, the upper and lower edges are finished with single crochet, having a group of five picots in place of every tenth stitch.

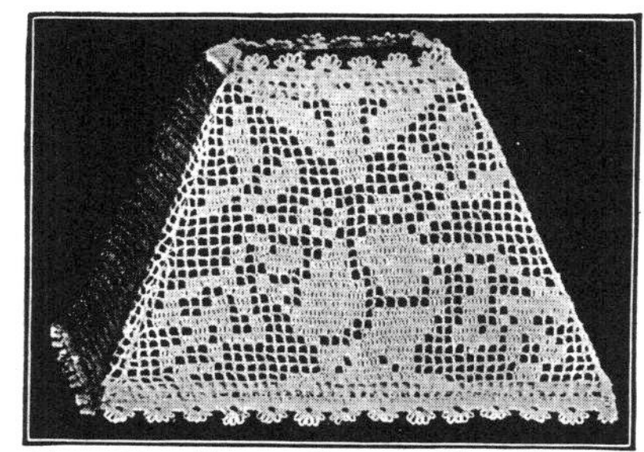

FIG. 16. CANDLE-SHADE (See Fig. 17)

FIG. 18. CENTREPIECE, 28 INCHES SQUARE. (See Figs. 19, 20)
Use No. 70 cotton and No. 14 hook

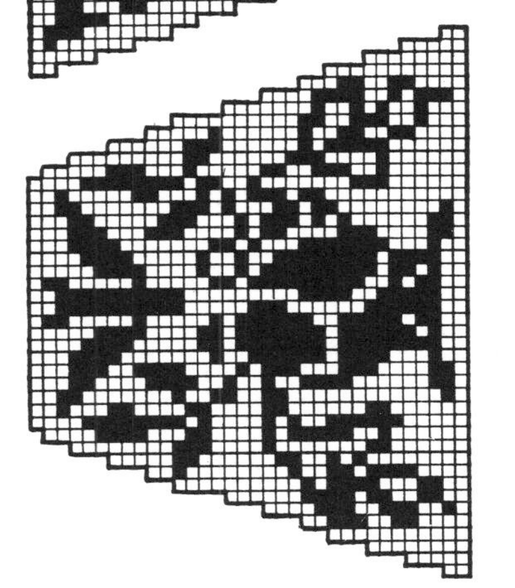

FIG. 17. PATTERNS OF FOUR SIDES OF CANDLE-SHADE. (See Fig. 16)

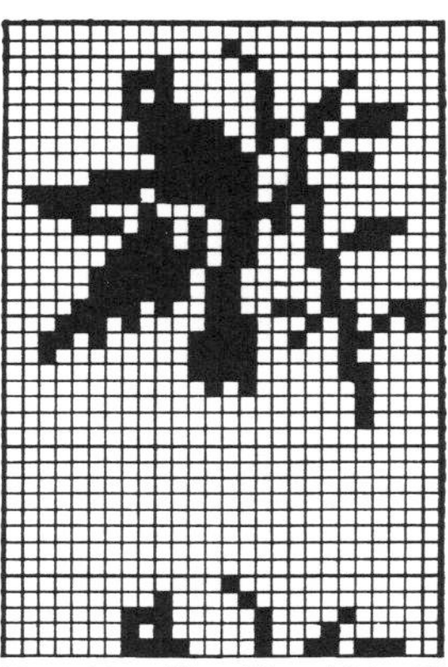

FIG. 19. (See Fig. 18.) 26 meshes. Work 2¾ x 11 inches

FIG. 20. (See Fig. 18.) 43 meshes Work, 4½ inches Square

FIG. 21

Figure 21. **CENTREPIECE. NEZ PERCE DESIGN.** *Materials.*—Two balls hard-twist crochet cotton No. 30; hook No. 11.

For the linen centre, trace a circle on a firm piece of linen, using a ten-inch plate, stitch along the line thus traced with the machine three times, then cut the linen close to the stitching and cover with very close single crochet (s c). Upon this work the pattern.

1st row—Double (d), with 1 chain (ch) between in every stitch (st) around. The model has 277 spaces (sp).

2d row—Double in each d and d in each ch of previous row. *3d row*—Double in every other d of 2d row with 2 ch between d. (These ch must be worked tightly.)

4th to 10th rows—Same as 3d row.

11th row—Widen circle by making 4 sp over the first 3 sp of previous row, then 6 sp over 6 sp; repeat all around.

12th row—Count number of sp in 11th row and divide by 8, to begin design. The number will depend upon the number of s c it took for foundation around edge of linen. The model has 300 sp, divided by 8 equals 37 and 38 sp for each motif, or 2 sp for top of design and 36 and 35 sp, respectively, between motifs. This row reads: 19 sp, 7 d, 36 sp, 7 d, 35 sp, 7 d, 36 sp, 7 d, 35 sp, 7 d, 36 sp, 7 d, 35 sp, 7 d, 36 sp, 7 d, 16 sp.

13th row—Work sp to within 1 sp of motif, then make 13 d (7 d over 7 d and 3 d to right and left of 7 d); repeat around. *14th row*—Work to within 2 sp of motif, then make 25 d; repeat around.

15th row—Work to within 2 sp of motif and make 13 d, 5 sp (d in every other d with 2 ch between, increasing the circle), 13 d, finishing 2 sp to left of motif. Between each motif widen 3 times by placing 3 sp over 2 at beginning and end of motif and midway between.

16th row—Work to within 2 sp of motif and make 16 d, 7 sp, 16 d; repeat around.

34 meshes

17th row—Work to within 2 sp of motif and make 19 d, 9 sp, 19 d; repeat around.

18th row—Work to motif and make 5 sp over 15 d, 4 d, 9 sp, 4 d; repeat around.

19th row—Work to within 1 sp of d of last row and make 10 d, 7 sp, 10 d; repeat around.

20th row—Work to within 2 sp of motif and make 19 d, 5 sp, 19 d; repeat around.

21st row—Work to within 2 sp of motif and make 28 d, 3 sp, 28 d; repeat around.

22d row—Work to motif and 9 sp over 28 d, then 10 d over 3 sp, and 9 sp more over 28 d of last row; repeat around.

23d row—Work to within 1 sp of motif and make 16 d (covering 10 d of 22d row and 1 sp to right and left). Between each motif in this row widen 3 times by placing 4 sp over 3; repeat around.

24th row—Work to within 1 sp of motif and make 22 d; repeat around.

25th row—Work to within 1 sp of motif and make 28 d; repeat around.

26th row—Work sp all around, widen once over each motif and once between.

27th row—Space all around. *28th row*—Space all around.

29th row—Five sp over 5 sp, then 5 d over next sp; repeat around. *30th row*—Same as 29th row.

31st row—Three sp over 3 sp and 11 d over next 2 sp and 5 d of 30th row; repeat around.

32d row—One sp, 18 d (7 over 2 sp and 11 more d, adding 1 d and widening for last time); repeat around.

33d row—Double all around.

34th row—Spaces all around.

SHELL FOR EDGE.—Chain 3, 3 d in same place, fasten with slip stitch to top of next d of last row, ch 3; repeat around.

Figure 22. PILLOW. — Use No. 20 hard-twist crochet cotton and No. 11 hook. Chain (ch) 270, turn.

1st row—Double crochet (d) in 10th from hook, 1 space (sp), (ch 2, miss 2, d in next), 7 d (including d after sp), * 2 sp, 7 d; repeat from * 20 times more (22 blocks of 7 d). Chain 3, turn.

2d row—Miss 1 d, 6 d in next 6, * 2 sp, 7 d; repeat from *, ending row with 2 sp, ch 3, turn.

3d row—Six d, 2 sp, * ch 10, miss 2 sp, 2 sp over next 7 d; repeat from *, having 20 chs of 10, after last 2 sp, make 6 d over 2 sp at end, ch 3, turn.

4th row—Six d, 1 sp, * ch 2, miss 1 of 10 ch, 7 single crochet (s c) in next 7 of ch, ch 2, d in d between next 2 sp; repeat from *, making 7 d at end, ch 5, turn.

5th row—Miss 3 d, d in next, 1 sp, * ch 10, d in next s c, 2 sp over 7 s c; repeat from * with 7 d at end, ch 3, turn. *6th row*—Like 4th row, ending with 2 sp.

Work 2 more rows with clusters of 4 sp, and 1 large sp, alternating. End each row with 7 d.

In *9th row*—After 2d ch of 10 make * 2 sp, 7 d; repeat 14 times, 2 sp, end row as before.

In *10th row*—Work large sp as shown, then 7 d and 2 sp over those of last row, finish with large sp as before.

From this point directions for the border will be omitted and only the design of spaces and double crochet inside of the blocks of border will be given. These will not include any spaces between the blocks of straight edge.

11th row—Fifty-four sp. *12th row*—Fifty-four sp.

13th row—Twenty-three sp, 10 d, 7 sp, 7 d, 5 sp, 16 d, 7 sp.

14th row—Six sp, 4 d, 5 sp, 4 d, 3 sp, 4 d, 2 sp, 4 d, 6 sp, 10 d, 14 sp, 4 d, 3 sp, 4 d, 4 sp.

15th row—Three sp, 10 d, 1 sp, 4 d, 13 sp, 4 d, 2 sp, 4 d, 2 sp, 4 d, 4 sp, 4 d, 3 sp, 4 d, 1 sp, 4 d, 4 sp, 4 d, 2 sp, 4 d, 3 sp.

16th row—Three sp, 4 d, 1 sp, 4 d, 1 sp, 4 d, 4 sp, 7 d, 9 sp, 4 d, 1 sp, 4 d, 1 sp, 4 d, 13 sp, 4 d, 2 sp, 7 d, 4 sp.

17th row—Six sp, 4 d, 2 sp, 4 d, 4 sp, 7 d, 2 sp, 7 d, 2 sp, 4 d, 3 sp, 4 d, 2 sp, 7 d, 5 sp, 4 d, 5 sp, 4 d, 3 sp, 4 d, 1 sp.

18th row—Two sp, 10 d, 3 sp, 13 d, 1 sp, 7 d, 4 sp, 4 d, 1 sp, 4 d, 1 sp, 4 d, 1 sp, 4 d, 1 sp, 4 d, 6 sp, 4 d, 1 sp, 4 d, 1 sp, 4 d, 1 sp, 4 d, 2 sp, 4 d, 4 sp.

19th row—Three sp, 4 d, 1 sp, 4 d, 2 sp, 13 d, 1 sp, 7 d, 8 sp, 10 d, 8 sp, 10 d, 3 sp, 4 d, 5 sp.

20th row—Five sp, 4 d, 4 sp, 10 d, 5 sp, 22 d, 6 sp, 7 d, 1 sp, 19 d, 6 sp.

21st row—Eight sp, 16 d, 2 sp, 4 d, 2 sp, 10 d, 1 sp, 16 d, 1 sp, 10 d, 2 sp, 7 d, 3 sp, 7 d, 4 sp.

22d row—Ten sp, 7 d, 2 sp, 10 d, 1 sp, 10 d, 1 sp, 10 d, 2 sp, 7 d, 1 sp, 22 d, 7 sp.

23d row—Ten sp, 13 d, 1 sp, 7 d, 3 sp, 7 d, 1 sp, 10 d, 1 sp, 7 d, 3 sp, 4 d, 9 sp.

24th row—Ten sp, 4 d, 2 sp, 7 d, 1 sp, 10 d, 1 sp, 7 d, 3 sp, 19 d, 1 sp, 10 d, 7 sp.

25th row—Six sp, 4 d, 1 sp, 10 d, 2 sp, 4 d, 1 sp, 7 d, 3 sp, 7 d, 1 sp, 10 d, 1 sp, 7 d, 2 sp, 4 d, 8 sp.

26th row—Nine sp, 4 d, 1 sp, 7 d, 1 sp, 10 d, 1 sp, 7 d, 1 sp, 7 d, 1 sp, 19 d, 3 sp, 4 d, 6 sp.

27th row—Eleven sp, 13 d, 3 sp, 4 d, 2 sp, 7 d, 1 sp, 4 d, 1 sp, 7 d, 2 sp, 4 d, 7 sp.

28th row—Seven sp, 4 d, 4 sp, 4 d, 1 sp, 4 d, 3 sp, 4 d, 1 sp, 4 d, 1 sp, 4 d, 15 sp.

29th row—Six sp, 4 d, 3 sp, 4 d, 4 sp, 7 d, 1 sp, 4 d, 1 sp, 7 d, 2 sp, 4 d, 4 sp, 4 d, 6 sp.

30th row—Seven sp, 13 d, 1 sp, 7 d, 2 sp, 4 d, 1 sp, 4 d, 5 sp, 7 d, 3 sp, 4 d, 6 sp.

31st row—Seven sp, 4 d, 2 sp, 19 d, 2 sp, 4 d, 1 sp, 4 d, 13 sp.

32d row—Nine sp, 13 d, 2 sp, 4 d, 1 sp, 19 d, 1 sp, 4 d, 4 sp, 4 d, 4 sp. *33d row*—Five sp, 10 d, 1 sp, 7 d, 5 sp, 4 d, 2 sp, 4 d, 1 sp, 4 d, 2 sp, 4 d, 7 sp.

34th row—Seven sp, 4 d, 2 sp, 4 d, 1 sp, 4 d, 1 sp, 4 d, 1 sp, 25 d, 4 sp, 7 d, 2 sp. *35th row*—One sp, 16 d, 1 sp, 31 d, 1 sp, 4 d, 2 sp, 13 d, 5 sp.

36th row—Four sp, 4 d, 5 sp, 4 d, 1 sp, 4 d, 1 sp, 25 d, 4 sp, 7 d, 2 sp. *37th row*—Five sp, 10 d, 1 sp, 7 d, 5 sp, 4 d, 2 sp, 4 d, 8 sp.

38th row—Eight sp, 4 d, 2 sp, 19 d, 1 sp, 4 d, 4 sp, 4 d, 4 sp. *39th row*—Seven sp, 4 d, 2 sp, 19 d, 3 sp, 4 d, 6 sp. *40th row*—Seven sp, 4 d, 6 sp, 7 d, 3 sp, 4 d, 6 sp.

41st row—Six sp, 4 d, 3 sp, 4 d, 4 sp, 10 d, 6 sp.

42d row—Nine sp, 7 d, 13 sp. *43d row*—Three sp, 4 d, 7 sp, 7 d, 9 sp. *44th row*—Ten sp, 10 d, 1 sp, 4 d, 4 sp, 4 d, 2 sp. *45th row*—Two sp, 4 d, 4 sp, 16 d, 8 sp.

46th row—Ten sp, 7 d, 4 sp, 4 d, 3 sp. *47th row*—Four sp, 16 d, 9 sp. *48th row*—Ten sp, 4 d, 1 sp, 4 d, 5 sp.

49th row—Four sp, 4 d, 2 sp, 4 d, 2 sp, 4 d, 5 sp.

50th row—Five sp, 4 d, 2 sp, 4 d, 3 sp, 4 d, 3 sp.

51st row—Two sp, 4 d, 5 sp, 7 d, 4 sp. *52d row*—Eleven sp, 4 d, 2 sp. *53d row*—Two sp, 4 d, 2 sp, 7 d, 5 sp.

54th row—Four sp, 4 d, 2 sp, 4 d, 1 sp, 4 d, 2 sp.

55th row—Two sp, 4 d, 2 sp, 4 d, 1 sp, 4 d, 2 sp.

56th row—Two sp, 4 d, 3 sp, 4 d, 3 sp. *57th row*—Four sp, 10 d, 1 sp. *58th row*—Eight sp. *59th row*—Six sp.

60th row—Six sp. *61st row*—Four sp. *62d row*—Four sp.

Continue the border as shown until it reaches a point, making 7 d in last 2 rows.

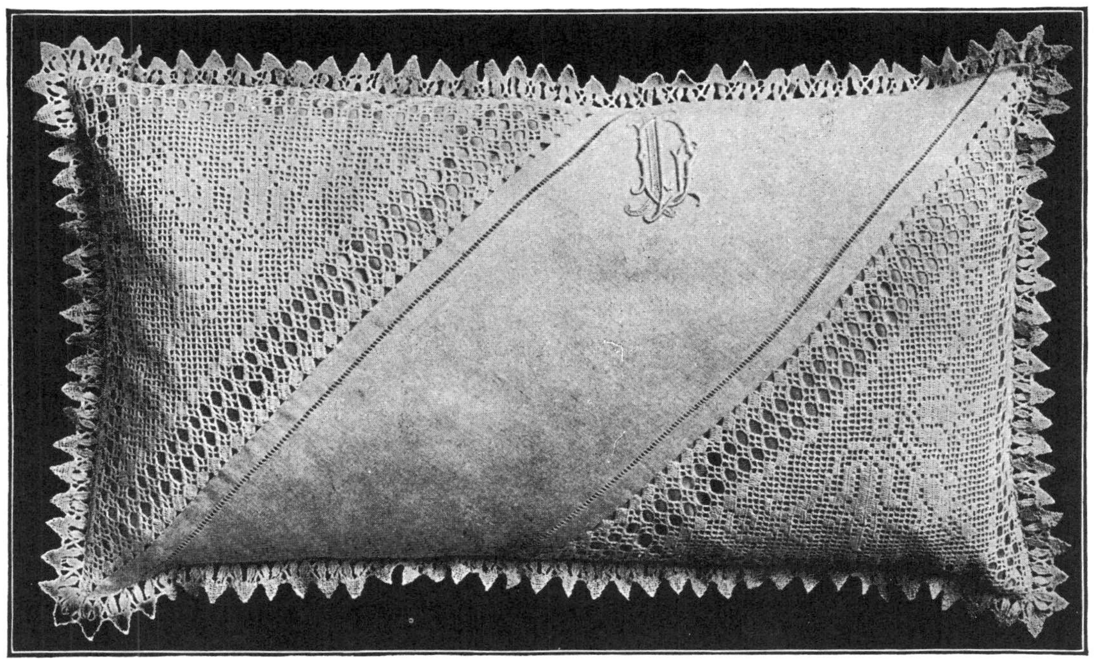

FIG. 22. SOFA PILLOW. (See directions for working on this page)

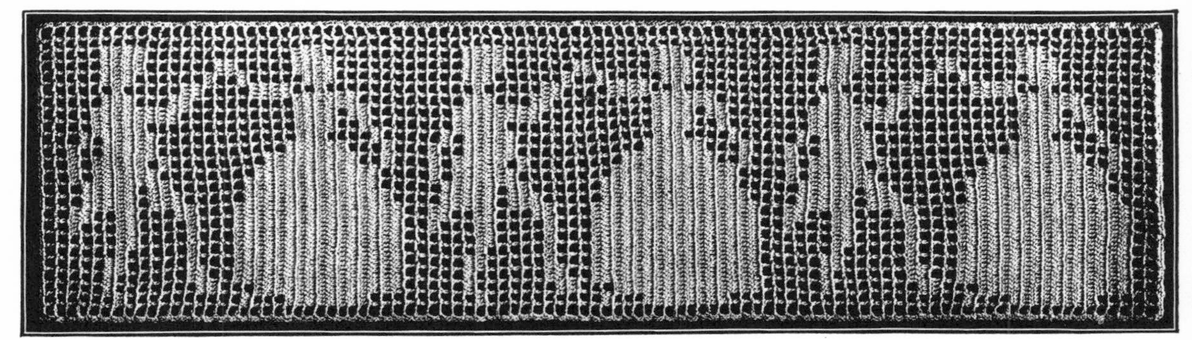

FIG. 23 24 meshes

FIG. 24. TEA CLOTH. (See Directions and Details on page 13)

Figure 24. TEA CLOTH. — Embroidery and crochet are very attractively combined in this handsome cloth. The diagram (Fig. 25) gives the measurements of the cloth, and the crochet can be easily carried out by the aid of the details. The embroidery is worked with cotton in satin-stitch. For the crochet use No. 30 hard-twist crochet cotton and a No. 11 hook.

To crochet the insertion, chain 11. The first row consists of 7 d (see Fig. 26), every other row being widened two meshes at each end. For widening at the beginning of a row, ch 8, turn, allowing 3 ch for 1 d, work 1 d into each of the next 5 ch and the last d of the preceding row, 7 d in all. To add solid meshes at the end of a row, when there is no foundation on which to work, treble are used, the first t being fastened into the same place as the last d in the row, and each succeeding t fastened through two loops at the bottom of the preceding t, 6 t being made in all. The 25th row begins at C (see diagram, Fig. 25) and ends at D. At this point it would be well to compare the crochet with working model (Fig. 26). Complete two sides of the diamond, ending at E. Figure 27 shows the corner. Cut thread, join at F and work the other two sides of the diamond like the first two, ending at G. Join G and E with 11 ch. Cut thread and join two spaces from the end of the line at H. Work the final triangular piece like the first, completing the insertion.

The illustration is a sufficient guide for working the edging, but the beginner will need directions for the corner. It will prevent confusion if the crochet is begun with the first row of this detail (Fig. 29) and the corner made first.

The pattern begins with the row marked A in Fig. 28, and it will help to compare the crochet with working model, Fig. 29, as the work proceeds.

1st row—Chain 60, turn, 2 spaces (sp), 16 d, 4 sp, 10 d, 2 sp, 7 d.

2d row—Slip stitch back over 4 d of the seven in last row, 7 d, 7 sp, 4 d, 7 sp.

3d row—Six sp, 4 d, 1 sp, 16 d, 2 sp, 7 d.

4th row—Slip stitch back over 4 d, 7 d, 2 sp, 10 d, 2 sp, 4 d, 5 sp.

5th row—Five sp, 4 d, 4 sp, 7 d, 2 sp, 7 d, ch 5.

6th row—Seven d, 2 sp, 4 d, 4 sp, 4 d, 4 sp.

7th row—Three sp, 4 d, 1 sp, 4 d. 6 sp, 7 d, ch 5.

8th row—Seven d, 4 sp, 7 d, 1 sp, 4 d, 1 sp, 4 d, 1 sp.

9th row—Four d, 3 sp, 13 d, 3 sp, 7 d.

10th row—Seven d, 2 sp, 4 d, 1 sp, 10 d, 2 sp.

11th row—Three sp, 4 d, 2 sp, 4 d, 2 sp, 7 d.

12th row—Slip stitch back over 4 d, 7 d, 1 sp, 10 d, 2 sp.

13th row—Six sp, 7 d. *14th row*—Seven d, 3 sp.

15th row—Three sp, 7 d. *16th row*—Slip stitch back over 4 d, 4 d, 1 sp.

17th row—Seven d. *18th row*—Slip stitch back over the 7 d just made, ch 5, 7 d (these are made at right angles to those made so far, the last three are fastened in the side of the row of 7 d instead of along the top). Fasten a d in the side of the step forming a space, ch 2, fasten a d in the corner of the step. This forms the first space on the next row.

19th row—Seven d, ch 5. *20th row*—Seven d, 3 sp, ch 2, fasten to middle of step, slip stitch up to corner.

21st row—Nine d, 1 sp, 7 d, ch 5.

22d row—Seven d, 2 sp, 4 d, 2 sp, 4 d, ch 2, fasten to middle of step, slip stitch up to corner.

23d row—Nine d, 1 sp, 4 d, 2 sp, 7 d.

24th row—Seven d, 3 sp, 13 d, 1 sp, a d in middle of next step, ch 2, a d in corner.

25th row—Four d, 1 sp, 7 d, 4 sp, 7 d.

26th row—Slip stitch back over 4 d, 7 d, 7 sp, 4 d, 1 sp, a d in middle of next step, ch 2, a d in corner.

27th row—Four d, 1 sp, 16 d, 2 sp, 7 d.

28th row—Slip stitch back over 4 d, 7 d, 2 sp, 10 d, 2 sp, 4 d, 2 sp, a d in middle of next step, ch 2, a d in corner.

29th row—Two sp, 4 d, 4 sp, 7 d, 1 sp, 7 d, ch 5.

30th row—Seven d, 2 sp, 4 d, 5 sp, 4 d, 4 sp, ch 2, fasten to corner, sl forward one space. *31st row*—Seven sp, 4 d, 7 sp, 7 d, ch 5. *32d row*—Seven d, 6 sp, 7 d, 8 sp. From here work by the illustration, Fig. 24.

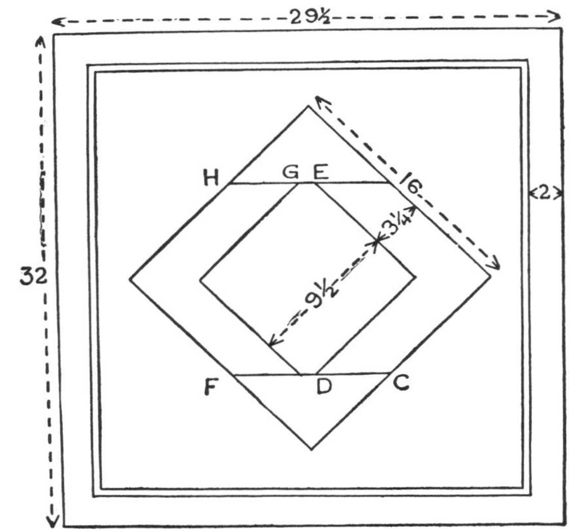

Fig. 25. Diagram of Tea Cloth on Page 12

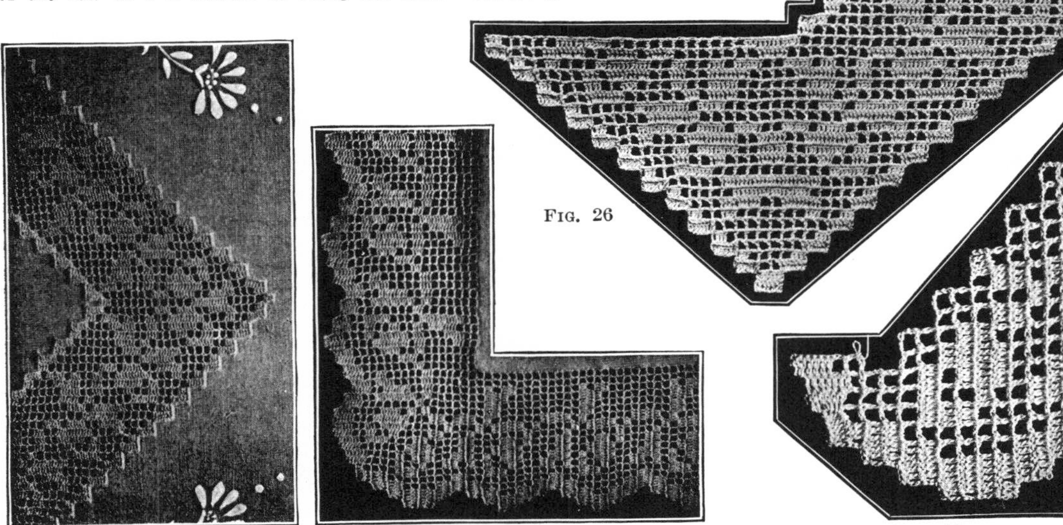

Fig. 26

Fig. 27

Fig. 28

A

Fig. 29

Fig. 30 33 meshes

Fig. 31. (See Puff Stitch, page 3) 15 meshes

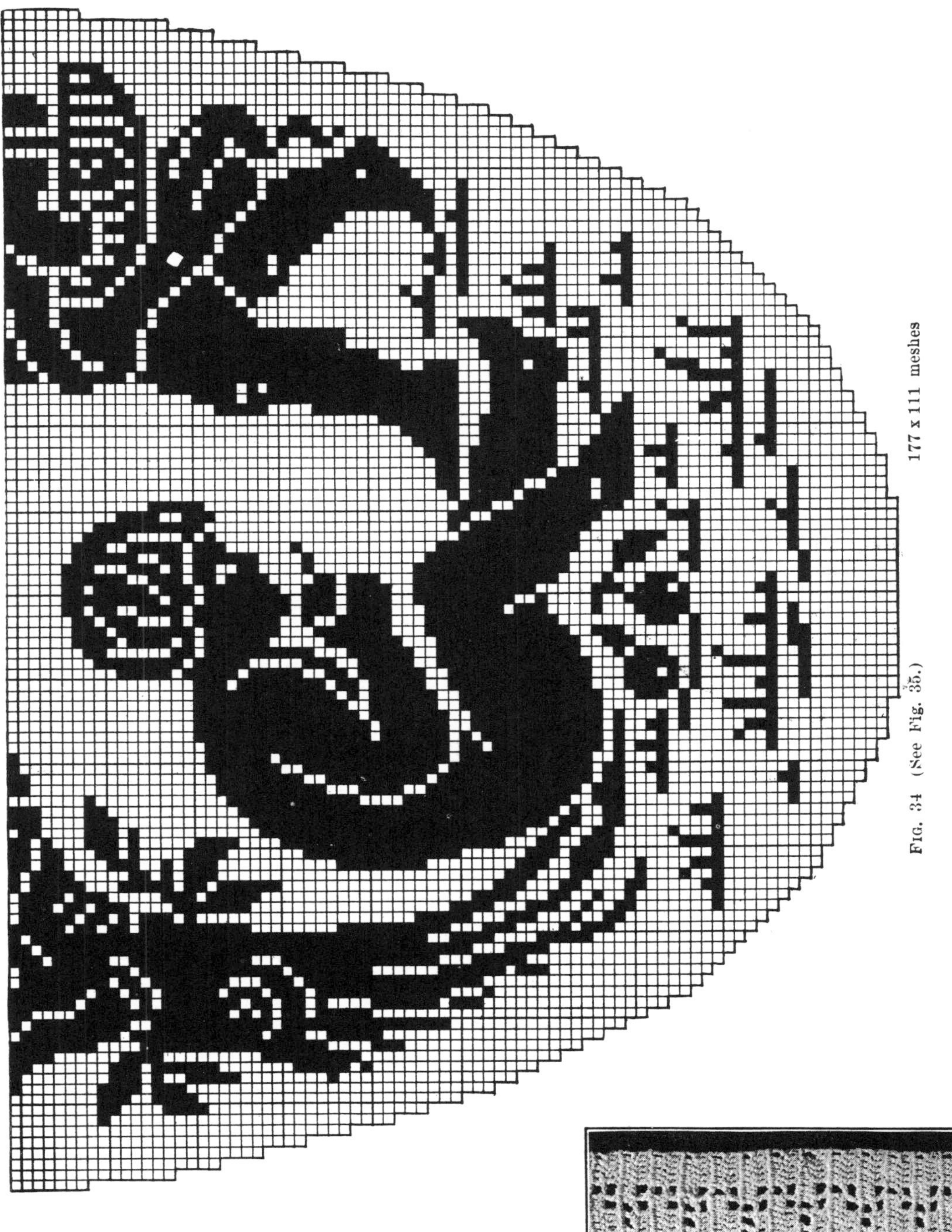

Fig. 34 (See Fig. 35.) 177 x 111 meshes

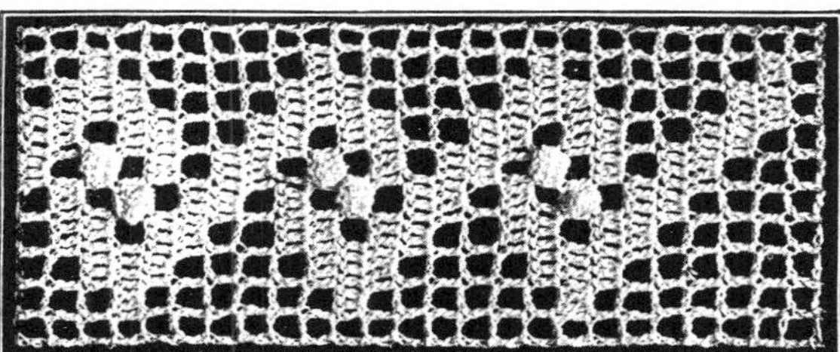

Fig. 32. (See directions for Puff Stitch on page 3.) 10 meshes

Fig. 33 18 meshes

FIG. 35. (See Fig. 34)

TRAY. — The crochet model was done with No. 100 crochet cotton and No. 14 hook. The work measures 10 x 15 inches.

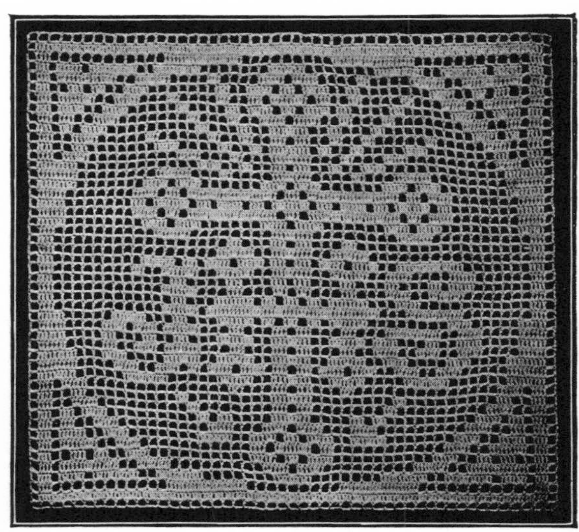

FIG. 36 49 meshes

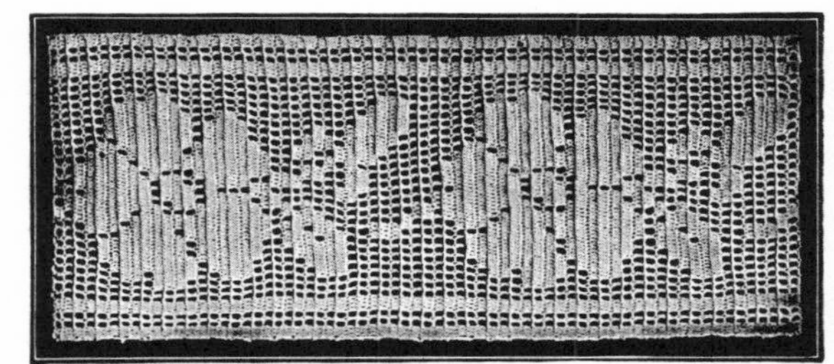

FIG. 37. (See Fig. 40)

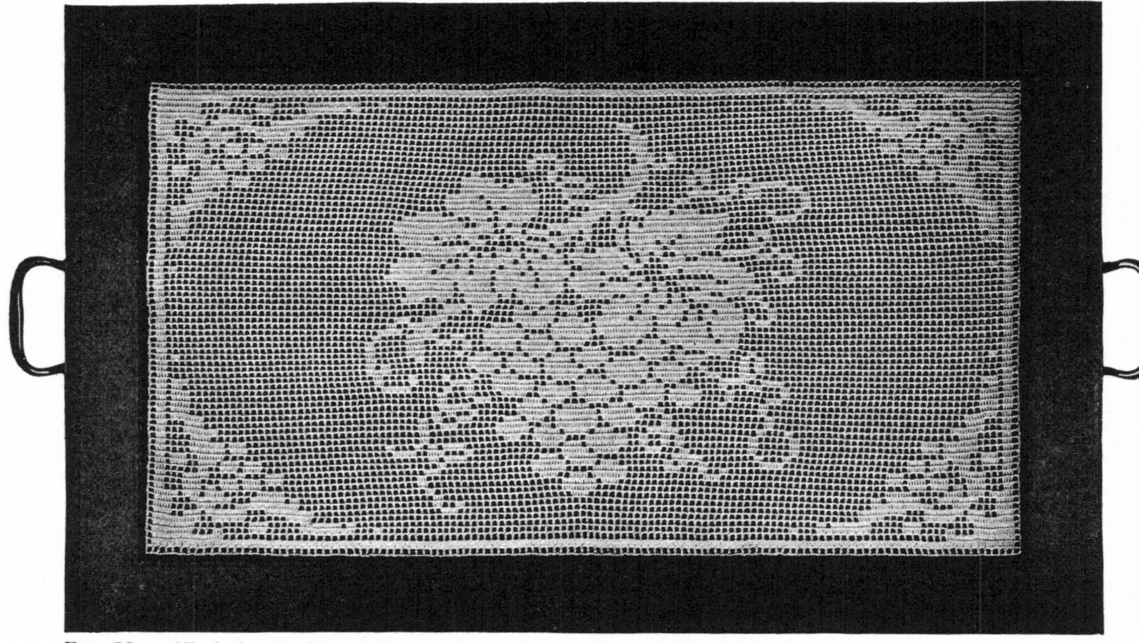

FIG. 38. (Worked with No. 70 hard-twist crochet cotton and No. 14 hook) 129 x 77 meshes

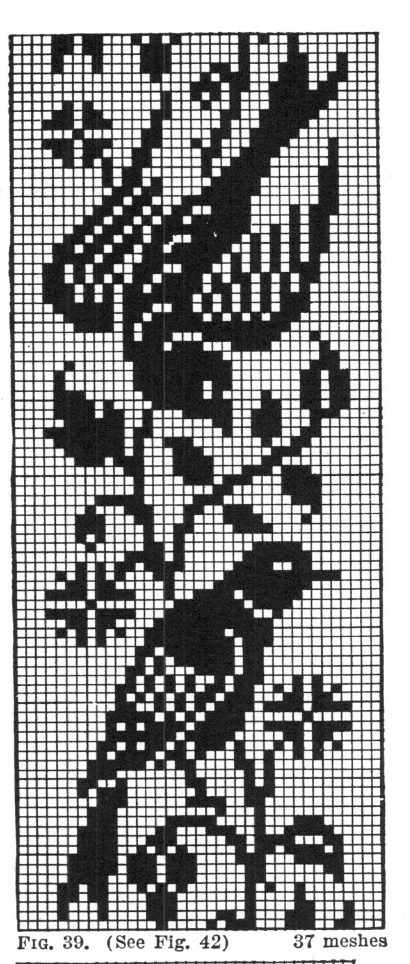

Fig. 39. (See Fig. 42) 37 meshes

Fig. 42. (See Fig. 39)

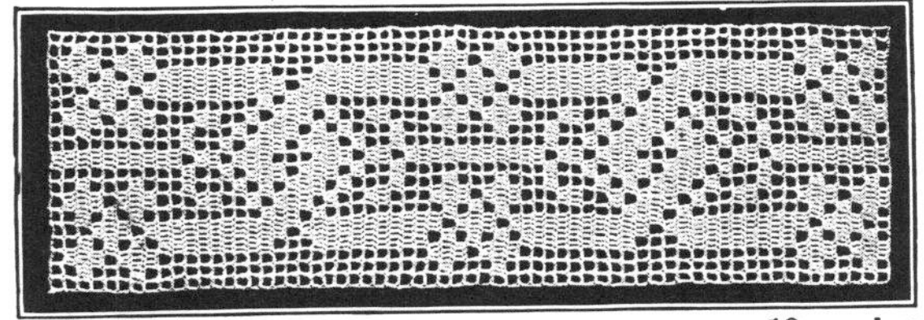

Fig. 43. 19 meshes

Fig. 40. (See Fig. 37) 32 meshes

Fig. 44. (Model worked with No. 50 hard-twist crochet cotton and No. 12 hook) 85 meshes

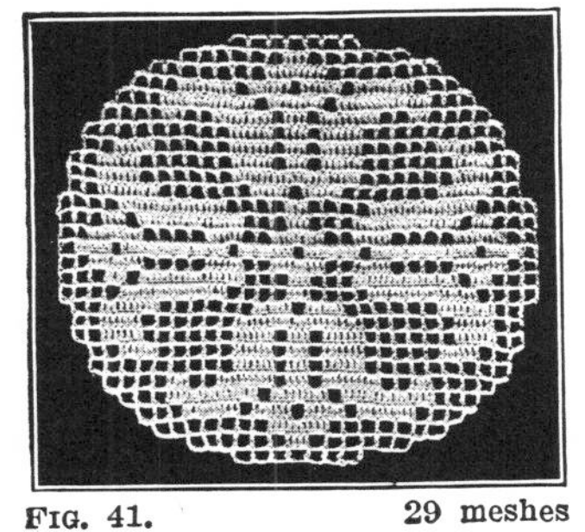

Fig. 41. 29 meshes

Figure 48. LAMP-SHADE.—This shade is made of linen, with eyelet embroidery and inserts of filet crochet. The patterns of the three medallions and six triangles are given (see Figs. 49 and 51), and the crochet was done with No. 60 hard-twist crochet cotton and No. 12 hook. The shade is 39 inches around and 7¾ inches high, and is trimmed with bobbin lace, tassels, and crochet pendants. The lining is of colored silk. A perforated pattern of the embroidery, also the stamped linen, can be supplied by the publishers.

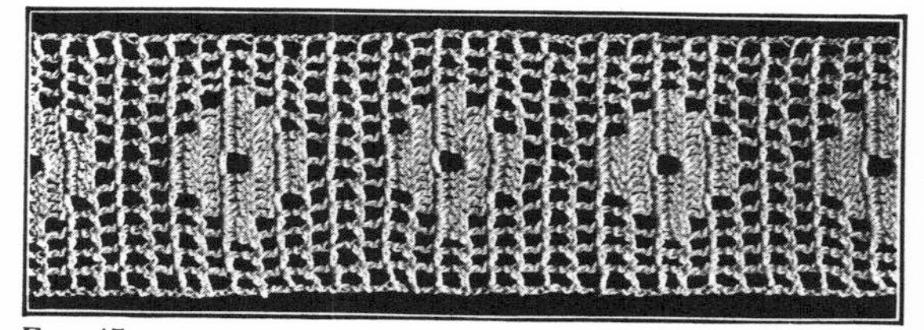

FIG. 45 12 meshes

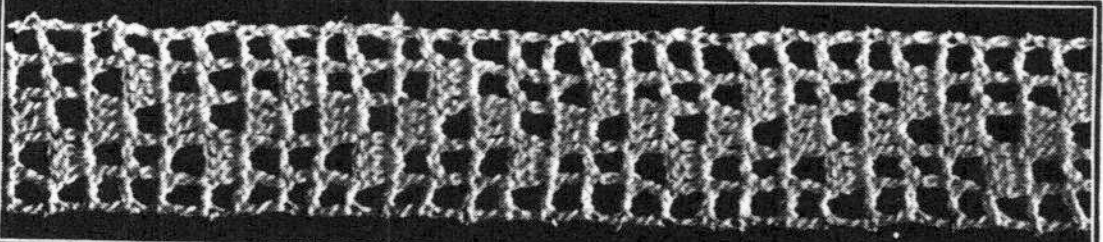

FIG. 46 5 meshes

FIG. 48. LAMP-SHADE. (See Figs. 49, 51)

FIG. 47 40 meshes

FIG. 49. (See Fig. 48) 62 meshes

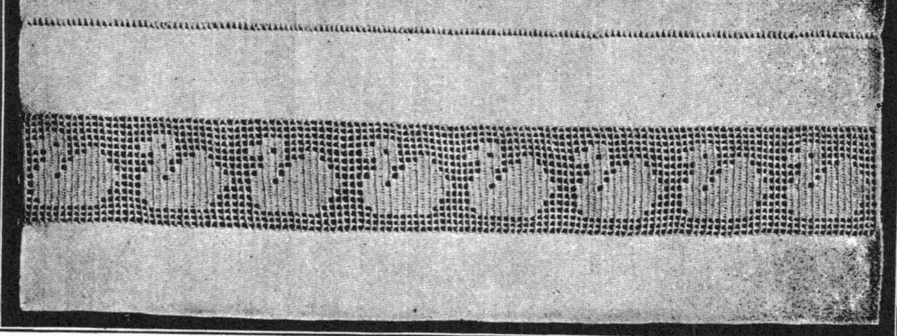

FIG. 50. (No. 60 cotton, No. 12 hook) 15 meshes

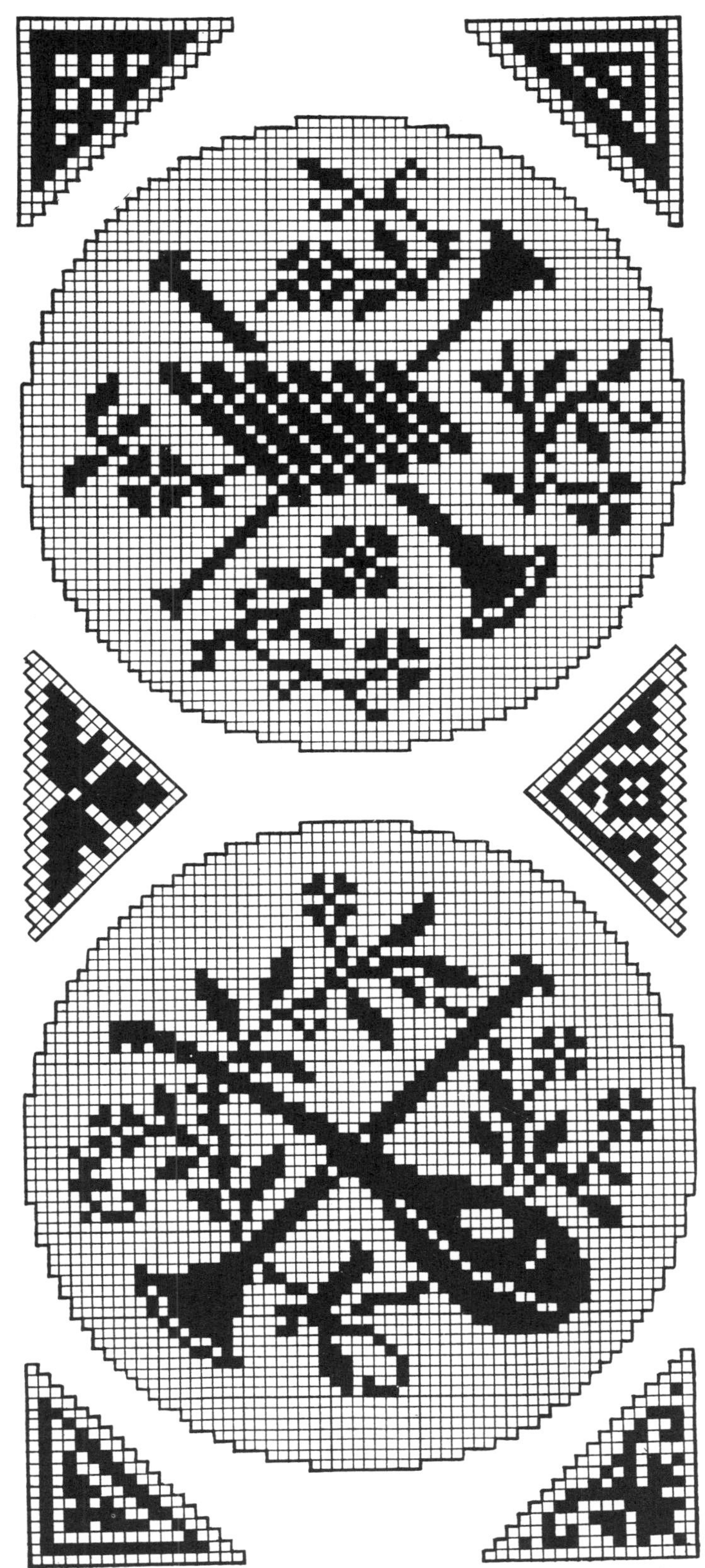

Fig. 51. Eight Block Patterns for Lamp-Shade. (See **Fig. 48**)

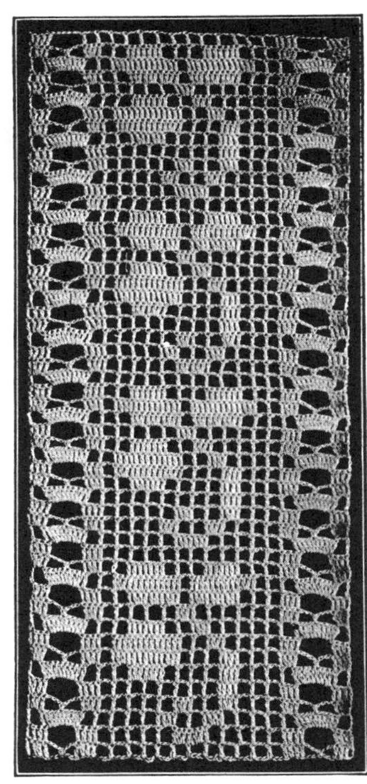

Fig. 52. (See Fig. 53) 20 meshes

S	D	S	D	S	D	S	D	S	D	S	D
X	4	F	4	12	4	F	4				
X	4	B	4	5	7	5	4	B	4		
1	10	5	4	2	4	5	10	1			
X	4	F	4	3	4	2	4	5	4	F	4
X	4	B	4	8	4	3	4	B	4		
1	10	4	4	4	7	3	10	1			
X	4	F	4	1	13	3	4	3	4	F	4
X	4	B	4	4	4	2	13	1	4	B	4
1	10	3	7	2	4	6	10	1			
X	4	F	4	6	4	5	4	F	4		
X	4	B	4	2	10	1	10	3	4	B	4
1	10	3	13	1	13	2	10	1			
X	4	F	4	2	7	3	7	3	4	F	4

Fig. 53. (See Fig. 52)

The groups of 10 d at the edges of this strip are all fastened into the block, where it is usual to fasten only seven.

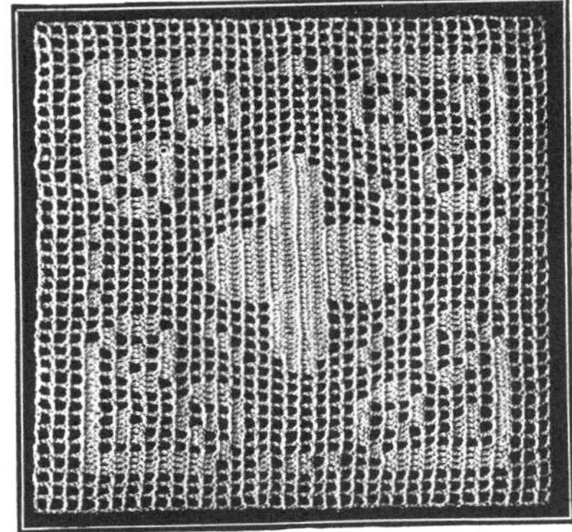

Fig. 54 36 meshes

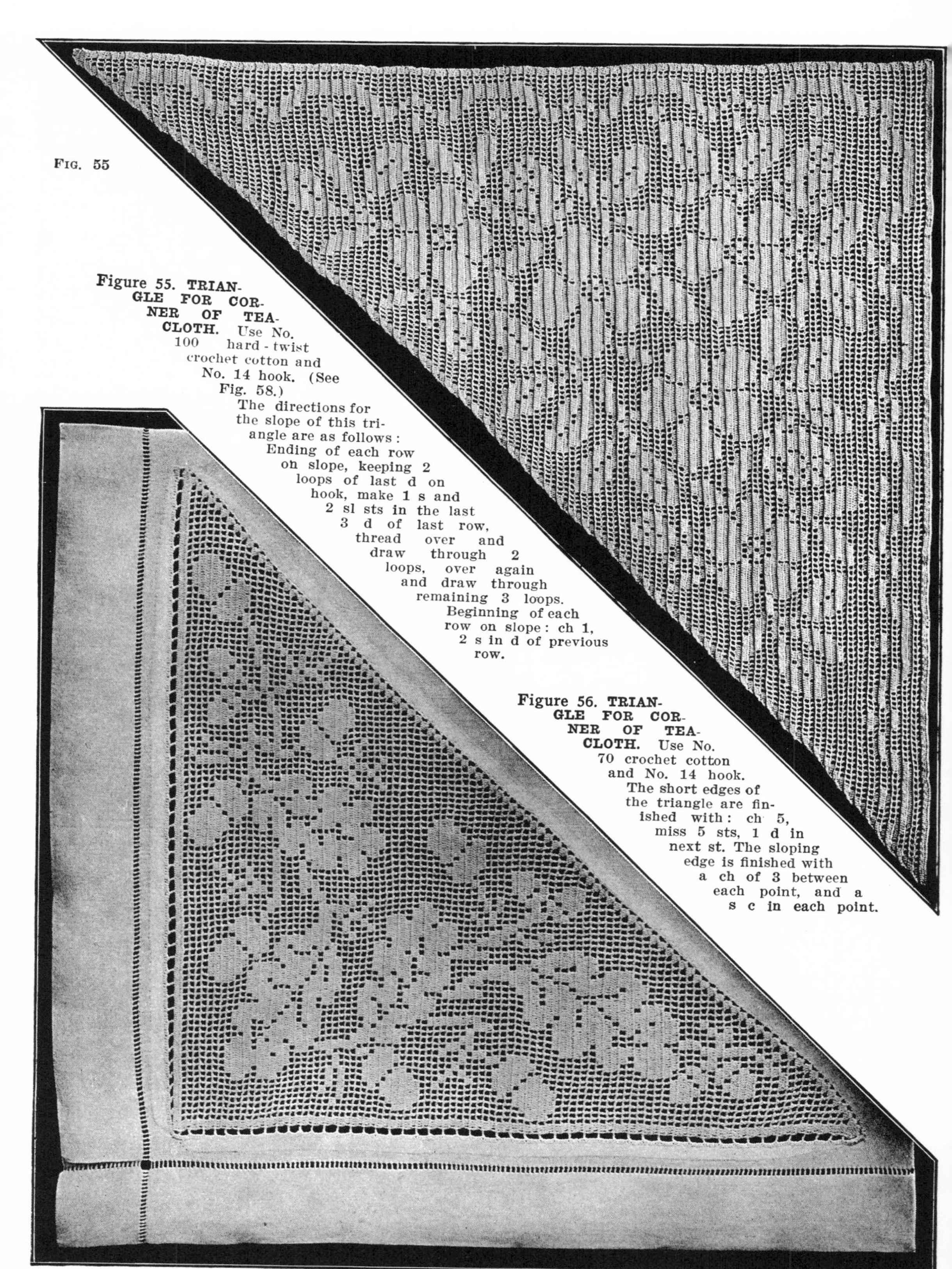

FIG. 55

Figure 55. TRIANGLE FOR CORNER OF TEA-CLOTH. Use No. 100 hard-twist crochet cotton and No. 14 hook. (See Fig. 58.)

The directions for the slope of this triangle are as follows: Ending of each row on slope, keeping 2 loops of last d on hook, make 1 s and 2 sl sts in the last 3 d of last row, thread over and draw through 2 loops, over again and draw through remaining 3 loops. Beginning of each row on slope: ch 1, 2 s in d of previous row.

Figure 56. TRIANGLE FOR CORNER OF TEA-CLOTH. Use No. 70 crochet cotton and No. 14 hook. The short edges of the triangle are finished with: ch 5, miss 5 sts, 1 d in next st. The sloping edge is finished with a ch of 3 between each point, and a s c in each point.

FIG. 56. (See directions above)

100 meshes

As Filet Crochet is very similar to Darned Netting most of the designs in the Priscilla Netting Book may be used for crochet. The patterns are arranged in block and space effects similar to Figure 58. Any one desiring a larger range of designs than are given in this book should have the Filet Crochet Book, No. 1, and the Netting Book also.

Fig. 57 — 87 meshes

Fig. 58. (See Fig. 55) — 138 meshes

Figure 60. TABLE-CLOTH.—This heavy white linen cloth has an insertion of filet crochet worked with No. 100 hard-twist crochet cotton and a No. 14 hook. The edge is hemstitched and the insertion is put in with rolled hems. After the crochet is finished shrink it thoroughly. Then the linen, also thoroughly shrunk, is to be cut and fitted to the crochet.

To work the insertion, Fig. 62, make 1149 chain. Refer to the diagram, Fig. 60, and begin at A. Work 41 rows, ending at B. Turn, and work 299 short rows, according to Fig. 62, ending at E. Cut thread and fasten at F. Work the third side of the insertion like the second, ending at K. From here, a chain of 902 is made and its end fastened at E. The thread is again cut and joined at L. The last side is then worked like the first, according to Fig. 62.

Figure 59. IMITATION HEMSTITCH IN CROCHET FOR TOWELS, ETC.—This pretty crochet will be found very attractive for the opposite end of a towel decorated with filet crochet.

Make a ch of the required length ; turn and work singles into each stitch of chain, cut thread and fasten into other end of work ; ch 4, 2 t (holding last st of each t on needle, making 3 st in all) ; draw thread through all and fasten snugly with ch st. * Chain 2, 3 t, holding last st of each on needle (making 4 in all) ; draw thread through all and fasten snugly with ch st. * Repeat between * for length of work. Cut thread, and beginning at other end of work make 3 singles in each open space. When sewing the crochet into the towel the open edge should always be sewed in first, otherwise the work will not be even. The model was done with No. 70 crochet cotton and a No. 14 hook.

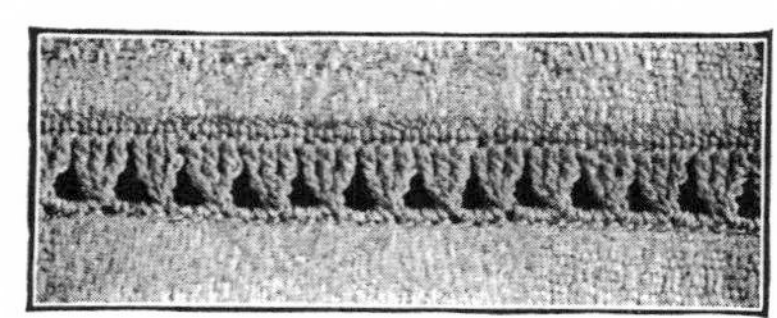

Fig. 59. Crochet Hemstitch

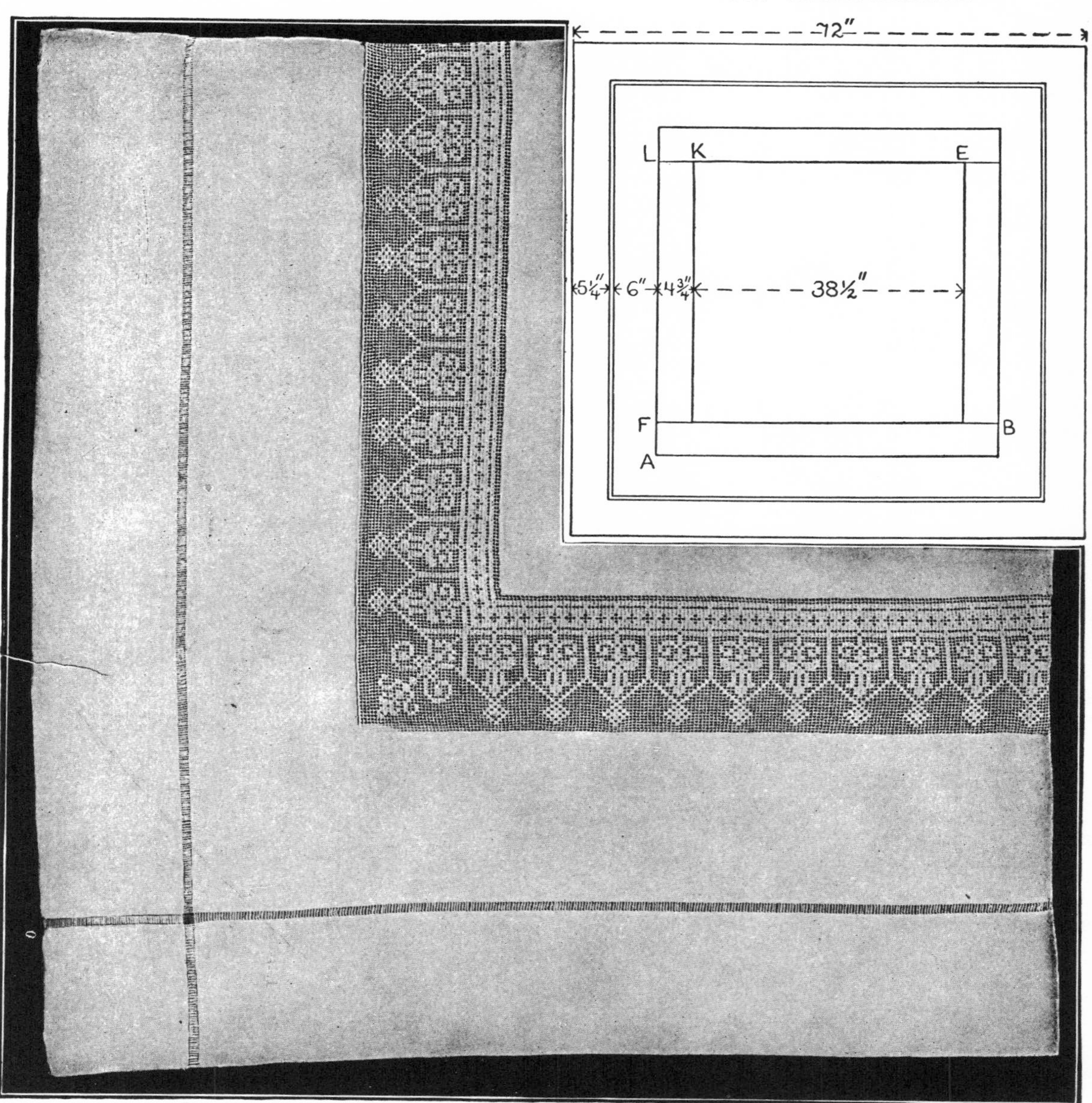

Fig. 60. Corner of Table-Cloth and Diagram for Working. (See Fig. 62)

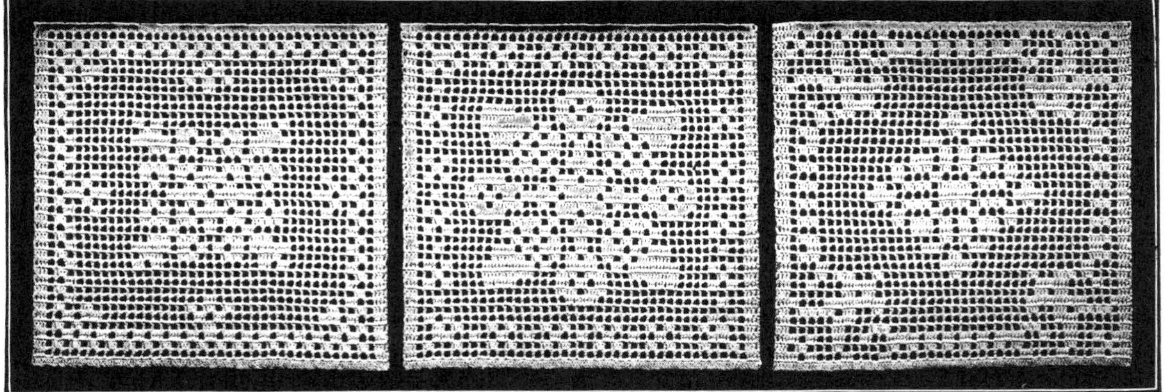

Fig. 61 39 meshes

Squares in filet crochet like those shown in Fig. 61 have many and varied uses. They may be finished with a picot edge and used as doilies, and four or nine squares joined make a nice centrepiece.

They may be used together for an all-lace bedspread or joined with alternate squares of plain or embroidered linen. The linen could be French-hemmed or hemstitched, and a touch of color added in simple outline embroidery or cross-stitch. Crochet squares are lovely inserted in the ends of towels, when made small, in the corners of table-covers, or used as borders of insertion around square cloths. Besides these designs many other patterns suitable for both filet crochet and cross-stitch are given in the Priscilla Filet Crochet Book No. 1, and many of the block patterns in the Priscilla Netting Book are also suitable for the purpose.

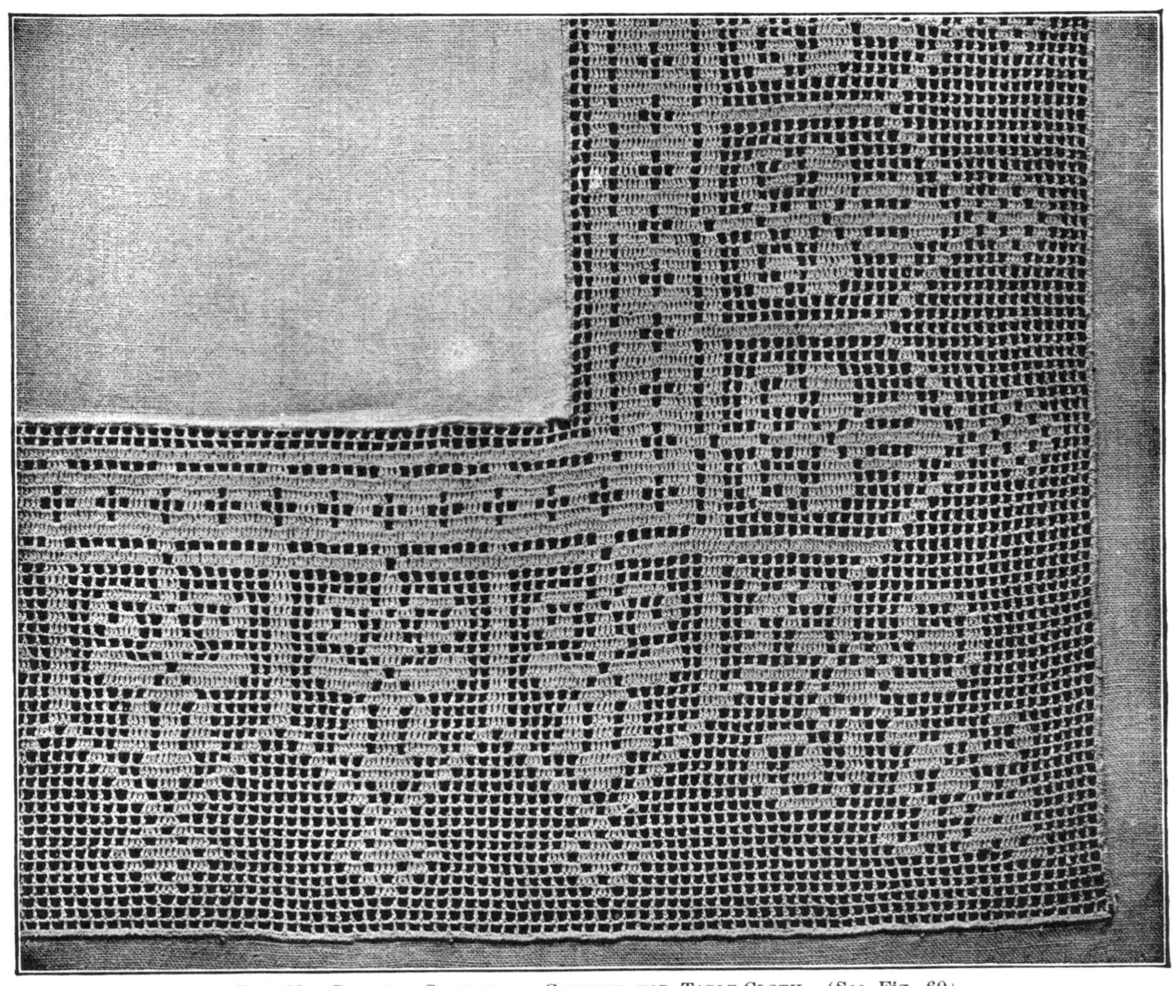

Fig. 62. Reduced Section of Crochet for Table-Cloth. (See Fig. 60)

Fig. 63. (See Fig. 68)
The model was worked with No. 70 hard-twist cotton and No. 14 hook

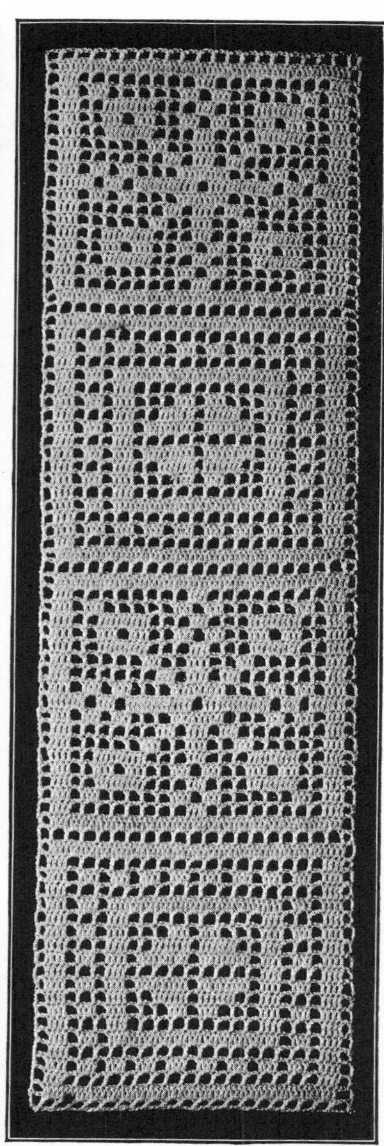

Fig. 66 21 meshes

A bedspread made of strips of crochet like Fig. 66 and plain linen is very attractive; and the lily edging and insertion used in the same way work up into an exquisite spread.

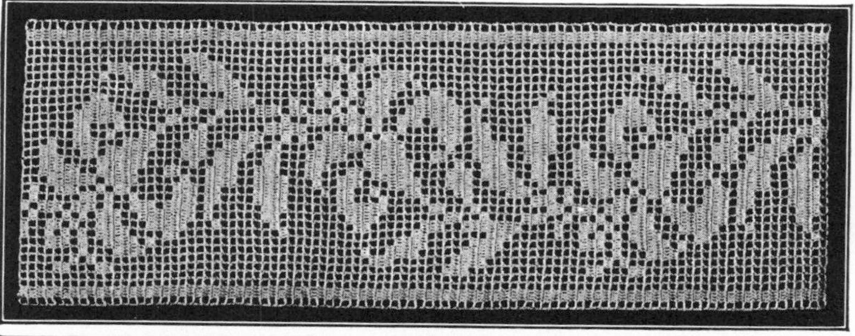

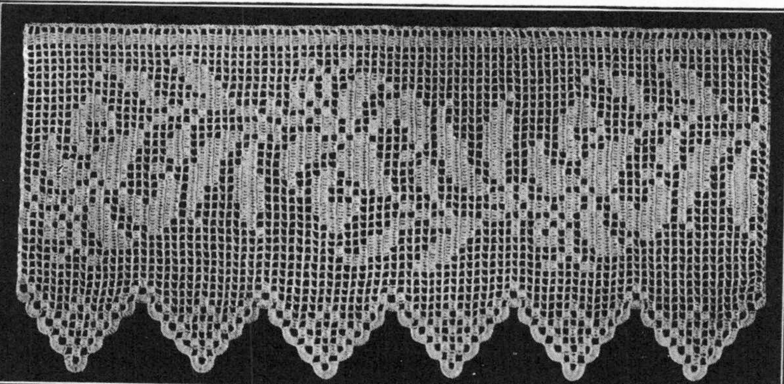

Figs. 64, 65. Edging and Insertion 33 meshes

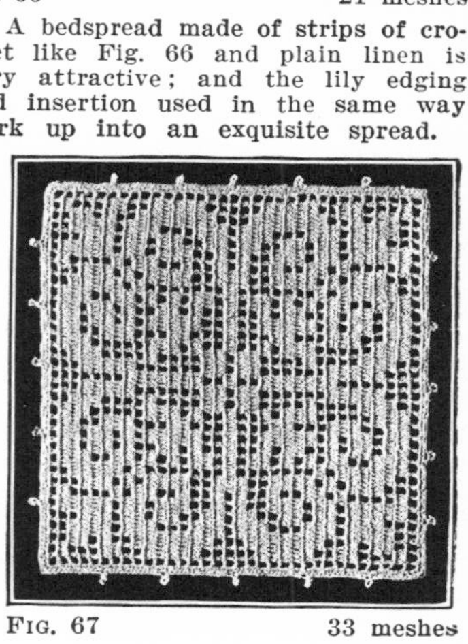

Fig. 67 33 meshes

Fig. 68. (See Fig. 63) Spring 91 x 127 meshes

The panel above and the one called "Autumn," on page 27, are both suitable for pillow-tops, chair-backs, door-panels, and bedspreads. For a pillow, insert the crocheted panel in linen, which may be either plain or embroidered, and finish the edges with a filet crochet edging or Cluny lace. The size of the panel when finished will be governed by the thread used. (See page 3 for the number of meshes to an inch in threads of different sizes.) When the panels are made for chair-covers a nice finish for the edges is a row of plain double crochet with picots, or a simple picot edging.

FIG. 69. (See Fig. 75.) The model was worked with No. 70 hard-twist cotton and No. 14 hook

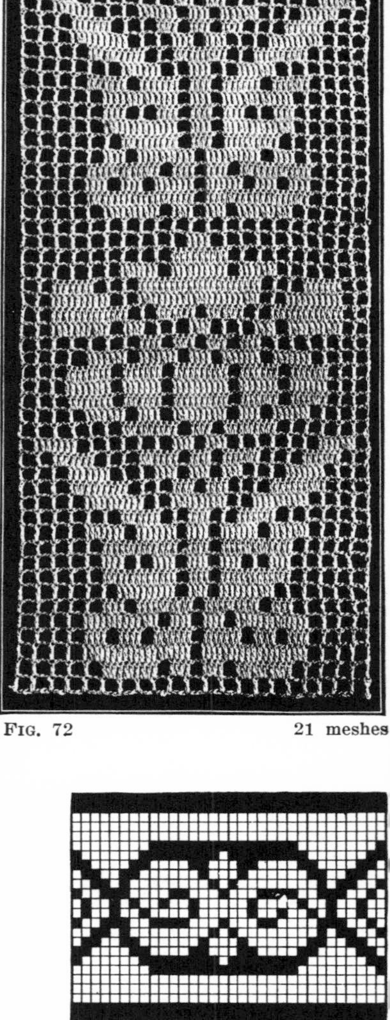

FIG. 72 21 meshes

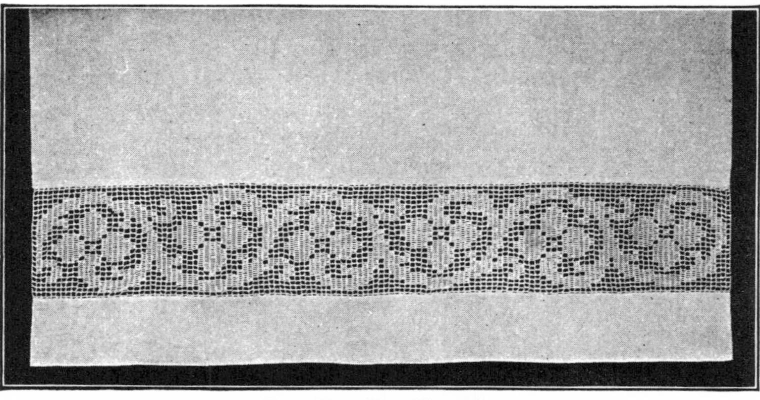

FIG. 70. (See Fig. 71)

FIG. 73. (See Fig. 74) 24 meshes

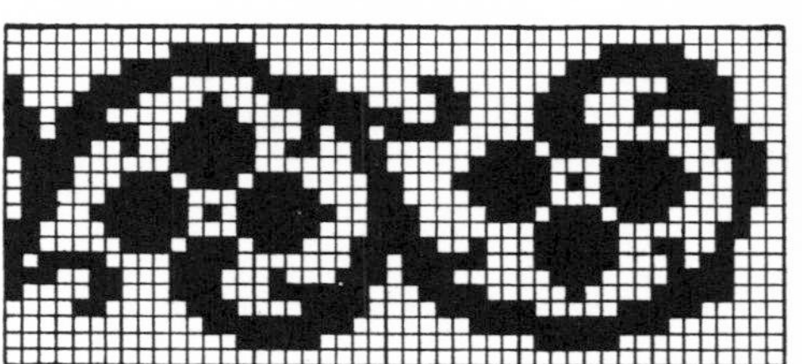

FIG. 71. (See Fig. 70) 21 meshes

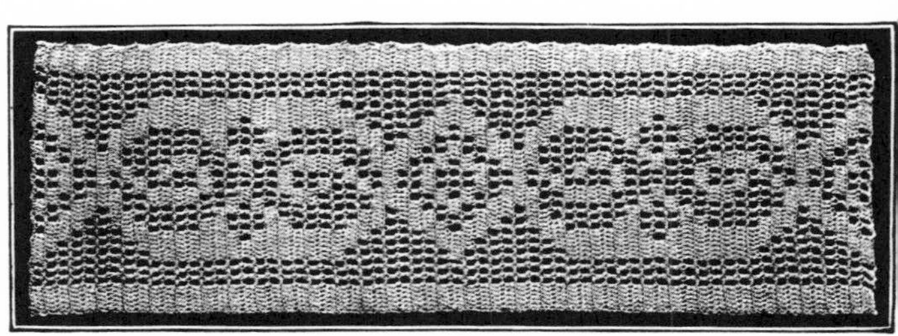

FIG. 74. (See Fig. 73)

FIG. 75. (See Fig. 69) AUTUMN 91 x 127 meshes

This panel and "Spring," shown on page 25, are very attractive used on bedspreads, inset in the linen and bordered by a filet insertion of the proper width. Another pretty arrangement for a spread is to use either panel in the centre, four crocheted squares in the corners, and on the sides, between the corners, the motto, "Early to Bed," etc., in Cameo crochet, which is given in the Priscilla Bedspread Book with full directions for working. This insertion could also be done in ordinary filet crochet or cross-stitch, as preferred. The two designs could be adapted for door-panels.

FIG. 76. (See Fig. 77 and directions for Edging)

Figure 76. EDGING FOR SCARF.—Chain (ch) 72.

1st row—Double crochet (d) in 9th ch from hook and make 21 more spaces (sp) (2 ch, d in 3d ch), 4 d in last 4 ch; turn.

2d row—Chain 11, 1 d into each of 9th, 10th, and 11th ch from hook and 1 d into next d, ch 2, 4 d in sp after 4 d of 1st row, 21 sp; turn.

3d row—Chain 5, 1 d in 1st d (for 1 sp), 19 more sp, 4 d, ch 5, 1 treble (t) over 2 ch between two groups of d, ch 5, 4 d into loop at end of row; turn.

4th row—Chain 11, 1 d into each of the 9th, 10th, and 11th ch from hook and 1 d into next d, ch 5, 3 s c over t of last row, using 1 ch at each side of t, ch 5, 4 d, 19 sp; turn.

5th row—Chain 5, 1 d in 1st d (this will hereafter be included in the number of sp beginning the row), 3 more sp, 4 d, 13 sp, 4 d, ch 5, 5 s c over 3 s c of last row, using 1 ch at each side, ch 5, 4 d into loop; turn.

6th row—Chain 11, 1 d into 9th, 10th, and 11th ch and 1 d into next d, ch 2, 4 d over 5 ch, ch 5, 3 s c over 5 s c, ch 5, 4 d over 5 ch, 13 sp, 4 d, 5 sp; turn.

7th row—Five sp, 4 d, 6 sp, 7 d, 6 sp, 4 d over 5 ch, ch 4, 1 t in 3 s c, ch 4, 4 d over 5 ch, ch 5, 1 t over 2 ch, ch 5, 4 d in loop; turn.

8th row—Chain 11, 1 d in 9th, 10th, and 11th ch, 1 d in d, ch 5, 3 s c, ch 5, 4 d over 4 ch, ch 2, 4 d over 4 ch, 4 sp, 4 d, 1 sp, 13 d, 4 sp, 4 d, 6 sp; turn.

9th row—Six sp, 4 d, 3 sp, 25 d, 4 sp, 4 d, ch 5, 5 s c, ch 5, 4 d in loop; turn.

10th row—Chain 11, 1 d in 9th, 10th, and 11th ch, 1 d in d, ch 2, 4 d over 5 ch, ch 5, 3 s c, ch 5, 4 d, 5 sp, 13 d, 1 sp, 13 d, 2 sp, 4 d, 6 sp; turn.

11th row—Seven sp, 13 d, 2 sp, 13 d, 3 sp, 10 d, 1 sp, 4 d, ch 4, 1 t in s c, ch 4, 4 d over 5 ch, ch 5, 1 t over 2 ch, ch 5, 4 d in loop; turn.

12th row—Chain 11, 1 d in 9th, 10th, and 11th ch, 1 d in d, ch 5, 3 s c, ch 5, 4 d, ch 2, 4 d, 3 sp, 13 d, 3 sp, 10 d, 3 sp, 4 d, 1 sp, 10 d, 4 sp; turn.

13th row—Three sp, 25 d, 1 sp, 16 d, 1 sp, 16 d, 3 sp, 4 d, ch 5, 5 s c, ch 5, 4 d in loop; turn.

14th row—Chain 11, 1 d in 9th, 10th, and 11th ch, 1 d in d, ch 2, 4 d over 5 ch, ch 5, 3 s c, ch 5, 4 d, 2 sp, 37 d, 1 sp, 4 d, 1 sp, 16 d, 5 sp; turn.

15th row—Four sp, 13 d, 2 sp, 7 d, 2 sp, 13 d, 1 sp, 22 d, 2 sp, 4 d, ch 4, 1 t over s c, ch 4, 4 d over 5 ch, ch 5, 1 t over 2 ch, ch 5, 4 d in loop; turn.

16th row—Chain 11, 1 d in 9th, 10th, and 11th ch, 1 d in d, ch 5, 3 s c over t, ch 5, 4 d over 4 ch, ch 2, 4 d over 4 ch, 4 sp, 22 d, 5 sp, 16 d, 2 sp, 10 d, 3 sp; turn.

17th row—Three sp, 31 d, 1 sp, 19 d, 3 sp, 13 d, 3 sp, 4 d, ch 5, 5 s c, ch 5, 4 d; turn.

18th row—Chain 5, 4 d over 5 ch, ch 5, 3 s c, ch 5, 4 d, ch 2, 4 d in sp, 3 sp, 19 d, 2 sp, 13 d, 2 sp, 7 d, 2 sp, 13 d, 4 sp; turn.

19th row—Five sp, 7 d, 1 sp, 16 d, 1 sp, 28 d, 5 sp, 4 d, ch 5, 1 t over 2 ch, ch 5, 4 d in 5 ch, ch 4, 1 t over s c, ch 4, 4 d over 5 ch; turn.

20th row—Chain 5, 4 d over 4 ch, ch 2, 4 d over 4 ch, ch 5, 3 s c over t, ch 5, 4 d in sp, 2 sp, 10 d, 2 sp, 16 d, 1 sp, 34 d, 3 sp; turn.

21st row—Four sp, 13 d, 2 sp, 16 d, 1 sp, 7 d, 1 sp, 13 d, 3 sp, 4 d, ch 5, 5 s c, ch 5, 4 d; turn.

22d row—Chain 5, 4 d over 5 ch, ch 5, 3 s c, ch 5, 4 d over 5 ch, ch 2, 4 d, 3 sp, 7 d, 1 sp, 10 d, 1 sp, 13 d, 2 sp, 7 d, 7 sp; turn.

23d row—Four sp, 22 d, 1 sp, 16 d, 1 sp, 16 d, 1 sp, 4 d, ch 5, 1 t over 2 ch, ch 5, 4 d over 5 ch, ch 4, 1 t over s c, ch 4, 4 d; turn.

24th row—Chain 5, 4 d over 4 ch, ch 2, 4 d over 4 ch, ch 5, 3 s c, ch 5, 4 d, 1 sp, 10 d, 1 sp, 25 d, 1 sp, 13 d, 5 sp; turn.

25th row—Six sp, 10 d, 1 sp, 22 d, 2 sp, 7 d, 1 sp, 4 d, ch 5, 5 s c, ch 5, 4 d over 5 ch; turn.

FIG. 77. (See Fig. 76) 62 meshes

26th row—Chain 5, 4 d over 5 ch, ch 5, 3 s c, ch 5, 4 d over 5 ch, ch 2, 4 d, 1 sp, 7 d, 2 sp, 16 d, 2 sp, 7 d, 7 sp; turn.

27th row—Eight sp, 4 d, 3 sp, 7 d, 3 sp, 7 d, 1 sp, 4 d, ch 5, 1 t over 2 ch, ch 5, 4 d over 5 ch, ch 4, 1 t over s c, ch 4, 4 d; turn.

28th row—Chain 5, 4 d over 4 ch, ch 2, 4 d over 4 ch, ch 5, 3 s c over t, ch 5, 4 d, 4 sp, 7 d, 13 sp; turn.

29th row—Eighteen sp, 4 d, ch 5, 5 s c, ch 5, 4 d; turn.

30th row—Chain 5, 4 d over 5 ch, ch 5, 3 s c, ch 5, 4 d over 5 ch, 19 sp; turn.

31st row—Twenty sp, 4 d over 5 ch, ch 4, 1 t, ch 4, 4 d; turn. *32d row*—Chain 5, 4 d over 4 ch, ch 2, 4 d over 4 ch, 21 sp. Repeat from beginning.

EDGE TO FINISH.—Fasten thread in 1st d, 3 s c in next 3 d, ch 3, * 3 s c in first loop, ch 1, 6 t with picot (5 ch, s c in 1st ch) between each t in next loop; repeat from * to loop on side of point, ch 1, 6 t with picot between each t in loop on other side of point and continue down side.

Finished scarf is 1 yard 19 inches long without edge. Use No. 50 hard-twist cotton and No. 12 hook.

FIG. 78. SQUARE WITH ROSE BORDER. OLD SWEDISH DESIGN

Use hard-twist crochet cotton No. 50 and a No. 12 hook. Make a very snug chain, about a yard in length. At end of this chain make a shell of * 3 d, 3 ch, 3 d for the first corner, then 52 spaces *. Repeat from * to * for the three remaining sides. Cut off extra chain, join carefully and proceed with the first row of the pattern, placing shell in shell at each corner, not forgetting to turn the work when starting each new row.

The edge finish consists of 2 s c in each square with 1 s c in each d, while at every 4th d a picot of 5 ch occurs. This finish is used on both inside and outside edges of the border square. A picot is used at each corner.

FIG. 79. (See Fig. 81.) Use No. 40 hard-twist cotton and No. 11 hook

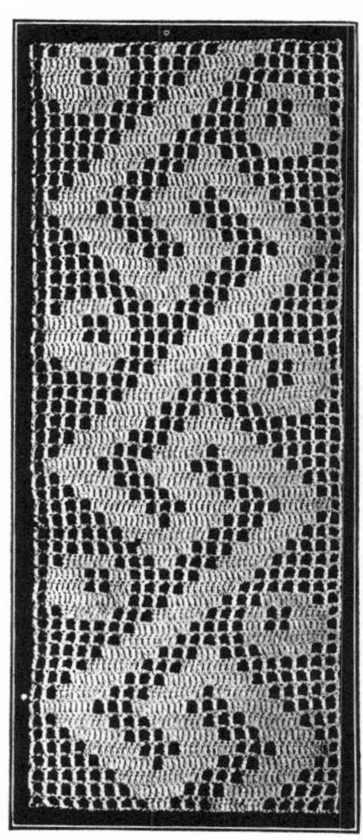

FIG. 80. 20 meshes

FIG. 81. (See Fig. 79) 93 meshes

Figures 82 and 86. FILET CROCHET BRODÉ. — This novelty is a step between the old-fashioned Filet Brodé and the Filet Crochet which is an imitation of it. The foundation is crocheted mesh instead of the ordinary netting, and the design is darned in as in Filet Brodé.

Figure 82. — This strip of Filet Crochet Brodé is done in coarse écru thread, about No. 20, and No. 7 hook, the mesh being made with 2 ch, 1 d. The piece is 221 meshes in length and 40 meshes in width. The foundation chain is 126 stitches. The weaving is done in the common filet stitch, *point de reprise,* which is simple weaving back and forth, over and under the mesh. A coarse, soft, white cotton is used for the weaving, which closely fills the mesh.

Figure 86. (See Figs. 83, 84, 85)—The beautiful insertion for the towel is worked with No. 40 hard-twist crochet cotton and No. 11 hook.

The mesh is made with 3 ch, 1 t. The t is made with 2 loops over the hook, and is worked off in twos, three times. To turn at the end requires 7 ch. The wide insertion is 11 meshes wide, 52 ch for foundation; the narrow insertion is 5 meshes wide; ch 28 for foundation, turn, t in the 12th ch from hook. After the 35th row, 39 ch are added, which widens the row to 13 meshes. The woven letter is 11 meshes high. The weaving in the insertion is done with soft mercerized cotton, in *point de reprise,* and the meshes should be well filled. Finish edges with s c.

FIG. 82. FILET CROCHET BRODÉ

FIG. 83. (See Fig. 86)

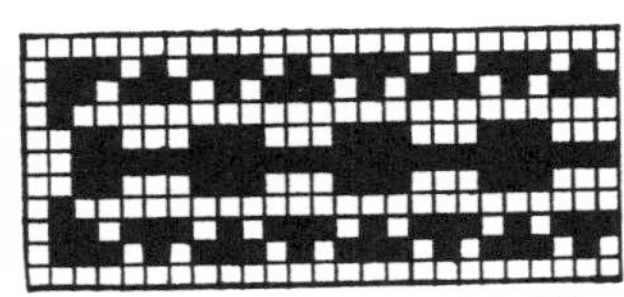

FIG. 84. (See Figs. 85, 86)

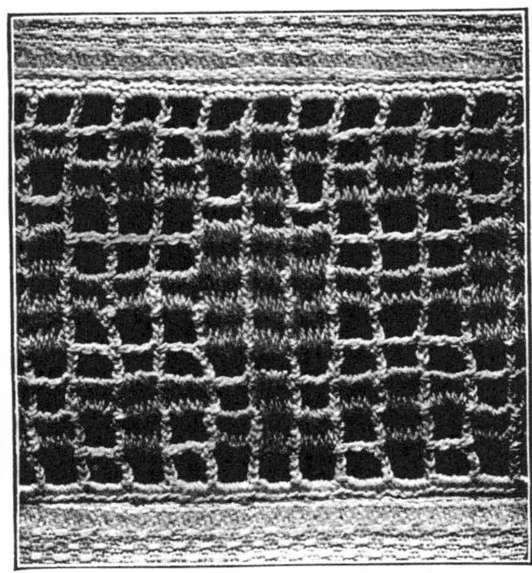

FIG. 85. (See Figs. 84, 86)

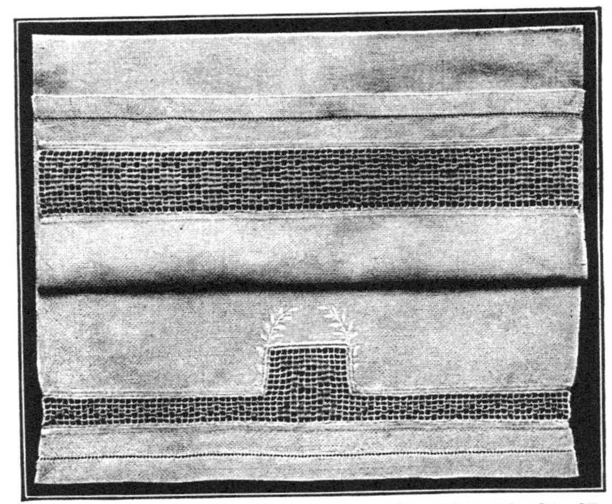

FIG. 86. FILET CROCHET BRODÉ. (See Figs. 83, 84, 85)

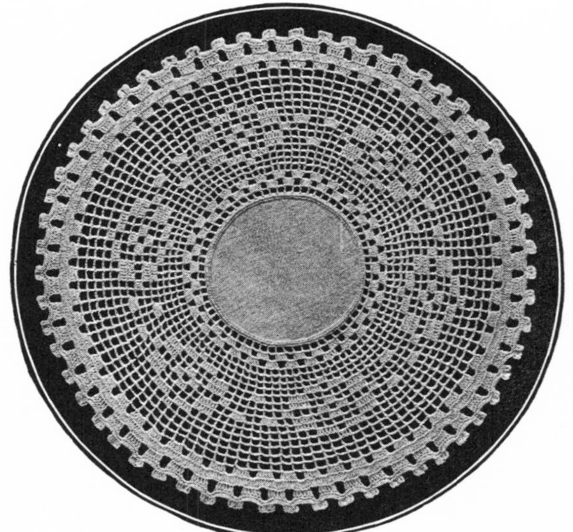

FIG. 87. DOILY

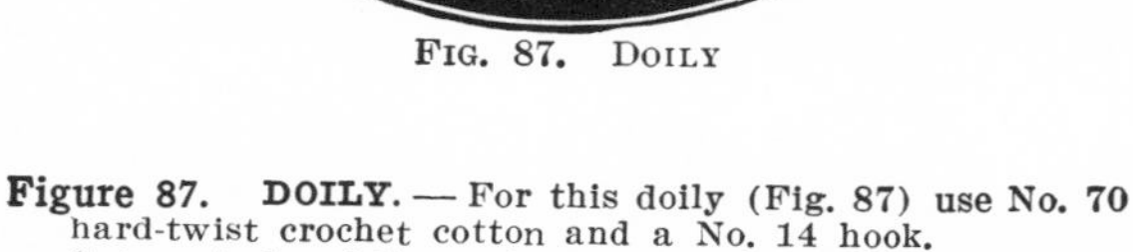

Figure 87. DOILY. — For this doily (Fig. 87) use No. 70 hard-twist crochet cotton and a No. 14 hook.

Cut a circle of linen three inches in diameter for the centre of doily, and finish edge with narrow hem. The directions as given require the edge to be sewed to the linen centre, but if desired the work can be begun by crocheting 192 slip stitches through the hem. Chain (ch) 192, join in ring.

1st row—Chain 6, double crochet (d) in third ch, * ch 3, skip 2 ch, d in next stitch (st) *. Repeat between *, making 64 spaces (sp) in row.

2d row—Chain 3, 4 d, * ch 3, 5 d *. Repeat between * around row.

3d row—Chain 3, 4 d in first sp, * ch 3, 5 d in next sp *. Repeat between * around row.

4th row—Chain 6 *, d in third st, ch 3 *. Repeat between *, making 96 sp in row.

5th row—Like 4th row.

6th row—Chain 6, make 5 sp, 4 d in next sp, * 15 sp, 4 d *. Repeat between * until last 9 sp, join with first 6 to complete row.

7th row—Chain 6, 3 sp, * 7 d over 2 sp, 1 sp, 7 d over 2 sp, 11 sp *. Repeat between * and complete as before.

8th row—Chain 6, 1 sp, * 7 d over 2 sp, 5 sp, 7 d over 2 sp, 3 sp, 7 d over 1 sp, 3 sp *. Repeat between *.

9th row—Chain 6, 1 sp, * 7 d, 2 sp, 5 d, 2 sp, 7 d, 8 sp *. Repeat between *.

10th row—Chain 6, * 4 d, 3 sp, 5 d, 1 sp, 5 d, 3 sp, 4 d, 6 sp *. Repeat between *.

11th row—Chain 6, 1 sp, * 7 d over 2 sp, 2 sp, 5 d, 2 sp, 7 d over 2 sp, 2 sp, 7 d over 1 sp, 2 sp, 7 d over 1 sp, 2 sp *. Repeat between *.

12th row—Chain 6, 1 sp, * 7 d, 5 sp, 7 d, 10 sp *. Repeat between *.

13th row—Chain 6, 3 sp, * 7 d over 2 sp, 1 sp, 7 d over 2 sp, 14 sp *. Repeat between *.

14th row—Chain 6, 5 sp, * 4 d over 1 sp, 18 sp. Repeat between *, closing row with 12 sp, which join to the first six.

15th row—Row of sp with ch of 4 in each sp.

16th row—Like 15th row.

17th row—Like 16th row.

18th row—Chain 8, 5 d in first sp, * ch 4, 6 d in next sp but one *. Repeat between *.

19th row—Double crochet over every d (making 4 d in every sp) around row.

20th row—Chain 8, * 6 d, ch 4 *. Repeat between *.

21st row—Single crochet (s) over every d (making 4 s in every sp) around row.

22d row—* Chain 3, 4 d, ch 4 over each sp and 7 s between *. Repeat between *.

NOTE. — The rows begin at right of one of the figures. Join each row evenly. Keep right number of spaces between the figures.

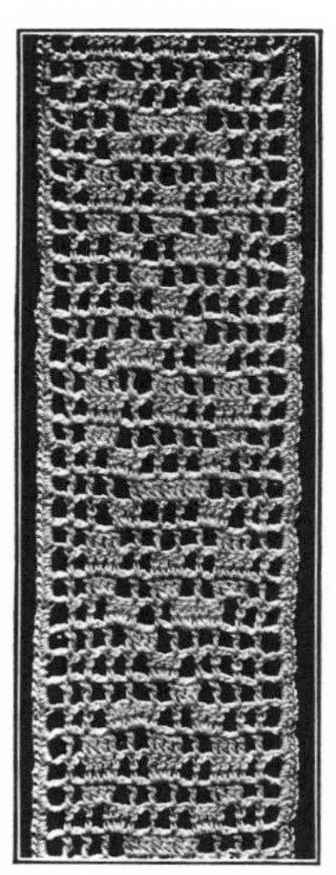

FIG. 88 11 meshes

FIG. 90. (See Fig. 94)

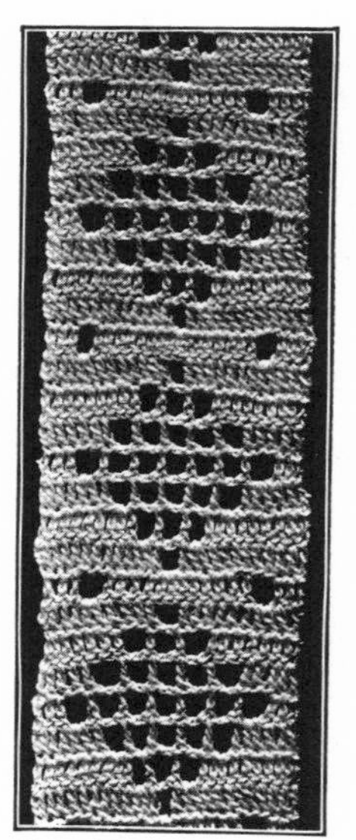

FIG. 89 9 meshes

The insertions on this page, Figs. 88, 89, and 91, will be found particularly attractive for towels, and Fig. 95 could serve a like purpose. The stork, Fig. 93, would be charming on a baby pillow.

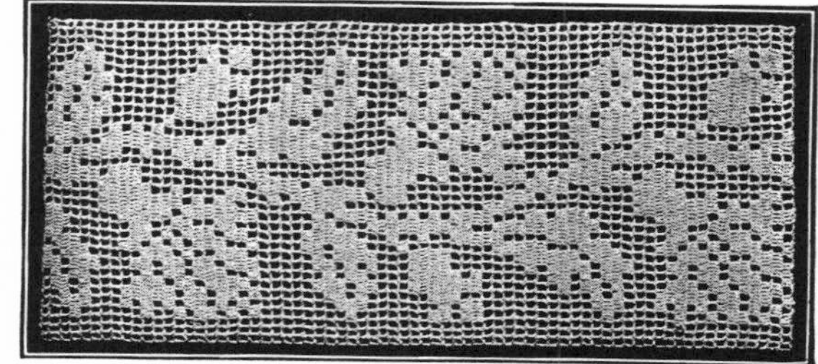

FIG. 91 33 meshes

Figure 94. LUNCHEON CLOTH.—Use No. 60 hard-twist crochet cotton and a No. 12 hook. The model cloth is 40 inches square. The hemstitched hem is 2 inches wide, and beyond that is the crochet insertion, 3¼ inches wide and set in 4 inches from the edge of the cloth. Then comes a strip of linen 3¼ inches wide, followed by the crochet insertion, which is ⅞ of an inch in width. The linen in the centre is 17¼ inches square.

First crochet the two insertions and shrink thoroughly, and after shrinking the linen, cut and fit it to the crochet.

The crochet is in four identical units with the ends joined in the course of the work to form a square. Each unit is 27 spaces wide and 202 spaces long. A little more than one-half a unit (one side) is given in the block pattern, Fig. 90, page 32. When one unit is finished, start the second on the double at the one hundred and ninety-second line.

The inner insertion is worked in the same way, with butted ends, and is 6 spaces wide and 126 spaces long (see Fig. 92).

FIG. 92. (See Fig. 94)

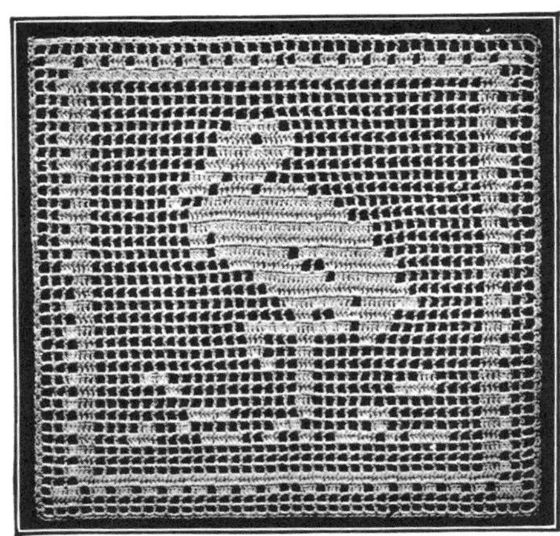

FIG. 93 40 meshes

FIG. 94. LUNCHEON CLOTH. (See Figs. 90 and 92)

Figure 96. BURNS' "SELKIRK GRACE" LUNCH CLOTH.

"Some hae meat that canna eat,
An' some wad eat that want it,
But we hae meat and we can eat,
An' sae the Lord be thankit. Amen."

This familiar verse of the Scotch poet has been very ingeniously arranged for insertion in a lunch cloth, as shown in the illustration.

The crochet in the model cloth was done with No. 50 hard-twist crochet cotton and a No. 12 hook. The insertion is worked the short way, and is 2¼ inches wide. The hem is 2¾ inches wide, and is hemstitched at the corners. The completed cloth is 45 inches square.

Work one strip and corner of the insertion, then complete the second strip and corner and sew to the first strip, and so on. The block pattern of the insertion is shown in Fig. 97, the letters indicating the connections. **If a larger cloth is wanted a coarser cotton should be used.**

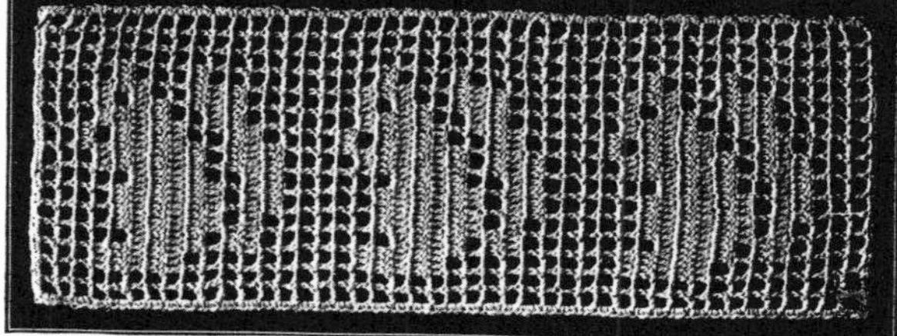

FIG. 95 — 15 meshes

FIG. 96. BURNS' "SELKIRK GRACE" LUNCH CLOTH. (See Block Pattern, page 35)

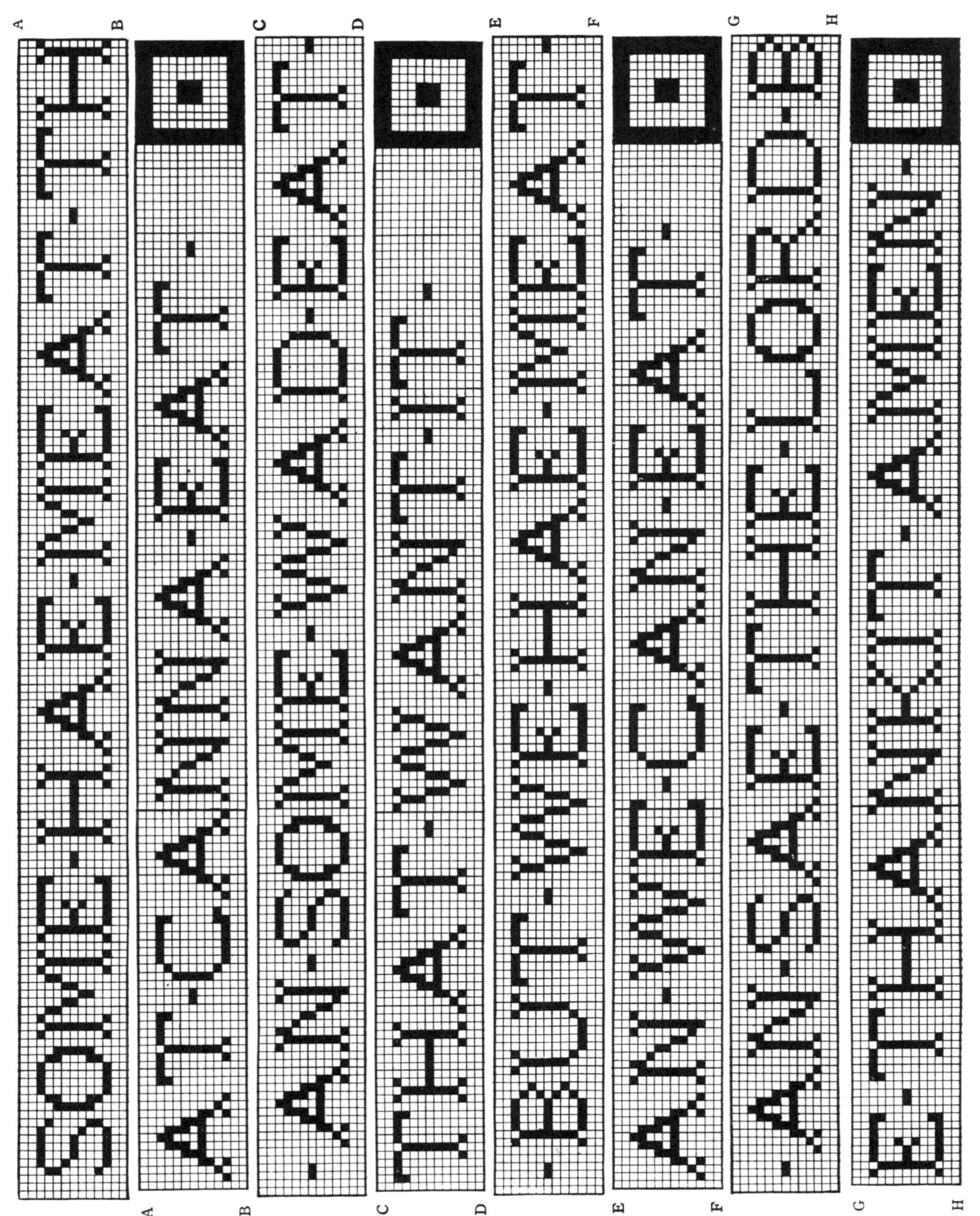

Fig. 97. Pattern of Insertion for "Selkirk Grace" Lunch Cloth. (See Fig. 96) 13 meshes

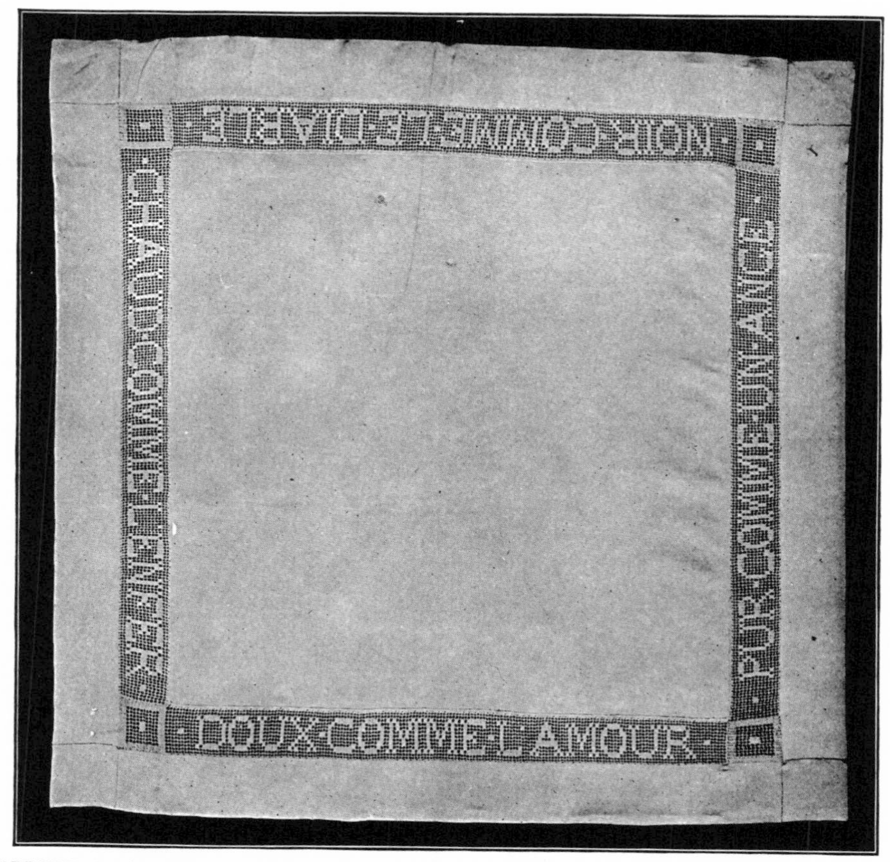

Figure 98. **TALLEYRAND COFFEE CLOTH.—**

"Doux comme l'amour
Pur comme un ange
Noir comme le diable
Chaud comme l'enfer."

This unique coffee cloth shows Talleyrand's famous lines used as an insertion. The block pattern is shown on this page and the next (Fig. 99), each strip of insertion being 13 rows wide and 169 rows long. The crochet in the model cloth was done with No. 50 hard-twist crochet cotton and a No. 12 hook. The cloth is 33 inches square, and has a hem 2¾ inches wide, hemstitched at the corners. The insertion is 2¼ inches wide, and is worked the narrow way. Complete one strip and corner, then work second strip and corner and sew to the first strip, and so on. Coarser cotton could be used if a larger cloth is preferred. The letters in the pattern indicate connections.

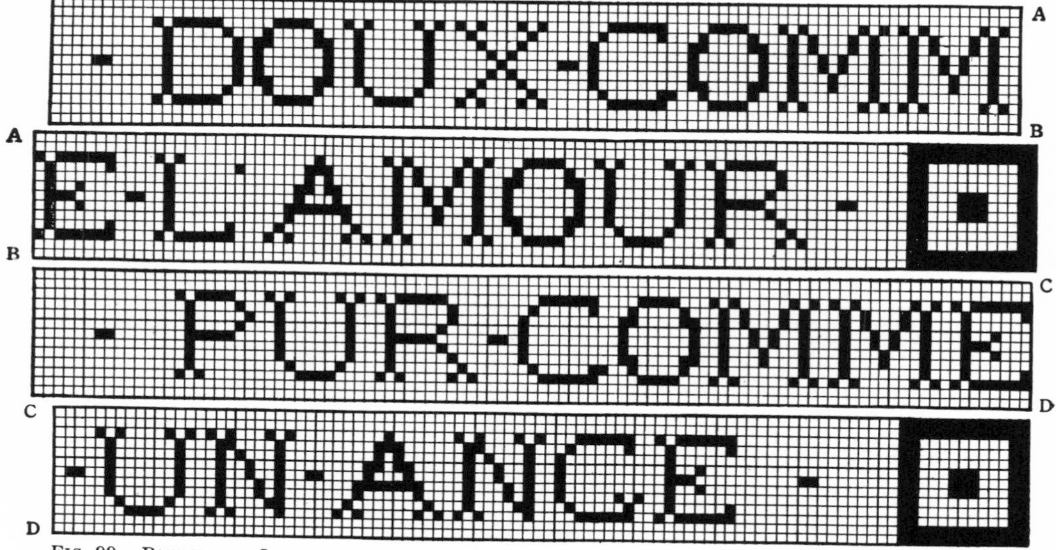

FIG. 99. PATTERN OF INSERTION FOR COFFEE CLOTH. (See page 37)

13 meshes

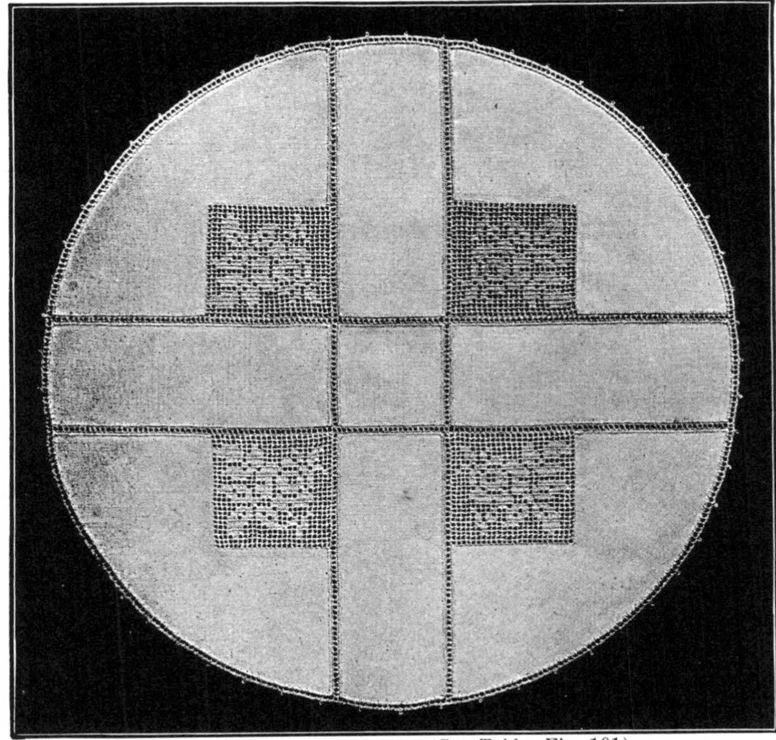

Fig. 100. Centrepiece. (See Table, Fig. 101)

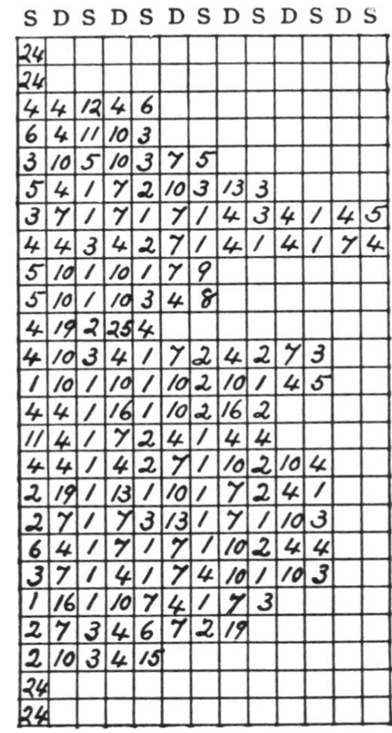

S	D	S	D	S	D	S	D	S	D	S	D	S
24												
24												
4	4	12	4	6								
6	4	11	10	3								
3	10	5	10	3	7	5						
5	4	1	7	2	10	3	13	3				
3	7	1	7	1	7	1	4	3	4	1	4	5
4	4	3	4	2	7	1	4	1	4	1	7	4
5	10	1	10	1	7	9						
5	10	1	10	3	4	8						
4	19	2	25	4								
4	10	3	4	1	7	2	4	2	7	3		
1	10	1	10	1	10	2	10	1	4	5		
4	4	1	16	1	10	2	16	2				
11	4	1	7	2	4	1	4	4				
4	4	1	4	2	7	1	10	2	10	4		
2	19	1	13	1	10	1	7	2	4	1		
2	7	1	7	3	13	1	7	1	10	3		
6	4	1	7	1	7	1	10	2	4	4		
3	7	1	4	1	7	4	10	1	10	3		
1	16	1	10	7	4	1	7	3				
2	7	3	4	6	7	2	19					
2	10	3	4	15								
24												
24												

Fig. 101. Table for Working Fig. 100

Figure 100. CENTREPIECE. — This centrepiece of heavy linen has four square insets worked with linen thread No. 40 and a No. 11 hook. The diameter of the centrepiece is 26 inches and the insets are 4½ inches square (see table for working, Fig. 101). The centre strips are 4 inches wide.

To make up, cut a circular paper pattern 26 inches in diameter, and mark on it the two cross strips, 4 inches wide. Cut three patterns—one for quadrant, one for centre square, and one for the half strip; cut the linen by these patterns. Insert the crochet in the quadrants, allowing for one-quarter-inch hem. Finish edges of all nine pieces with s c, except edge of crochet work. Crochet strips of spaces and sew them to the linen and crochet, thus joining the nine parts as shown in the illustration. Work a row of spaces around the centrepiece, and finish by a row of s c, with a picot every 7 spaces.

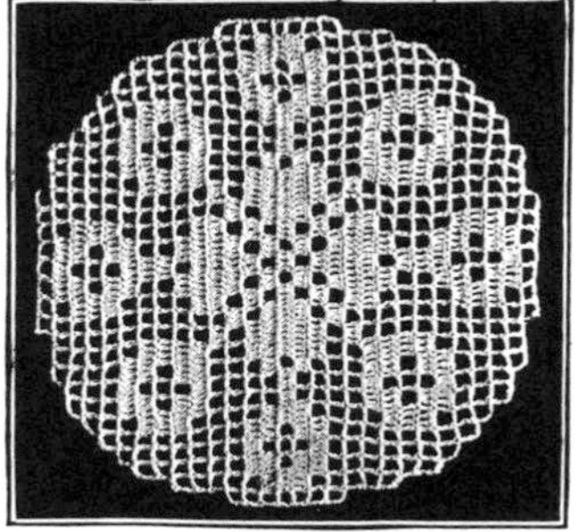

Fig. 102 29 meshes

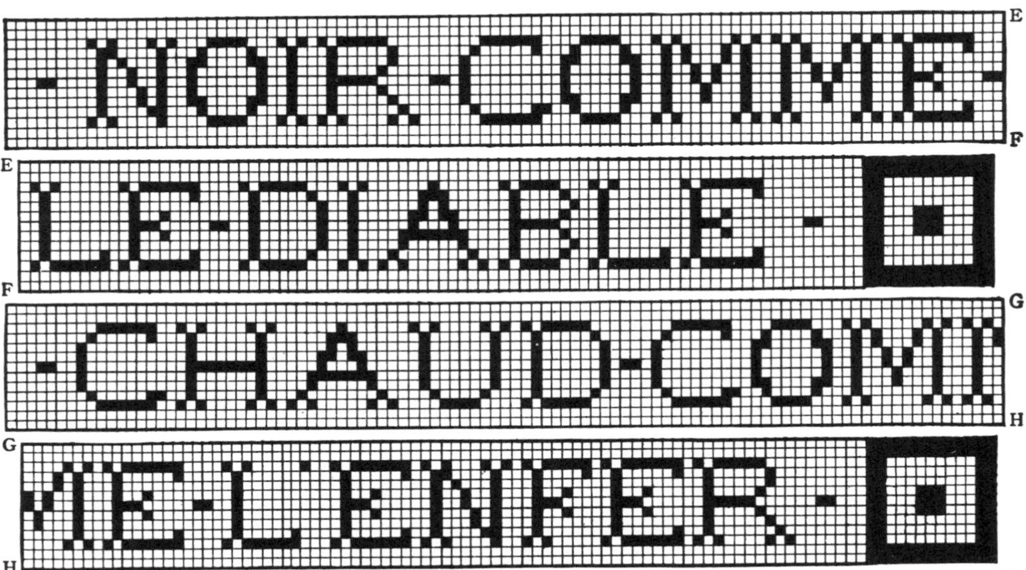

Fig. 99 — Continued. Insertion for Coffee Cloth 13 meshes

Figure 103. BORDER OF TEA CLOTH. *Explanation of Terms.*—Chain (ch). Stitch (st). Slip stitch (sl). Single crochet (s c). Double crochet (d). Treble crochet (t). Space (sp); for a space, ch 2, miss 2, d in next st.

MATERIALS.—Hard-twist crochet cotton No. 40 or 50, steel hook No. 11 or 12.

Begin work at point marked "A" (see Fig. 103) with a ch of 154. The 1st row is worked from outside edge toward inside. Beginning in 4th st from hook, make 7 d in 7 ch, 4 sp, 7 d in next 7 (the given number of d's in a cluster always includes the d at end of last sp), 8 sp, 7 d, 18 sp, 7 d, 8 sp, 7 d, 2 sp, ch 5, turn.

2d row—Double crochet in 2d d, ch 2, 7 d in 7 d, 8 sp over 8 sp, 7 d in 7 d, 18 sp, 7 d, 8 sp, 7 d, 4 sp, 7 d, turn.

3d row—Slip stitch in each of 7 d, ch 3 (for a d), 6 more d (2 in each sp and 1 in each d between sps), 4 sp, 7 d, 34 sp, 7 d, 4 sp, ch 5, turn.

4th row—Begin with 4 sp and work in d and sps as shown, following design from illustration, turning at ends as described. When the fifth block (blk) on edge is finished (at end of 10th row) ch 10, turn, miss 4 ch, 6 d in next 6 and 1 d in next d; finish row as shown. Begin next blk on edge in same way.

Follow design from illustration for 41 rows. The 41st row is worked toward inside edge. The diagonal edge is begun with 42d row. *The chain forming straight edge across corner is not a part of the work now, but is added later.* Follow directions carefully at this point in order to get the blocks across the diagonal corner started right.

After 41st row, ch 10, turn, miss st next the st on hook, and sl in next 7 ch. This leaves 2 ch. (If the worker finds the sl on a ch difficult, s c may be substituted with nearly the same effect.) Miss the 2 ch at end, ch 2, d in next d, ch 2, 7 d in 7 d; finish as usual.

At end of next row, after last 4 sp, make 7 d in the 7 sl, ch 9, turn, miss st next st on hook, 6 sl in next 6, miss next 2 ch, 7 d in 7 d; finish as usual.

At end of next row, after sps, d in d next sl, 6 d in 6 sl, ch 9, turn and begin with 6 sl, miss next 2 ch, 7 d in 7 d. Follow design as shown until there are 24 blks on diagonal edge.

For first side of mitred corner, when turning to make 2d row of 24th blk on diagonal edge, ch 3, miss 1 d, 6 d on next 6, 2 sp, 7 d; finish as shown.

Work again to inside edge and after 7 d over the 2 sp, ch 3, turn.

Miss 1 d, 6 d on next 6, 8 sp; finish as shown.

Work again to inside edge, ending with the 4 sp just before last blk on edge, ch 5, turn.

Doubles after first space, 3 sp; finish as shown.

Work again to inside edge, ending with 7 d before last 2 sp on edge.

The next 14 points or "steps" on edge are like the 3d, having 2 sp at each side of point.

Next point is a blk of 2 rows of 7 d, same as first and second points. Then 19 points of sp as before, 1 point of 7 d, 4 points of sp, and 1 point (at outer end), of 7 d.

After 2d row of 7 d of this point, turn, sl across last 7 d, ch 10, turn.

The rows are now worked at right angles to the others. Miss 4 ch st, 6 d in next 6 ch, 1 d in next d, ch 2, d between 2 rows of d at side of last blk, d in d between 2 sp at side of next point, ch 2, d in centre of 5 ch at point, ch 2, turn, 7 d in last 7 d, ch 10, turn.

Make 6 d on 10 ch as before, d in next d, 4 sp, 6 d, sl between 2 sp at side of next point, sl to centre of 5 ch at point, turn.

Six d in 6 d, 4 sp, 7 d in 7 d, ch 10, turn. Six d on ch, d in next d, 4 sp, 7 d, 3 sp, d in d between 2 sp at side of point, ch 2, d in 5 ch at point as before, ch 2, turn.

Double in d after next sp, 2 more sp, 7 d, 4 sp, 7 d, This finishes the 6 blks across square scallop at corner. Turn. Slip stitch across last 7 d, ch 3 (for a d), 6 more d, 4 sp, 7 d, 2 sp, 6 d, sl between 2 sps on side of next point, sl up to point, turn.

Six d, 2 sp, 7 d, 4 sp, 7 d, turn, sl across last 7 d. Chain 3 (for a d), 6 d, 4 sp, 7 d, 3 sp, d in centre of side of point, ch 2, d at point, ch 2, turn.

Three sp over next 3 sp, 7 d, 4 sp, 7 d, turn and sl over 7 d.

Further directions are unnecessary, as the design may be easily copied from illustration, and joinings are as described. When joining to a point made by a blk, make a d at side of blk, ch 2, d at end of blk, turn for next row. When corner is all joined, the blks are again taken up on diagonal edge, turning at end of 1st row of each blk with a ch of 3.

To make the straight edge across blks on diagonal edge, join thread at end of corner, (ch 7, s c in next blk); repeat. The star indicates the mitre line.

FIG. 103. BORDER OF TEA CLOTH

Figure 104. **BORDER OF DOILY.**

Explanation of Terms. — Chain (ch). Stitch (st). Slip stitch (sl). Single crochet (s c). Double crochet (d). Treble crochet (t). Space (sp); for a space, ch 2, miss 2, d in next st.

MATERIALS. — Hard-twist crochet cotton No. 40 or 50, steel hook No. 11 or 12. Make 50 ch for foundation.

1st row (see "A," Fig. 105)— Miss 3 ch, d in next 4 ch, 3 sp, 7 d, 2 sp, 7 d, 3 sp, 4 d, 1 sp, ch 8, turn.

2d row—Double crochet in last d of 1st row, 1 sp, 4 d, 3 sp, 7 d, 2 sp, 7 d, 3 sp, 4 d, turn.

3d row—Slip stitch across 4 d, ch 3 (for a d), 2 d in next sp and 1 d in next d, 4 sp, 7 d, 6 sp, 4 d, ch 2, d in 3d of 8 ch, ch 10, turn.

4th row—Double crochet in 3d ch st (counting back from last d of 3d row) ch 2, d in last d of 3d row, 6 more d, 6 sp, 7 d, 3 sp, 4 d, turn.

5th row—Beginning same as 3d row, finish as shown in illustration, ending with 10 ch.

6th row—Beginning same as 4th row, finish as shown.

7th and 8th rows—Work as shown, and after last 4 d of 8th row, ch 10, turn.

9th row—Miss st next one on hook, sl in next 4, miss next 3, d in next 2, also d in last d of 8th row. Continue with sps and d as shown, finishing row as before.

10th row—Work as shown, after last 4 sp, making 4 d in 4 sl at end, ch 10, turn.

11th row—Beginning same as 9th row, finish as shown.

12th row—Work as shown, ending with 4 d in 4 sl. *13th row*—Chain 6, miss 4 ch, d in next 2 ch and in next d, finish as shown.

Continue working design from illustration (Fig. 105), making edges as directed.

In *17th row* work only to first sp, over last 7 d of 16th row. After first sp ch 5, turn. Work back to outside edge.

The *19th row* ends with first sp over last 7 d of 18th row; ch 5, turn. Continue working as shown in detail of corner (Fig. 105), making outside edge as described for first scallop.

In *39th row* work to first sp over 7 d of 38th row. After this sp, ch 5, turn, d in next d, ch 2, 4 d on edge, turn, sl across 4 d, ch 3, 3 d, ch 10, turn. This finishes half of corner.

To begin next half of corner, miss 1 ch, sl in next 4 ch, miss next 3 ch, d in next 2 ch, and in next d, ch 2, sl in centre of 5 ch at next point, sl across next 2 sp and in next 3 d to corner of 7 d; ch 2, turn, 3 sp over 3 sp of last row, 1 sp over 4 d on edge, 4 d in 4 sl, ch 6, turn. Miss 4 ch, 2 d in next 2, 1 d in next d, 3 sp, 7 d, sl in 5 ch at corner, sl across 2 sp and 3 d, to corner of 7 d. The work shown in detail of corner (Fig. 105) ends at this point. The design may be followed from the cut of completed doily, Fig. 104.

The thread is again joined near the lower edge (Fig. 105) and just enough work done to show method of working the inside edge (where border is joined to centre) on second half of corner.

For extra row on inside edge, join thread to a corner, (ch 3, d in next sp, ch 3, s c in next corner); repeat.

1st row on outside edge—Join in centre between two scallops, ch 3 for a t, 1 t in same place, ch 2, s c in next blk, * ch 4, s c in next blk; repeat from *, making a s c in centre of blk at point, and 2 t between scallops.

2d row—Chain 5, sl back in second ch for a picot, ch 2, s c in next loop; repeat.

This border for doily matches the border of cloth, Fig. 103.

FIG. 104. DOILY TO MATCH TEA CLOTH, FIG. 103. (See detail, Fig. 105)

THREAD. Most of the work in this book was done with hard-twist crochet cotton. The table on page 3, which gives the size of the thread and of the corresponding hook and the number of meshes per inch, was made upon this basis. The size of thread made by different manufacturers varies. For instance, a No. 40 linen thread is nearly as coarse as a No. 20 cotton thread. Therefore, if crochet is made with any other than hard-twist cotton, it will probably require a different sized hook and make different sized meshes than are given in the table.

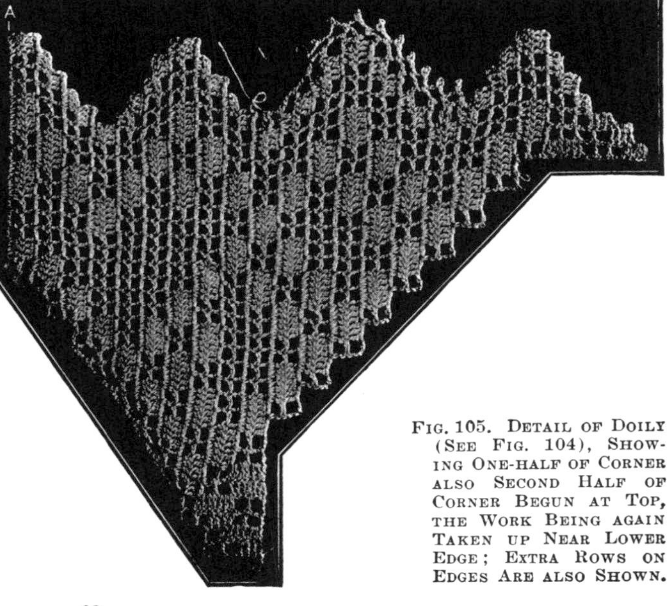

FIG. 105. DETAIL OF DOILY (SEE FIG. 104), SHOWING ONE-HALF OF CORNER ALSO SECOND HALF OF CORNER BEGUN AT TOP, THE WORK BEING AGAIN TAKEN UP NEAR LOWER EDGE; EXTRA ROWS ON EDGES ARE ALSO SHOWN.

Figure 107. TOWEL WITH INSERTION IN CAMEO CROCHET (see Fig. 106 and page 3).—This new and beautiful form of filet crochet has the solid portion of the design worked in color. There must be a separate colored thread carried for every group of blocks in the row, which are separated by open spaces worked in white, since the color cannot be carried over the white.

In changing from white to color, ch 2, tie the colored thread in the top of the next d in previous row; ch 2 with color, pulling the last st of ch through both the colored loop and the white. When crocheting with the color, carry the white along, crocheting over it. The white thread must be pulled tightly or it will show through the colored stitches. When taking up the white again, the last colored d is not finished, but the white thread is pulled through the last two loops of color. The color is now dropped, to be picked up again on the next row when the process is repeated. The insertion was worked with hard-twist crochet cotton, white No. 40, blue No. 30, and No. 11 hook. See page 3 for illustration of work in full size.

Figure 108. FLOWER INSERTION. — This design can be worked from the illustration.

For the scallops, 1 single crochet in edge, chain 9, miss 2 spaces, single crochet in next; repeat for entire length of edge; turn, 4 single crochet, 1 picot, 4 single crochet, in each loop of 9 chain. This charming pattern would combine prettily with the floral edging, Fig. 116, page 42, for towels and scarfs, and the separate units could be adapted in many attractive ways.

[CONCLUDED FROM PAGE 3]

on after the pattern is completed. Sometimes the edge of single crochet is varied by making a picot at every 10th or 12th stitch.

The ability to crochet *square* should be learned and cultivated, as resulting in superior work and greater range of design.

When crocheting for any length of time, the fingers may become chafed. To avoid this, a good plan is to use a finger from an old glove.

LAUNDERING.—Although a new piece of work does not usually need to be laundered, it adds greatly to its appearance. The crochet should be squeezed, not rubbed, in good soap-suds. It should then be rinsed well without twisting.

When crochet is to be combined with linen, both the linen and crochet should be thoroughly shrunk. The crochet is then pinned on the cloth and the cloth cut to fit the crochet. This is the only way to ensure a perfectly smooth piece of work.

After a piece is finished, it should be pressed on a thickly padded board, under a damp cloth.

Fig. 106. (See Fig. 107)

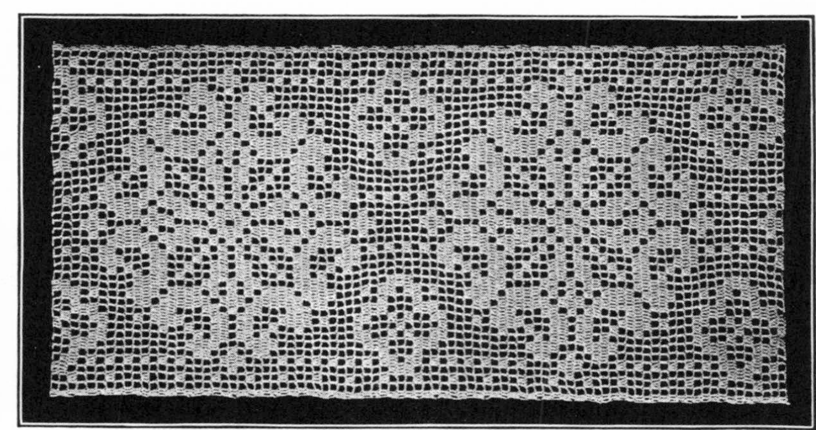

Fig. 109

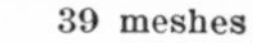

39 meshes

Figure 109 is a very handsome insertion that is adaptable for a bedspread with alternate strips of linen. The large unit would also work up into a square and could be used for a spread with linen squares; a suitable edging could be arranged from the insertion by the addition of scallops. The adaptations of the units of designs are various, and their possibilities should be studied by workers in search of new combinations.

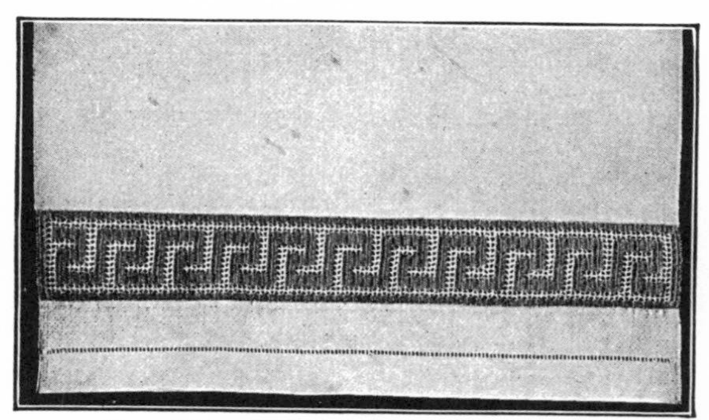

Fig. 107. Towel with Cameo Crochet
(See page 3 and Fig. 106)

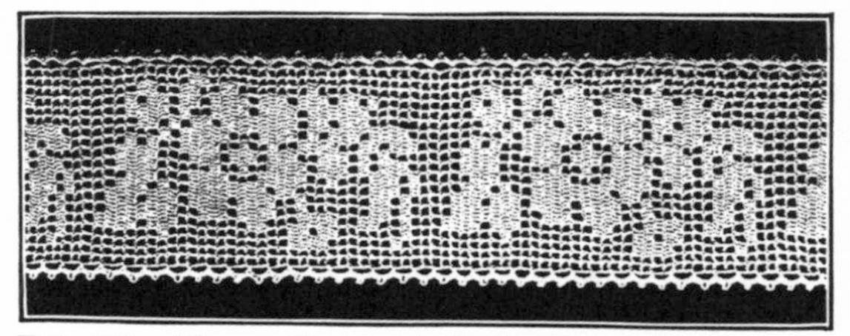

Fig. 108. (For scallop, see text above) 19 meshes

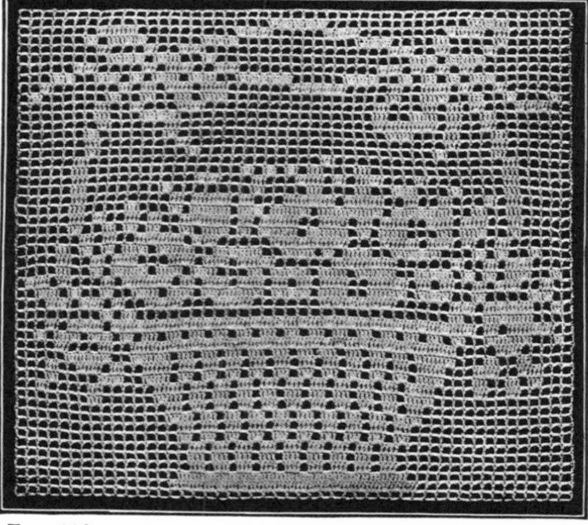

Fig. 110 49 x 50 meshes

FIG. 111. DOILY IN FANCY FILET CROCHET
(See Detail, Fig. 112, and Table, Fig. 113)

DESIGNS. Workers wishing to copy or alter patterns for filet crochet, or, having some artistic ability, to make original designs, and finding it tedious to rule a great many squares, may buy paper already ruled. It is sold under the name of cross-section paper, and can be bought where artists' materials are sold.

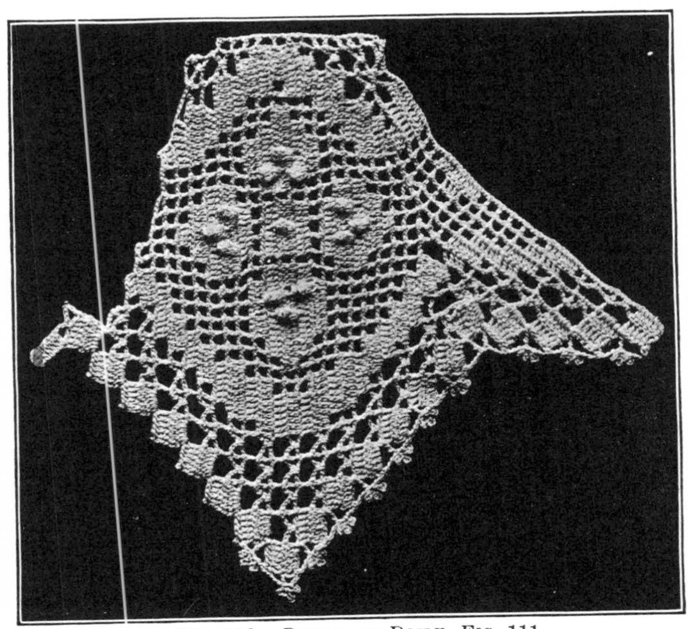

FIG. 112. DETAIL OF DOILY, FIG. 111

	D	S	D	S	D	S	D	S	D	S	D
	7	F2	X	1	7	6	10	3	10	B	F
	B	1	B	X	7	4	4	6	7	B3	7
E2	7	F2	X	1	7	10	4	1			
E4	X	6	10	B3	7						
E2	7	F3	7	3							
E3	4	1	B3	X	7						
E2	7	F2	C5	Fasten to beginning of previous row							
	4	1	B2	X	7						
E2	7	F									
	X	B	7	W							
	5	F	C5								

12th row—Seven d in 7 d of previous row, W.

13th row—Five d, F 2, ch 2, 1 d in nearest corner, ch 2, 1 d in nearest angle, 7 d over the one space and 4 d. Chain 2, 1 d, fasten to d one space up from next angle. Chain 2, fasten to next space up. Slip stitch forward over three following spaces. Turn, ch 2, 1 d, forming a space.

D	S	D	S	D	S	D
X	5	10	B2	7	W	
5	F2	X	1	7	10	2

Two s c, sl st forward over space and half of block, turn, ch 2, 1 d, forming a space.

	D	S	D	S	D	S	D	S	D	S	D	S	D	S	D	S	D
	7	4	4	6	7	B2	7	W									
	5	F2	X	1	7	6	10	3	10	F2							
	X	B2	7	3	7	R	8	6	7	B2	7	W					
	5	F2	X	1	10	6	4	R	5	R	5	4	10	F			
	X	B	7	6	10	8	7	1	B2	X	7	W					
	5	F3	10	3	10	7	7	3	7	1							
	10	2	8	R	4	1	10	1	5	R	10	3	7	B3	7	W	
	5	F4	7	2	9	R	9	1	4	R	5	1	6	R	9	2	7
	10	2	8	R	4	1	10	1	5	R	10	3	7	B4	7		
E2	7	F3	10	3	10	7	7	3	7	1							
	X	B	7	6	10	8	7	1	B3	X	7						
E2	7	F2	X	1	10	6	4	R	5	R	5	4	10	F			
	B2	X	7	3	7	R	8	6	7	B3	7		Turn			E2	

FIG. 113. TABLE FOR FIG. 111

The first row of the table begins at the outside edge of the crochet. The last row ends at the outside edge. The crochet was made with hard-twist crochet cotton No. 20 and hook No. 11.

EDGE. — Fasten at point of scallop, ch 3, 1 t in angle, 3 picots, ch 3, 1 s c in corner, work 6 times down side of scallop, ch 3, 1 t in each angle, ch 3, s c in corner, ch 3, 1 t in angle, 3 p, ch 3, 1 s c in corner, work 6 times up sides of scallop, ch 3, 1 d in middle of point, 3 p, ch 3, 1 s c in corner; repeat.

The blocks in relief are marked R in the Table, and are made as follows: A double, fasten 7 more d in the same place, join top of last d to top of first d with a sl st on the wrong side of the work.

This 16-inch doily has a 5-inch linen centre. The crochet may be worked from the accompanying Table, but the detail, Fig. 112, may prove a sufficient guide for the experienced worker. This detail shows a complete scallop, the method of changing direction, the row of spaces with which the inside edge is finished, and the picot edging used on the scallops. The meaning of the letters in the Table will be found on page 3. The figure with the letter shows the number of times the direction is repeated. Thus: E2 means slip stitch over two spaces, B3 means make three blocks, etc.

S	D	S	D	S	D	S	D	S	D	S	D	S	D	S
25														
1	4	1	28	1	28	1	4	1						
3	4	7	10	7	4	3								
1	16	13	16	1										
1	4	1	4	1	4	13	4	1	4	1	4	1		
1	4	1	10	6	4	6	10	1	4	1				
1	4	9	10	9	4	1								
1	4	5	10	1	4	1	4	1	10	5	4	1		
1	4	5	4	1	4	1	10	1	4	1	4	5	4	1
1	4	5	13	1	4	1	13	5	4	1				
1	4	7	7	1	4	1	7	7	4	1				
1	7	3	10	2	10	2	10	3	7	1				
2	4	2	7	1	13	1	13	1	7	2	4	2		
1	7	3	10	2	10	2	10	3	7	1				
1	4	7	7	1	4	1	7	7	4	1				
1	4	5	13	1	4	1	13	5	4	1				
1	4	5	4	1	4	1	10	1	4	1	4	5	4	1
1	4	5	10	1	4	1	4	1	10	5	4	1		
1	4	9	10	9	4	1								
1	4	1	10	6	4	6	10	1	4	1				
1	4	1	4	1	4	13	4	1	4	1	4	1		
1	16	13	16	1										
3	4	7	10	7	4	3								
1	4	1	28	1	28	1	4	1						
25														

FIG. 114. TABLE FOR FIG. 118

FIG. 117 113 meshes

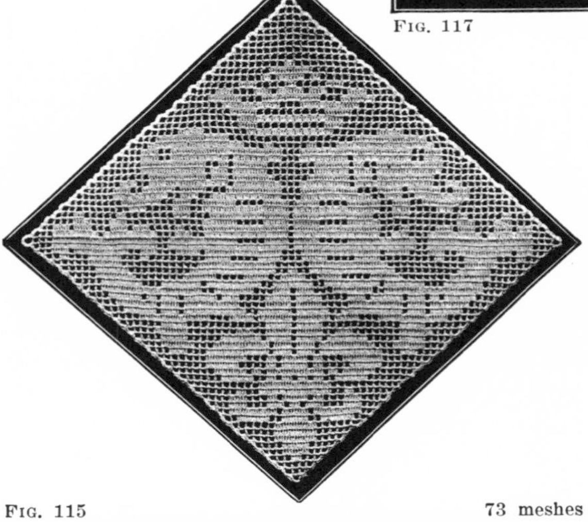

FIG. 115 73 meshes

FIG. 118. (See Fig. 114)

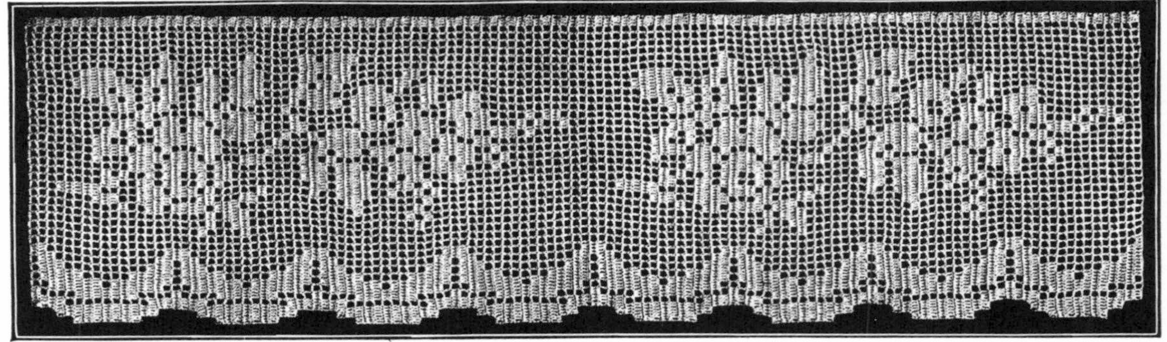

FIG. 116 38 meshes

Figure 122. TOWEL WITH EMBROIDERED CROCHET. (See Figs. 119 and 121.) The crochet insertion for this towel is worked according to the design, Fig. 119. Use No. 30 hard-twist crochet cotton and No. 11 hook. The model is embroidered with colored mercerized cotton, as shown in Fig. 121, the coloring being as follows: In the centre of the medallion work a flower in French knots, one yellow French knot in the centre, with seven of the same shade around it, and twelve of a lighter shade around those. The illustration, Fig. 121, shows how the green leaves are placed, these being done in chain-stitch caught down with a short stitch over the loop at the end. Smaller French-knot flowers, blue, pink, and lavender, with yellow centres, are worked in the middle of each of the three solid figures that are grouped together. On the two-inch hem of the towel there is a design of the same flowers with stems in outline. The hem is double hemstitched and the same on both ends of the towel.

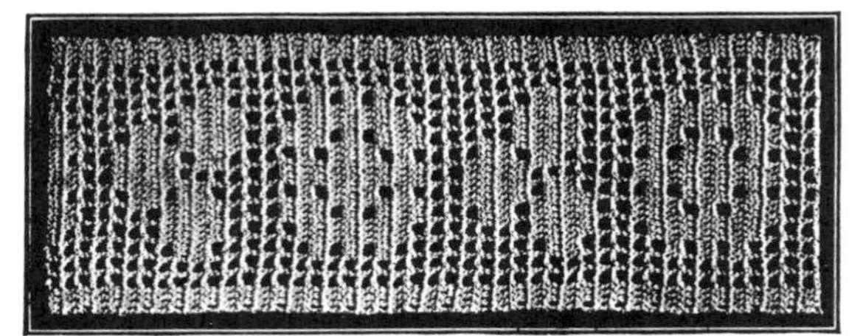

Fig. 119. Pattern of Fig. 122 — 15 meshes

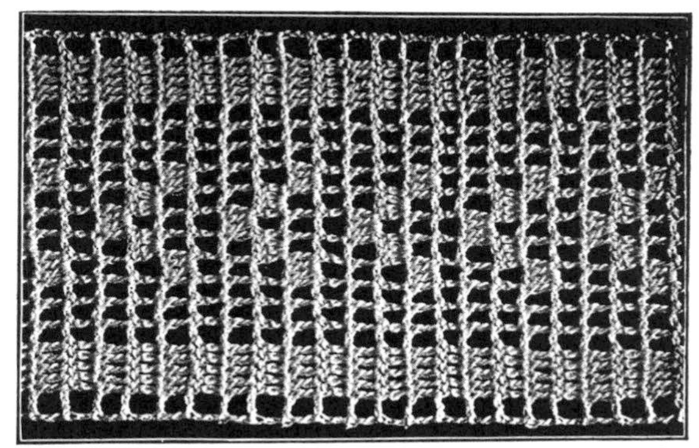

Fig. 120½ — 15 meshes

In the above insertion, Fig. 120½, a slight variation from the usual filet crochet is shown in the wide mesh of 5 d, forming the horizontal stripe at the top and bottom of the design. But the working of the pattern without mistake has been made possible by the reproduction of the work in full size, thus making the counting of the stitches an easy matter. The insertion will be found very attractive for towels, and if done in carpet warp would be handsome for a bedspread.

Fig. 120 — 87 meshes

Fig. 121. Insertion for Towel, Fig. 122

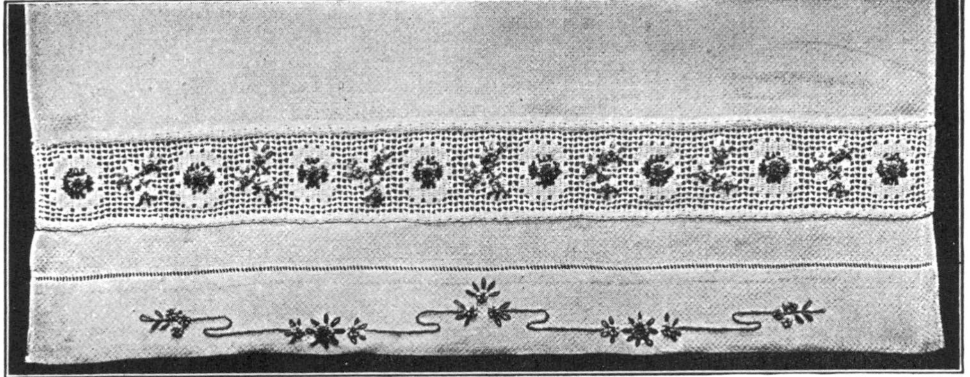

Fig. 122. Towel with Embroidered Crochet. (See Figs. 119 and 121)

DIRECTIONS FOR FRONTISPIECE

Figure 1. TEA CLOTH. (Frontispiece.) *Materials.*—Hard-twist crochet cotton No. 100, hook No. 14, and linen for centre. Shrink linen and crochet, then hemstitch a square to fit edging. The triangles may be buttonholed to the linen or closely whipped, as preferred.

EXPLANATION OF TERMS.—*Chain* (ch). *Stitch* (st). *Slip stitch* (sl). *Single crochet* (s c). *Double crochet* (d). *Treble crochet* (t). *Space* (sp) ; for a "space", ch 2, miss 2, d in next st. *Long space* (l sp) ; for a "long space," ch 5, miss 5 (if over a festoon miss festoon), d in next. *Festoon* (fest) ; for a festoon, if over a long space, ch 3, s c in long space, ch 3, d in next d ; if festoon is over a ch or over doubles, ch 3, miss 2, single in next, ch 3, miss 2, d in next. *Block* (blk). A chain of 3 before a cluster of doubles equals 1 d ; thus "3 ch, 6 d," are counted as 7 d in working next row. Both in triangles and edging in working doubles into doubles only the back thread of stitch is taken up, except in working inside edge of edging when both threads are taken up.

Figure 123. INSERTED TRIANGLE. (See Fig. 124.)—Chain 7, turn.

1st row—Double crochet in 4th from hook and in next 2 ch, ch 7, turn.

2d row—Four d in 4 d, ch 3, turn, (3 ch and 3 d count as 4 d in 1st row).

3d row—Miss 1 d, 3 d in next 3 d, 2 d under next 2 of 7 ch, 1 d into next ch st, ch 2, t in same st with last d, ch 7, turn.

4th row—* Double crochet in t, 1 sp, 7 d, * ch 3, turn.

5th row—Miss 1 d, 3 d in next 3, 1 sp, * 7 d, (last 3 made as in 3d row,) ch 2, t in st with last d, ch 7, turn.

6th row—From * to * of 4th row, 1 sp, 4 d, ch 3, turn.

7th row—Miss first d, 6 d, 2 sp, from * to end of 5th row.

8th row—From * to * of 4th row, 2 sp, 7 d, ch 3, turn.

9th row—Twelve more d, 2 sp, from * to end of 5th row.

10th row—From * to * of 4th row, 2 sp, 7 d, 1 sp, 4 d, ch 3, turn.

11th row—Six d, 1 fest, 7 d, 2 sp, from * to end of 5th row.

12th row—From * to * of 4th row, 2 sp, 7 d, one l sp (ch 5, miss fest, d in next d), 1 sp, 4 d, ch 3, turn.

13th row—Six d, 2 fest, 7 d, 2 sp, from * to end of 5th row.

Continue working in same way until there are 13 fest in 35th row. In 36th row there are 13 l sp.

The figure of design is begun in the 37th row.

37th row—Make edge as usual, then 8 fest, 19 d (making 5 d in each l sp and 1 in each d), 3 fest; finish lower edge as usual.

38th row—Edge, 3 l sp, 19 d, 8 l sp, edge.

39th row—Edge, 5 fest, 7 d, 1 fest, 7 d, 6 sp, 7 d, 1 fest, 7 d, 1 fest, edge.

40th row—Edge, one l sp, 7 d, one l sp, 7 d, 6 sp, 7 d, one l sp, 7 d, 5 l sp, edge.

The design may readily be followed from the illustration from this point. The last row (88th) being made entirely of d's. Work across diagonal side with s c.

Figure 126. EDGING. (See Fig. 125.)—Begin at "A." (See Fig. 126.) Chain 143, turn.

1st row (*worked from outside edge to inside*)—Double in fourth st from hook and in next 5, 2 sp, 7 d, 19 fest, 7 d, ch 3, turn.

2d row—Miss 1 d, 3 d in next 3, 1 sp, 19 l sp, 7 d, 2 sp, 7 d, ch 8, turn.

3d row—* Miss 3 ch st next hook, 5 d in next 5, 1 d in next d, 2 sp, 7 d, * 20 fest. 7 d, ch 3, turn.

4th row—Three d (as in 2d row), 1 sp, 20 l sp, 7 d, 2 sp, 7 d, ch 8, turn.

5th row—From * to * of 3d row, 5 fest, 55 d, (make 5 d in each l sp and 1 in each d), 7 fest, 7 d, ch 3, turn.

6th row—Three d, 1 sp, 7 l sp, 55 d, 5 l sp; finish same as 4th row.

Continue working design from illustration and making edges as described. After 16th row, ch 3, turn, and work 6 d, 2 sp, 7 d over those of preceding row. Continue in same way until there are 6 rows of d across point. After 6th row, turn, sl across last 7 d, ch 3, 6 d, 2 sp, 7 d; finish as shown. Turn after 23d row and sl across 7 d and work as before.

At end of 31st row begin mitred corner. Make only 4 d at lower end of 31st row instead of the usual 7, turn and sl back over the 4 d, ch 8, turn.

32d row—Double crochet in next d (after next fest), one more l sp, 7 d (including the d after sp) ; finish as shown.

33d row—Work through last 7 d of row, then 1 fest, ch 8, turn.

34th row—Seven d in 7 d ; finish as shown.

35th row—Work through last 7 d of row, 1 fest, ch 8, turn.

36th row—Same as 34th row. *37th row*—Same as 35th row.

38th row—Same as 34th row. *39th row*—Same as 35th row.

40th row—Same as 34th row. *41st row*—Same as 35th row.

42d row—Same as 34th row.

43d row—After last 25 d of row, 1 fest, ch 8, turn.

44th row—Twenty-five d in 25 d ; finish as shown.

45th row—After last 4 fest, ch 8, turn.

46th row—Double crochet in next d, 3 more l sp ; finish as shown.

Work next 6 rows from illustration, turning at inside edge as described for 34th and 35th rows.

57th row—Ends with 7 d, ch 3, turn.

58th row—Miss 1 d, 6 d in next 6 ; finish as shown.

59th row—Ends with 19 d, ch 3, turn.

61st row—Ends with 5 fest, ch 8, turn, d in next d ; finish as shown.

63d row—After 3 fest, ch 8, turn.

65th row—After 1 fest, ch 8, turn.

67th row—After 2 sp, ch 5, turn.

68th row—Double crochet in next d, 1 more sp, 7 d, turn, and sl back over 7 d. This completes first half of corner.

To finish the corner begin as follows:

1st row—Chain 8, turn, miss 3 ch next hook, 5 d in next 5, sl in d between 2 sp, sl in next 3 ch, (to corner of point), turn.

2d row—Six d in 6 d (counting 3 ch as 1 d), ch 8, turn.

3d row—Five d on ch as in 1st row, 1 d in next d, 2 sp, 6 d, sl in 3d of 8 ch forming next point, sl in next 3 ch sts, turn.

4th row—Six d in 6 d, 2 sp, 7 d, ch 8, turn.

5th row—* Five d as in 1st row, 1 d in next d, 2 sp, 7 d, * 1 fest on next 7 d, ch 3, miss 2, s c in next, ch 3, sl in 3d of 8 ch of next point, sl in next 3 of 8 ch, ch 5, turn.

6th row—Double crochet in next d, ch 5, 7 d in 7 d, 2 sp, 7 d, ch 8, turn.

7th row—From * to * of 5th row (of second half of corner), 3 fest, ch 3, miss 2, s c in next, ch 3, sl in 3d and next 3 of 8 ch of next point, (as in 5th row), ch 5, turn.

8th row—Double crochet in next d, 3 more l sp, 7 d ; finish as shown.

9th row—Work through second 7 d, 5 fest; finish same as 7th row, except that the 4 sl sts are made on last 4 of 19 d, ch 5, turn.

10th row—Double crochet in next d, 5 more l sp; finish as shown.

11th row—Ends with 19 d, ch 3, s c between 2 rows of 19 d, ch 3, 4 sl on last 4 of 7 d, ch 5, turn.

12th row—Nineteen d on 19 d ; finish as shown.

13th row—Ends with 7 d ; then finish as 11th row.

14th row—Seven d in 7 d ; finish as shown.

Continue working as shown in the illustration, joining rows worked *inward*, same as 5th, and beginning rows worked *outward* with long space as shown.

The *39th row* ends with a 3 ch and a sl at outer end of the 4 sl (over 4 d) at end of 31st row of first half of corner. Turn and again sl back over the 4 d at end of 31st row, turn.

40th row—One sp, 2 l sp, 7 d, 2 sp, 7 d ; finish as shown.

41st row—Work toward inside edge and after last 7 d of row, make 1 fest, 7 d, (the 7 d are made in the sp and across end of 4 d), ch 3, turn.

42d row—Miss 1 d, 3 d in next 3, 1 sp, one l sp, 7 d ; finish as shown. This row begins straight edge after corner is finished. From this point the design may be readily copied without directions. After working the first large figure after the one at corner, the second one may be worked from illustration showing corner, if the first one is reversed. That is, the 1st row of second figure is same as last row of first, and so on th ough entire figure.

The difference between this fancy filet crochet and the ordinary kind is in the background, which is more open and lacy, and while the solid parts are the same, four or some multiple of four, small blocks are always used together, except perhaps on an edge. The large details show very plainly how the work is done and how the corners are mitred.

The triangles may be used for a variety of purposes besides the one suggested here. They may be set into sofa-pillows, scarfs, curtains, and bedspreads, or the entire spread could be made of the triangles joined together. This would be after the fashion of a patchwork quilt, the patches consisting of crocheted triangles.

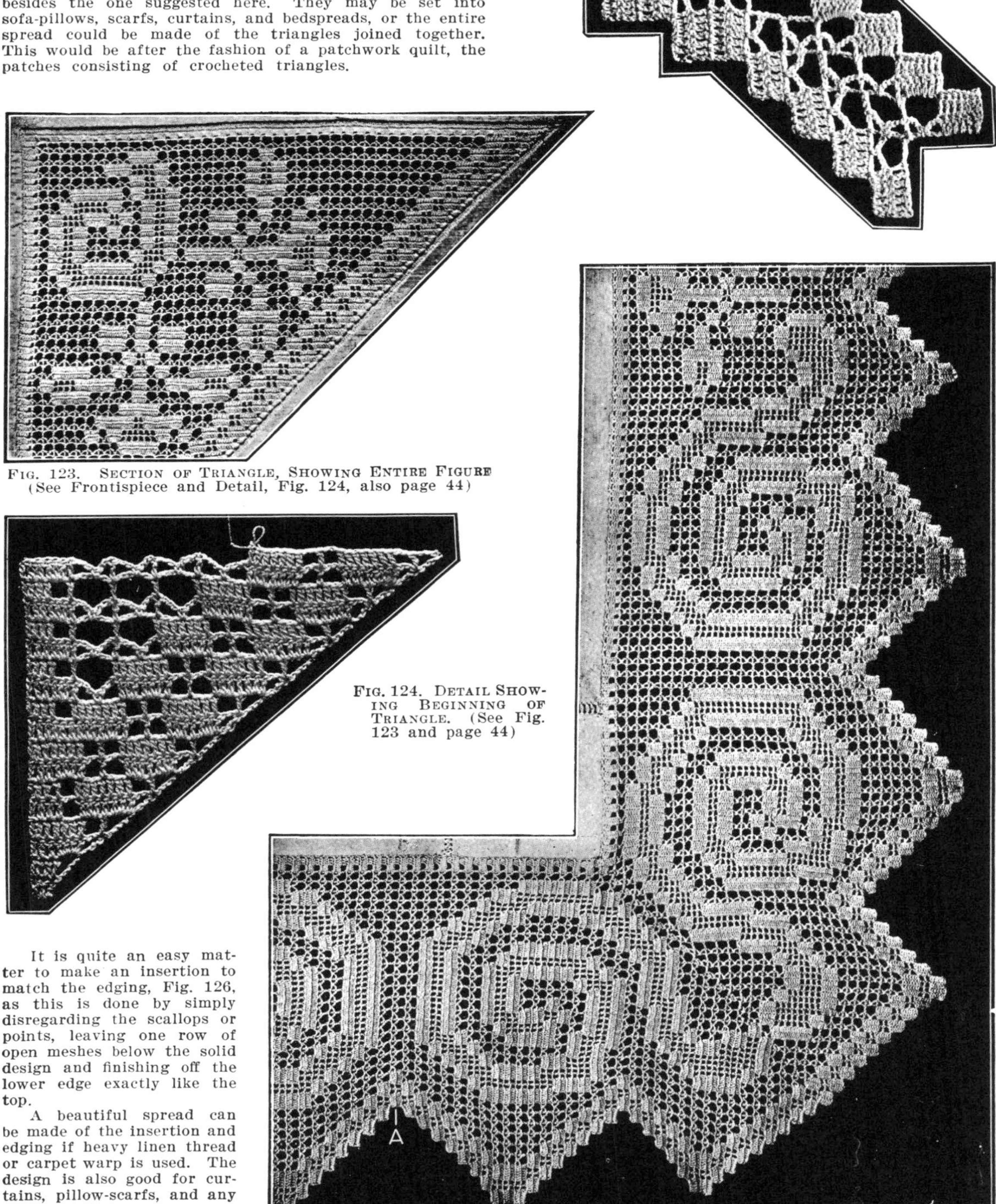

FIG. 125. SMALL SECTION OF INSIDE OF MITRED CORNER OF EDGING, SHOWING METHOD OF JOINING. (See Frontispiece and Fig. 126, also page 44)

FIG. 123. SECTION OF TRIANGLE, SHOWING ENTIRE FIGURE (See Frontispiece and Detail, Fig. 124, also page 44)

FIG. 124. DETAIL SHOWING BEGINNING OF TRIANGLE. (See Fig. 123 and page 44)

FIG. 126. SECTION OF EDGING FOR TEA CLOTH. (See page 44 and Fig. 125)

It is quite an easy matter to make an insertion to match the edging, Fig. 126, as this is done by simply disregarding the scallops or points, leaving one row of open meshes below the solid design and finishing off the lower edge exactly like the top.

A beautiful spread can be made of the insertion and edging if heavy linen thread or carpet warp is used. The design is also good for curtains, pillow-scarfs, and any other household linens on which a crocheted edge may be used.

Fig. 127. (See Fig. 128) 159 x 97 meshes

FIG. 128. This was worked with No. 70 crochet cotton and No. 14 hook. (See Fig. 127)

Figure 131. **BABY SHOES.** (See Figs. 129 and 130.) *Materials.*—One ball hard-twist crochet cotton No. 150 and No. 14 hook. The two uppers and two soles are made separately and joined with d. The left shoe is given in Fig. 129, and the left sole in Fig. 130; the right upper and sole are made in the same way, and reversed when they are crocheted together.

SOLE. (See Fig. 130.) — Begin the heel at A with 21 ch, turn, d in the 9th ch from the hook; the *1st row* is 5 sp (2 ch, 1 d). *2d row*—Chain 11, d in 9th from the hook making 1 sp, 1 sp, 16 d, add 3 sp. (See page 3 for the method of adding spaces at the end of a row.) *3d row*—Chain 8, 1 d in last d of row before, making 1 sp, 10 d, 5 sp, 7 d, add 1 sp, etc. Make the second sole like the first, and reverse it in joining to the upper.

FIG. 129. BLOCK PATTERN OF BABY SHOE (Left). See Fig. 131. 63 x 89 meshes. See pattern of left sole, Fig. 130.

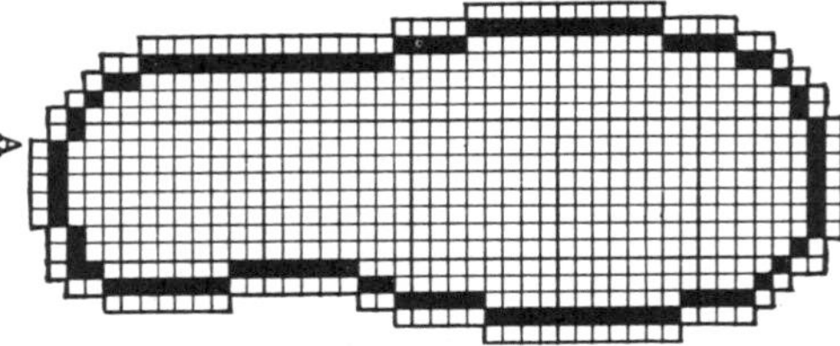

FIG. 130. PATTERN OF LEFT SOLE OF BABY SHOES 20 x 45 meshes. (See Figs. 129 and 131)

UPPER. (See Fig. 129.)—Begin at A, ch 27, turn, d in 9th ch from hook. *1st row*—Seven sp. *2d row*—Chain 18, d in 9th from hook, making 4 sp, 7 sp over 1st row, add 4 sp at the end of the row, etc.

Working back and forth, when B is reached, turn and make 7 rows between B and C. At C, ch 9 for the foundation of next 3 sp, ch 9 more and d into the 9th of the first ch; this will make the first of the 6 sp beyond C. The d will lie across the top of the sp, leaving the hook at the upper right-hand corner of the sp, turn the work and add 5 sp. This makes altogether 6 sp. Then ch 15, turn, d in 9th and make 3 sp over the ch, 6 sp over 6 sp, 3 sp over ch, and 3 sp over the body of the work, 7 d, etc. When D is reached, fasten and cut the thread; join it at E and work back and forth to F. Along the top of the upper (from D to F)

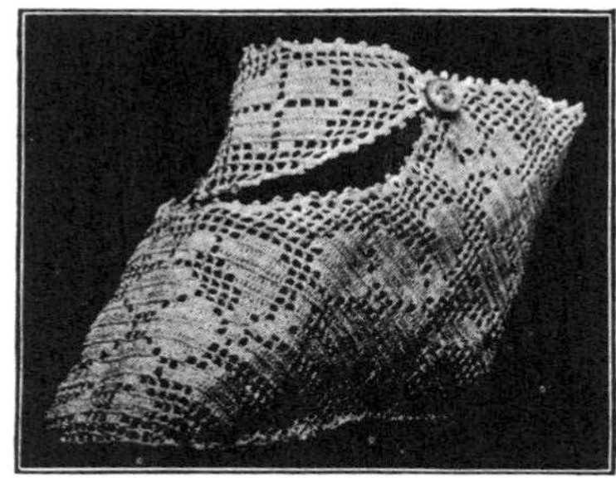

FIG. 131. BABY SHOE. (See Figs. 129 and 130)

FIG. 132. 93 meshes

work 3 s c in each sp along the edge, making a picot of 4 ch after every 6 sts. At H, ch 12 for a buttonhole-loop and cover with s c. Sew a tiny pearl button on the point opposite. With needle and thread, overcast the back seam of the upper, then holding the lower edge of upper to edge of sole, s c both edges together with 3 s c in each sp

FIG. 133. PANEL SUITABLE FOR A PILLOW. (Worked with No. 70 crochet cotton and No. 14 hook.) 123 x 93 meshes.

POLISH WING

Steve Brooking, Wojtek Matusiak, Piotr Sikora

303 Squadron North American Mustang

STRATUS

Wydawnictwo STRATUS sp. j.
Po. Box 123, 27-600 Sandomierz 1, Poland
phone. +48 15 833 30 41
e-mail: office@stratusbooks.pl
www.stratusbooks.pl www.mmpbooks.biz

ISBN 978-83-65281-80-7

Layout concept Bartłomiej Belcarz
Cover concept Artur Juszczak
Cover artwork Zbigniew Kolacha
Proofreading Roger Wallsgrove
DTP Artur Juszczak
Colour Profiles © John Melson
Edited by Roger Wallsgrove

PRINTED IN POLAND

The authors would like to thank the following veterans and their relatives for sharing photographs and documents:

Mark Baczkiewicz (for Stanisław Bączkiewicz), the late Jakub Bargiełowski, Jan Bartkowiak (for Zenon Bartkowiak), the late Stanisław Bochniak, Rodney Byles (for Marian Matejski), the Dowgalski family (for Eugeniusz Dowgalski), Bożena Gostkowska (for Witold Łokuciewski), Małgorzata Jagieniak (for Norbert Miszkowicz), the late Edward Jaworski, Ted Knobelsdorf (for Roman Knobelsdorf), the Kufluk family (for Romuald Kufluk), Ryszard Mach (for Bronisław Mach), Marek Malarowski (for Andrzej Malarowski), Jacek and Karol Mierzejewski (for Józef Mierzejewski), Richard Palimaka (for Józef Palimąka), the late Tadeusz Rybak, the Skrzydło family (for Władysław Skrzydło), Piotr Trąbiński (for Sylwester Patoka), Jan Wieckowicz (for Zbigniew Więckowicz), Paul Zdanowski (for Stanisław Zdanowski).

Other photographs courtesy of:
Bartomiej Belcarz, Dave Birch, Steve Brooking, Artur Domański, Andrzej Glass, Łukasz Gredys, Adam Jackowski, Mick Jennings, Tadeusz Królikiewicz, Zbigniew Legierski, Wojtek Matusiak, Micha Mucha, Lechosław Musiałkowski, Piotr Paszkowski, Wilhelm Ratuszyński, Piotr Sikora, Andy Thomas, Józef Zieliński, Wojciech Zmyślony, Ryszard Górecki collection, Muzeum Lotnictwa Polskiego – Cracow, Polish Institute and Sikorski Museum – London, Royal Air Force Museum – London.

Special thanks to Peter Devitt, Artur Domański, Robert Gretzyngier, Richard Palimaka, Andy Renwick and Wojciech Zmyślony for their help.

***Previous page:** A group of pilots with Mustang IV believed to be KH868 PD-E, in the summer of 1945. Standing on the ground, left to right: F/Lt Tomasz Rzyski, F/Lt Zenon Krzeptowski, F/O Bronisław Zborowski, W/O Leszek Bisanz. On the aeroplane, left to right: possibly F/O Borys Runc (on the wing root), F/O Włodzimierz Polaniak (standing above him), F/O Jan Schandler, Sgt Marian Matejski (visiting Lancaster pilot from No. 300 Sqn), F/Sgt Jan Kukuć, F/Lt Stefan Kleczkowski, F/Sgt Antoni Benski. The aircraft is armed with practice bombs on a pylon adapter rack. Note 'POLAND' in red below the Polish AF marking on the nose.*

***Front cover:** A trio of No. 303 Sqn Mustang IVs in flight soon after the unit re-equipped with the type in April 1945.*

***Back cover:** KH663 RF-M, one of a couple of camouflaged Mustang IVs used by No. 303 Sqn.*

303 SQUADRON NORTH AMERICAN MUSTANG

No. 303 'Kościuszko' Squadron

No. 303 Squadron has been, without a doubt, the most famous unit in the history of the Polish Air Force. It was formed in the summer of 1940 as the fourth Polish squadron in Britain (preceded by Nos. 300 and 301 Bomber, and No. 302 Fighter Squadrons). Officially, No. 303 Sqn came into existence on 2 August 1940. Its personnel mainly came from the former fighter units of the Warsaw-based 1st Air Regiment (1 *Pułk Lotniczy*) and the new unit took the traditions of the 111th 'Kościuszko' Fighter Flight (*111 Eskadra Myśliwska im. Tadeusza Kościuszki*).

The 'Kościuszko' tradition dated back to the Polish-Russian war of 1919–1921. During that conflict a group of American flyers volunteered to fly with Poland's air service, and thus to repay the debt of their nation towards the Poles who had fought in the American War of Independence in the late 18th century. That was why the Polish unit to which they were posted took on the name of Tadeusz Kościuszko, who distinguished himself in Poland's wars of the period, and was also a general in the American war. The badge of the unit reflected this, by using the red-and-white stripes and thirteen stars of the first American states, combined with the Cracow region peasant hat and crossed scythes prepared for combat (symbols of the Polish Rising against Russia, in which peasant infantry played an important role). In 1940 the Kościuszko badge and his name were taken on by No. 303 Squadron.

The unit was formed at Northolt in the outskirts of London and this would decide its subsequent history. Even before it completed its training, No. 303 Squadron found itself in the very centre of the Battle of Britain, as the air fighting shifted from the Channel and southern England to the London area. Unlike an average RAF pilot at the time, the Poles already had substantial experience from air combats over Poland and France. However, it was over England in the summer of 1940 that they were first able to engage the Germans on equal terms, flying the latest fighter types and profiting from an excellent early

[1]: No. 303 Sqn pilots in the summer of 1945 with one of their Mustangs. Left to right: F/O Tadeusz Sikorski, F/O Jan Schandler, F/O Włodzimierz Polaniak, F/Lt Stefan Kleczkowski, F/O Bronisław Zborowski, F/O Borys Runc, F/Lt Zenon Krzeptowski, F/Sgt Konrad Sztuka.

[2]: A souvenir photo taken at RAF Coltishall, probably at the time when No. 303 Squadron was about to leave for conversion onto Mustangs. Standing, left to right: W/Cdr Julian Kowalski (Polish station commander), G/Cpt Arthur H. Donaldson (RAF station commander) and S/Ldr Bolesław Drobiński (commanding No. 303 Sqn). Backdrop is provided by Spitfire F.IX MA683 RF-M. In the evening of 30 March 1945 W/O Skrzydło flew it from Ursel to Coltishall, this being the last Spitfire flight recorded in No. 303 Squadron Operations Record Book. W/Cdr Kowalski continued to be the Polish station commander at subsequent bases of No. 303 Sqn until its disbandment.

warning and control system. All these factors contributed to the enormous success of No. 303 Sqn. The squadron was praised by ACM Dowding, who commanded Fighter Command in that campaign, as the Command's top-scoring unit in the Battle.

Following its highly successful participation in the Battle, in mid-October No. 303 Squadron moved north, to Leconfield near the Yorkshire coast, away from the most intensive fighting area. There it became a training unit for a number of Polish pilots who had to be introduced into British air fighting procedures. At the same time the squadron flew coastal and shipping patrols to protect the convoys travelling along the East Coast.

During the war the same sequence was repeated several times: the squadron had a tour of combat duties at Northolt or another air base in Southern England, followed by several months of 'rest' at an airfield away from the frontline.

In January 1941 No. 303 Squadron returned to Northolt, which by now had become the main Polish fighter base in Britain. Here it re-equipped with the latest RAF fighter, the Supermarine Spitfire.

By mid-1941 fighter squadrons in Britain started to be grouped in fighter wings. Two such wings were formed within the exiled Polish Air Force. The 1st Wing was based at Northolt as the principal offensive formation of Polish fighters (the 2nd Wing was headquartered at Exeter at the time). Polish fighter squadrons rotated, joining the 1st Wing for tours of intensive operations and then leaving it for periods of rest.

With the *Luftwaffe* no longer attacking Britain in force, it was now the turn of the RAF and allied squadrons to attack enemy held territory. These operations became particularly intensive in the summer 1941, when Hitler invaded the USSR.

Between mid-July and early October 1941 No. 303 Squadron was again 'resting', this time at Speke near Liverpool. In October it returned to Northolt and until June 1942 it participated in combat operations over occupied Europe. In the summer of 1942 it started another period of rest, now at Kirton-in-Lindsey in the North-East of England, where the 2nd Polish Wing had moved by then. The Polish pilots were not only training their own younger colleagues there, but also American pilots. At the time USAAF units started to arrive in the European Theatre of Operations with personnel who had practically no operational experience. One of those fighter squadrons was based together with No. 303 for a while, and the Poles introduced the US pilots to the tricks of the fighter trade.

In August 1942 No. 303 Squadron moved south for a few days, to take part in the air operations connected with the ill-fated Dieppe landings. Although a defeat on the ground, the battle proved successful for the Polish flyers, once again No. 303 became the top-scorers among Fighter Command units.

In early 1943 No. 303 returned to the 1st Polish Wing, initially based at the satellite airfield at Heston, and from June 1943 at Northolt. The squadron continued intensive combat operations until mid-November 1943, usually flying escort missions for allied bombers over the occupied Europe (or even over Germany).

By then the 2nd Polish Wing had become an operational one, just like the 1st Wing. From late 1943 until 1945 the 3rd Polish Wing was established as a token backup formation, with two

[3]: An anonymous Mustang IV sits at Andrews Field after delivery on 5 April 1945. Note the exhaust glare shield (for night flying) mounted in front of the cockpit. In September 1944 when the RAF Mustang squadrons began to escort daylight operations for Bomber Command the RAF introduced Mod No 616 "Introduction of exhaust glare shield (for night flying)" but photographs show that most squadrons including No. 303 removed this after delivery.

squadrons, Nos. 303 and 316, equipped with different aircraft types and operating separately. Their main role was to accept newly trained pilots straight out of operational training units and prepare them for service with one of the two front-line wings. Therefore, while No. 316 Sqn converted to Mustang IIIs in 1944 (to match the 2nd Polish Wing), No. 303 continued to fly Spitfires (to support the 1st Polish Wing on Spitfire LF.IXs and then XVIs).

In November 1943 No. 303 moved for another period of 'rest', to a particularly distant place: Ballyhalbert near Belfast in Northern Ireland. In April 1944, while nominally still a 'resting' backup unit, it returned to Southern England and operated from Horne in anticipation of the Normandy landings. From D-Day on, the unit flew in support of the invasion forces. Later in 1944 it moved to Merston and then to Westhampnett, still supporting the ground forces on the Continent. In October it moved again, and changed its role. Based at RAF Coltishall in East Anglia, No. 303 Squadron was tasked with searching and destroying the German V2 rocket launch pads, Hitler's 'wonder weapon'.

During the twelve months from April 1944 to March 1945, No. 303 flew intensive operations on obsolete Spitfire variants (first Mk Vs and then early Mk IXs), suffering losses and casualties that were due not only to enemy action, but also to the poor condition of the worn-out machines.

Polish Mustang units

The first Polish unit to re-equip with the Mustang was No. 309 Squadron, a tactical reconnaissance unit, which flew the Allison-engined Mustang I between mid-1942 and February 1944, and then briefly in September 1944. In 1944 it eventually lost its reconnaissance role and became a dedicated fighter unit on Mustang IIIs.

Meanwhile, in the spring of 1944 the 2nd Polish Wing (No. 133 Wing in the 2nd TAF structure) converted from Spitfire Vs to Mustang IIIs. At the time the wing included two Polish squadrons: Nos. 306 and 315, plus No. 129 'Mysore' Sqn RAF. As described earlier, No. 316 Sqn converted to Mustang IIIs at the same time.

In April 1945, with the war in Europe about to end, the backup role of the 3rd Wing was no longer essential, and it was decided to equip both its squadrons, Nos. 303 and 316, with the same type: the Mustang. As by this time Mustang IIIs were no longer delivered to Britain, superseded by the Mk IV, it was this most recent Mustang variant that was supplied to No. 303 Sqn.

Although no other Polish AF squadron re-equipped with the Mustang IV, two more examples were used by the exiled Polish units.

The second P-51D delivered to Britain, KH642 (ex 44-11169), was used by W/Cdr Kazimierz Rutkowski, the leader of the 3rd Polish Wing, Various documents quote its code as KR or KWR, but no photographs have surfaced so far.

KM249 (ex–P-51K-10NT 44-12372) was transferred from No. 250 Sqn RAF to No. 318 Squadron in Italy in September 1945 'with a view of making flying more interesting for the pilots' (as the squadron Operations Record Book explained it). The only known photo shows it still with code letters LD-J of the former unit, and it is not clear if it ever received No. 318's code letters, LW. In February 1946 it was transferred back to No. 239 Wing HQ.

No. 303 Squadron on Mustangs

At the end of March 1945 No. 303 Squadron and No. 6303 Servicing Echelon started preparations for a move to RAF Andrews Field, where they would convert onto North American Mustang IVs. Their Spitfires were to be handed over to No. 441 Sqn RCAF. At the time No. 303 Sqn was commanded by S/Ldr Bolesław Drobiński, with F/Lts Mirosław Szelestowski and Stanisław Socha as 'A' and 'B' Flight commanders, respectively.

The first four Mustang IVs were delivered on 4 April. A few Allison-engined Mustang Is were also used by the squadron to speed-up its conversion. Squadron pilots undertook their first taxiing practices on the 5th, but it was not until 8 April that first flights were made. Formation flying commenced on the 12th. The first squadron-strength formation was flown on the morning of 20 April. There was no flying the following day, due to bad weather, and just a few training sorties were flown on the 22nd.

On 23 April 1945 No. 303 Squadron flew its first operation on the Mustangs, 'Ramrod' 1552 (escort for 150 Lancasters sent to bomb Flensburg). Eight pilots took off:

- S/Ldr Bolesław Drobiński (KM112 RF-D)
- F/Lt Mirosław Szelestowski (KH855 RF-A)
- F/O Mieczysław Maksymowicz (KM102 RF-G)
- P/O Zygfryd Nowiński (KM220 RF-B)
- W/O Zenon Bartkowiak (KH836 RF-R)
- F/Sgt Jerzy Kmiecik (KM239 RF-I)
- F/Sgt Józef Janicki (KM201 RF-Z)
- F/Sgt Marian Michalak (KM263 RF-T)

However, P/O Nowiński and F/Sgt Michalak had to turn back within an hour. The squadron was led by S/Ldr Drobiński in his personal Mustang IV KM112 RF-D. The Andrews Field Wing included at the time Nos. 303 and 316 Squadrons of the Polish Air Force and No. 122 Sqn RAF (Nos. 122 and 316 flying Mustang IIIs). The wing was led by W/Cdr Clifford Percival Rudland.

No. 303 sqn suffered its first Mustang accident on 24 April 1945, when F/O Krok's KH770 (probably coded RF-J) was damaged during landing.

The squadron's final operational mission, 'Ramrod' 1554, took place on 25 April 1945. That day several hundred Lancasters (including fourteen of the Polish No. 300 Squadron) bombed Obersalzberg near Berchtesgaden, Hitler's Alpine resort. They were escorted by Mustangs from No. 11 Group Fighter Command RAF and the VIII Fighter Command USAAF. The former included five Polish squadrons: Nos. 306, 309 and 315 (all on Mustang IIIs) from Coltishall, led by W/Cdr Kazimierz Rutkowski, and Nos. 303 and 316 from Andrews Field. The latter two again flew together with No. 122 Sqn RAF, the wing being led by W/Cdr Rudland. The following No. 303 Squadron pilots participated in this mission:

- S/Ldr Bolesław Drobiński (KH836 RF-R),
- F/Lt Janusz Franckiewicz (KH663 RF-M),
- F/Lt Stefan Kleczkowski (KM209 RF-S),
- F/Lt Edward Bartys (KH868 RF-E),
- F/O Tadeusz Sikorski (KH866 RF-P),
- F/O Stanisław Zdanowski (KH825 RF-C),
- P/O Zygfryd Nowiński (KM239 RF-I),
- W/O Władysław Sznapka (KH855 RF-A),
- W/O Alojzy Rutecki (KM220 RF-B),

[4]: No. 303 Sqn padre, S/Ldr Wilhelm Stempor (right) with unidentified civilians on a Mustang IV. The Polish national marking is visible on the nose and the squadron badge on the fuselage (directly above the gun ports). The horizontal bar of the code letter next to the badge shows the aircraft was photographed before the change of the squadron code to PD.

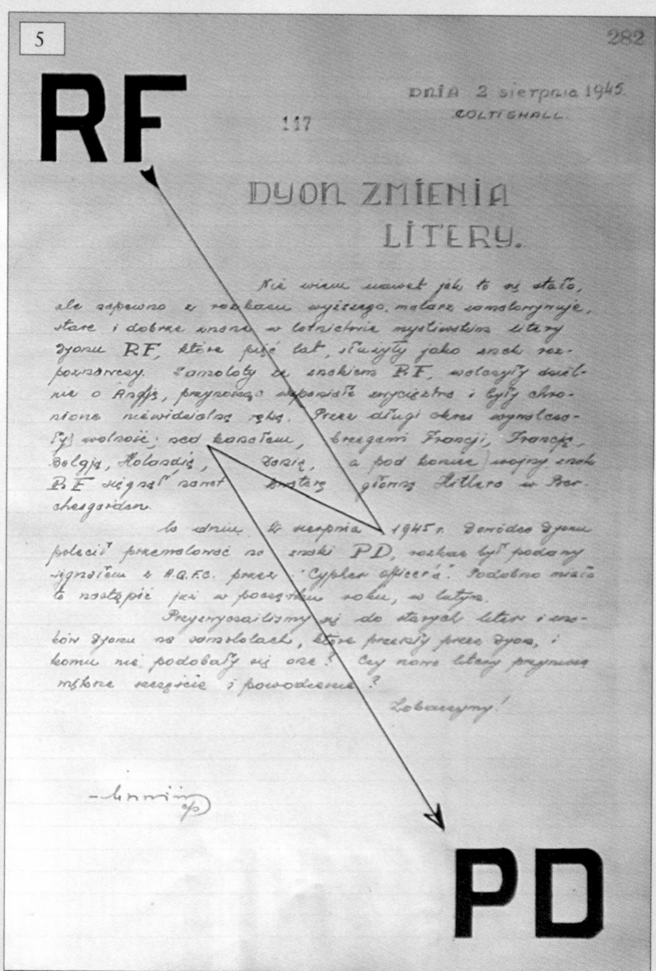

5 282

RF

DNIA 2 sierpnia 1945
COLTISHALL

117

DYON ZMIENIA LITERY.

Nie wiem nawet jak to się stało, ale zapewno z rozkazu wyższego, malarz samolotowy maluje, stare i dobrze znane w lotnictwie myśliwskim litery dyonu RF, które pięć lat, służyły jako znak rozpoznawczy. Samoloty ze znakiem RF, walczyły dzielnie o Anglję, przynosząc wspaniałe zwycięstwa i były chronione niewidzialną ręką. Przez długi okres symbolizowały wolność; nad Kanałem, brzegami Francji, Francję, Belgję, Holandję, Rzeszę, a pod koniec wojny znak RF sięgnął samej [illegible] górnej Hitlera w Berchesgaden.

W dniu 4 sierpnia 1945 r. Dowódca dyonu polecił przemalować na znaki PD, rozkaz był podany sygnałem z H.Q.F.C. przez "Cypher oficera". Podobno miało to nastąpić już w początku roku, w lutym.

Przyzwyczailiśmy się do starych liter i znaków dyonu na samolotach, które przeżyły przez dyon, i komu nie podobały się one? Czy nowe litery przyniosą również szczęście i powodzenie?

Zobaczymy!

PD

- W/O Władysław Skrzydło (KH769 RF-Y),
- F/Sgt Marian Michalak (KM238 RF-U).

The squadron took off from Andrews Field between 07.05 and 07.10 and at the end of the mission landed at B.86 (Helmond) between 11.55 and 12.00 to refuel. The Mustangs landed back at Andrews Field about 17.00. As satisfactory as it was for all the pilots, the operation was largely uneventful, although there were mishaps both during take-off and landing. W/O Skrzydło suffered an accident when taking off, while F/O Sikorski's Mustang was damaged during landing at B.86. Both aircraft had to be sent away for repairs and did not return to No. 303 Squadron.

Bad weather then prevented any operational or training flying until the end of the month, apart from four Mustangs attempting a short formation practice on 28 April. While taking

[5]: This page from the squadron diary dated 2 August 1945, provides a prominent record of the change of codes from RF to PD. The reason for the change was neither known nor understood by the squadron. It caused great disappointment across the unit and was generally considered an unnecessary nuisance, if not deliberately malicious. The change occurred soon after the British government ceased to recognise the Polish Government in Exile and the Polish squadrons were absorbed into the RAF (although the diary entry says that it had been, apparently, originally scheduled for February 1945). The RF code letters had been carried with pride by No. 303 Squadron throughout their combat career from their time as the most successful fighter squadron in the Battle of Britain. For reasons best known to the RAF the RF code was subsequently carried by No 1510 Radio Aids Training Flight!

[6]: No. 303 Squadron pilots and ground officers photographed on 3 October 1945 during gunnery and bombing practice at No. 1 Armament Practice Station, RAF Fairwood Common. Seated, left to right: F/O Borys Runc, F/O Tadeusz Broniecki (Engineering Officer), F/Lt Edward Bartys, F/O Bronisław Zborowski, F/Lt Andrzej Malarowski, S/Ldr Bolesław Drobiński, F/Lt Mirosław Szelestowski, F/Lt Stanisław Zdanowski, F/O Zenon Krzeptowski, F/O Julian Krok, F/Lt Stefan Kleczkowski; standing in the first row, left to right: W/O Władysław Skrzydło, F/O Tadeusz Sikorski, F/Sgt Jerzy Kmiecik, F/Sgt Józef Janicki, F/O Jan Schandler, P/O Edward Martens, F/O Zygfryd Nowiński, W/O Władysław Sznapka; standing in the second row: F/Sgt Antoni Benski, F/Sgt Jan Kukuć, F/Sgt Konrad Sztuka, F/Sgt Leszek Bisanz, W/O Zenon Bartkowiak, W/O Eugeniusz Dowgalski; on the propeller: F/O Ryszard Górecki. A stencilled number can be seen painted on the left hand propeller blade (see enlargement). The number seems to be 12386 which was part of the USAAF serial number 44-12386 of a P-51K Mustang assigned to the RAF as KM263 (PD-T). The Technical Order instructions for the shipping of aircraft by sea state that the aircraft serial should be stencilled on all parts removed from the aircraft during preparation which would include the propeller.

off F/O Krok suffered an accident and KH855 RF-A was seriously damaged. Fortunately the pilot escaped unhurt. This was No. 303 Squadron's fourth Mustang damaged within a month since it started conversion onto the type. The Mustang, as formidable a fighter as it was, was a much less forgiving aircraft than any of the Spitfire variants the unit had used before. After a day of bad weather, extensive flying training on Mustangs commenced on 2 May.

8 May marked the end of the war in Europe. It was a day of joy for all, but for the Poles there was much less joy than for the British. Even though Poland was free of German occupation, it was now controlled by Stalin, who had nominated a puppet regime in Warsaw, while his army and secret police persecuted the Poles loyal to the exiled Polish Government in London.

On 14 May 1945 the squadron received orders to move back to Coltishall. The move took place two days later.

Flying training continued for the rest of the month. On 25 May F/Lt Socha was replaced by F/Lt Zdanowski as the 'B' Flight Commander.

On 6 July HM Government officially withdrew recognition of the Polish Government in Exile and recognised the puppet administration set up by Stalin in Poland. From then on, Polish squadrons and other elements of the Polish Armed Forces came under British control. Technically No. 303 Squadron (and all other units of the exiled Polish Air Force) became part of the RAF.

Training continued as before, and orders were received from HQ Fighter Command to change the No. 303 Squadron code from RF to PD. This was done on 2 August.

On the morning of 8 August W/O Skrzydło in Mustang IV KM115 PD-V collided with No. 306 Squadron's Mustang III HB866 (code unknown) of F/Lt Stefan Tronczyński during taxiing and both aircraft were damaged.

On 9 August the squadron commenced its move from Coltishall back to Andrews Field and the aircraft flew there on the afternoon of the 10th.

Intensive training flying continued, and on 20 August 303 Squadron suffered its first fatal accident on the Mustangs. During a bomber escort practice W/O Alojzy Rutecki (in KM113 PD-F) and F/Sgt Stanisław Magdziak (KM201 PD-Z) collided in clouds and were both killed, their aircraft crashing at Lickey End, Bromsgrove, Worcestershire. Magdziak had served with 303 since December 1944, while Rutecki was one of the most experienced pilots of the unit, having flown with it since February 1942.

[7]: A group of ground crew (LAC Józef Palimąka third from the left) with an anonymous Mustang of No. 303 Sqn, with the later PD code letters. The squadron badge near the cockpit and the Polish AF national marking on the nose suggest that this was one of the aircraft delivered before July 1945. Available photos show that no Mustang taken on charge by the unit after July 1945 had the white-and-red square painted on, and the same applies to the Kościuszko badge. No reason for that could be found in documents or personal accounts, but the timeframe suggests that this was connected with the British withdrawal of recognition of the exiled Polish Government, and the incorporation of Polish squadrons into the RAF.

On 26 August eight Mustangs of the squadron led by F/Lt Zdanowski escorted the battleship HMS *Queen Elizabeth* on her final voyage.

As in previous years, Squadron Day celebrations started on 31st August. Many former members of the unit joined these. In the evening F/Lt Malarowski led a section of three Mustangs to drop a wreath in the Channel, commemorating squadron members who lost their lives 'in the drink'. The main fete, which started with a solemn mass, and ended in a party for all ranks, took place on the actual Squadron Day, 1 September.

Squadron formation was practiced during 12–14 September, and on the 15th twelve Mustangs led by S/Ldr Drobiński took part in the Battle of Britain anniversary flypast over London. Whilst taxiing after landing from this show, W/O Skrzydło in KH663 PD-M collided with F/Lt Zdanowski in KH836 PD-R, seriously damaging both Mustangs.

Two days later, on 17 September, both squadrons of the 3rd Polish Wing (Nos. 303 and 316) and their accompanying Servicing Echelons moved from Andrews Field to No. 1 Armament Practice Station at Fairwood Common for training in air-to-air and air-to-ground gunnery, and dive bombing. While there, on 28 September F/O Schandler suffered an accident in Mustang IV KM209 PD-S which was very severely damaged. On 5 October 1945 both squadrons returned to Andrews Field.

In November 1945 the squadron took part in two exercises: 'Funfair' (6–13) and 'Johnny' (14–15). On 13 November a landing collision resulted in slight damage to two Mustangs: KH825 PD-C of F/Lt Szelestowski and KM220 PD-B of F/Lt Malarowski.

At the end of November No. 303 Squadron moved to RAF Turnhouse in Scotland. The Mustangs flew to the new location on the 28th, leaving Andrews Field at 13.30 and landing at Turnhouse at 16.20. The rail party left Andrews Field on 30 November, arriving at the destination on 1 December.

The new year started badly when F/O Schandler was killed on 2 January. He was flying the new PD-S, KH836, which stalled on take off, probably due to propeller pitch control failure, as the propeller was found in fully feathered position in the wreckage.

The stay at Turnhouse was only temporary, and on 4 January the squadron rail party left for RAF Wick in northern Scotland. Adverse weather delayed the Mustangs, and they flew on the 5th, landing at the destination at 12.20.

On 11 January Mustang IV KM238 PD-U was written off in a landing accident of W/O Łubieński, but the pilot escaped unhurt.

Between 13 and 21 January the squadron took part in Group Exercise 'Dodgem 14'.

KH744 PD-M was written off in accident on 25 January, this being the third Mustang destroyed with No. 303 Squadron during the month. Taxiing with F/Lt Sikorski at the controls, it was run into by F/O Zborowski in KH868 PD-E. Both pilots escaped unhurt and PD-E was damaged but repairable.

S/Ldr Łokuciewski, No. 303 Sqn's Battle of Britain veteran, took over command of the squadron at the beginning of February 1946, replacing S/Ldr Drobiński. At the same time F/Lt Szelestowski was replaced by F/Lt Kazimierz Budzik at the head of the 'A' Flight.

Training flying continued throughout February, and the squadron took part in Group Exercise 'Dodgem 18' on the 14th.

On 4 March 303 Squadron went for gunnery training to No. 3 Armament Practice Station at RAF Charter Hall.

Mustang IV KM297 PD-K was damaged during taxiing on 12 March with F/Lt Krok at the controls. It collided with a stationary vehicle on the runway.

Upon completion of training at Charter Hall the squadron moved to RAF Hethel at the end of the month, the air party flying on the 23rd, and the ground party travelling on 25–26 March.

W/O Konrad Sztuka was killed in a crash of KH747 PD-F at Ketteringham Park, Norfolk on 29 March. It was believed that his engine failed soon after take-off and he attempted to turn back to reach the airfield. He was the last pilot to lose his life while serving with No. 303 Sqn.

Training flying in May was mostly uneventful, except for the accident of F/O Haczkiewicz on the 8th, when he ditched 6 miles off Wells-on-Sea, Norfolk after the engine cut in KM102 PD-G. The pilot escaped unhurt. This was the last recorded aircraft accident in No. 303 Squadron.

On 5 June F/Lt Zdanowski was posted to Station HQ RAF Hethel and F/Lt Bronisław Mach was appointed to command the 'B' Flight.

On 2 July the squadron took part in Group Exercise 'Roster'. On 3 July a section led by F/Lt Malarowski performed an air display for local young people over Beccles Common, as part of the British Legion Silver Jubilee celebrations. As a special treat, Beccles schoolchildren were able to talk to the pilots on the radio during the flight.

Squadron Day was celebrated for the last time. On 31 August the Roll of Honour was read out during a parade at 18.15. The same evening three Mustangs led by F/O Górecki dropped a wreath in the Channel to commemorate squadron pilots who died in its waters. Górecki, who had survived 74 hours 'in the drink' in July 1941, was particularly suited to give this last farewell to his colleagues who were not as lucky as him. On 1 September a mass was said in No. 303 Squadron hangar, followed by a lunch for all squadron members and guests at 11.45. A party was organised in the evening.

On Saturday 14 September eight Mustangs of the squadron took part in the great Battle of Britain anniversary flypast, alongside 35 other fighter squadrons (including eight Polish).

No. 303 Squadron continued to fly its Mustangs on various training missions for another two months. A final farewell ceremony for the squadron was organised on 27 November. Many former members of the unit participated, including W/Cdr Zdzisław Krasnodębski, the first Polish commander of 303. In the most moving moment of the ceremony, S/Ldr Łokuciewski 'removed' the squadron badge from one of the Mustangs.

Two days later, on 29 November 1946, No. 303 Squadron Mustangs were ferried to Lyneham for disposal.

The squadron disbanded on 9 December. Although at that time it seemed like this was the end of the 'Kościuszko Squadron' traditions in the Polish Air Force, it was not so. See 'Polish Wings' no. 21 for the continued story…

[8]: KM112 PD-D photographed after the war with a visiting airman, LAC Romuald Kufluk. The Mustang was the personal mount of No. 303 Squadron commanders: first S/Ldr Bolesław Drobiński and then S/Ldr Witold Łokuciewski. For more photos of the aircraft, see pp. 36-39.

[9]: North American Mustang I, AM126/5, April–May 1945, RAF Andrews Field.

[10]: No. 303 Sqn appears to be the only RAF/PAF unit to have used Allison-engine Mustangs for conversion from the Spitfire. At the beginning of 1945 No. 133 (Polish) Wing at Andrews Field had several Mustang I aircraft (officially allocated to individual squadrons), used for initial training of newly arriving pilots. When No. 303 Squadron moved to Andrews Field these aircraft were transferred to them. Here one of the Mustang Is, believed to be AM126, is seen taxiing through a No. 306 Squadron dispersal at Andrews Field. The aircraft displays no Polish national marking, nor a squadron emblem. Available documents suggest that no squadron code was applied to these Mustang Is, just single-digit numbers. At least two pilots (F/Sgts Michalak and Benski) recorded the code number '5' for AM126 in their personal flying log books.

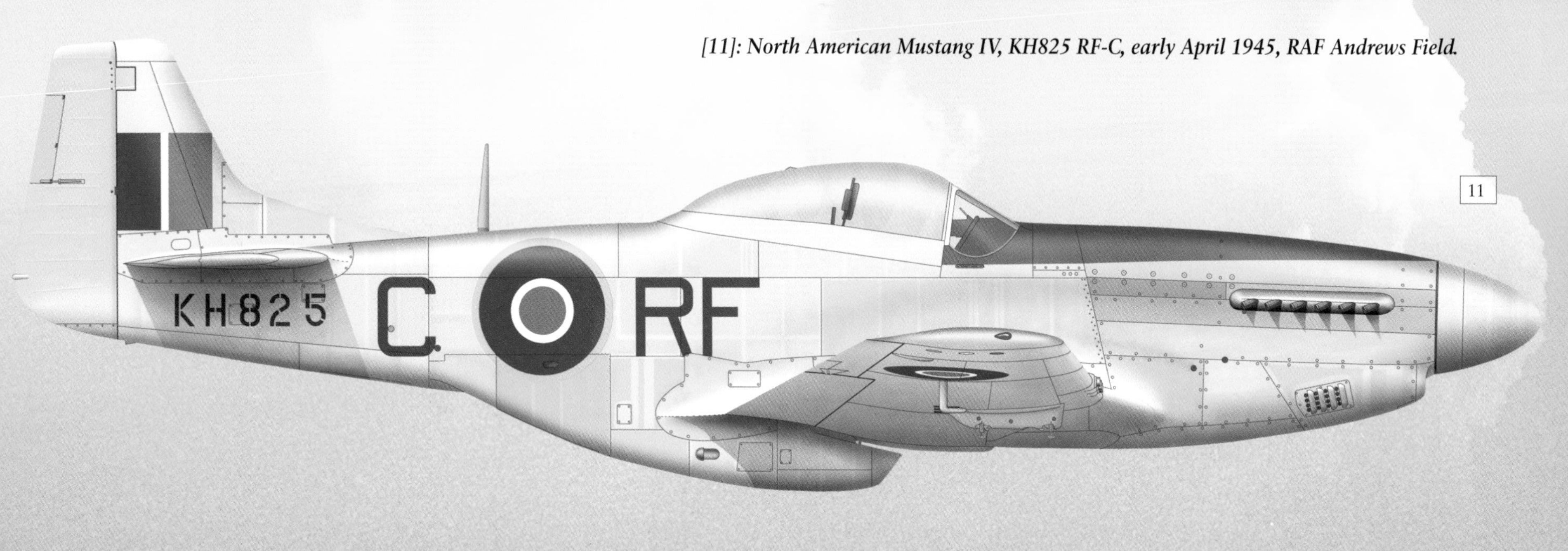

[11]: North American Mustang IV, KH825 RF-C, early April 1945, RAF Andrews Field.

12

[12]: In the first days of April 1945 Polish Air Force Film Unit crew visited RAF Andrews Field and recorded the first Mustang IVs in No. 303 Sqn markings. At that time they already had the RF codes painted on, but carried neither the 'Kościuszko' badge nor the Polish AF insignia. KH825 RF-C, a brand new Mustang IV, is seen landing at Andrews Field, with the flaps fully extended. With the exception of KH663 and KH669, all other Mustang IVs of No. 303 Sqn were built as P-51Ks according to the US nomenclature. P-51K aircraft are sometimes labelled 'Mk IVA' in British publications, but as far as can be ascertained no such designation was applied officially, both the P-51D and P-51K being simply called the Mk IV by the RAF.

[13, 17]: Mustang IV KH866 RF-P comes in to land and taxies at Andrews Field in the first days of April 1945. These two photos show clearly the standard layout of codes on No. 303 Sqn Mustangs, with the unit code RF near the cockpit and the aircraft letter between the roundel and the tail, on both sides of the fuselage. KH866 was lost by No. 303 within three weeks of delivery. On the 25th it was flown by F/O Tadeusz Sikorski during 'Ramrod' 1554 to Berchtesgaden. When landing at B.86 (Helmond) to refuel, the port wheel seized, causing the aircraft to swing violently off the runway, which resulted in damage to the starboard undercarriage leg and wing attachments. The aircraft did not return to No. 303 Squadron after repair, it was placed in store and eventually scrapped. This Mustang has been mis-identified in some publications as KH865, but that machine never served with the Polish unit. It has also been confused with the subsequent RF-P, KH669, delivered in early May 1945. That machine, however, was in fact one of the last camouflaged Mustang IVs.

[14]: F/Lt Bochniak (No. 308 Sqn) with a Mustang. This photo shows the louvered plate over the filtered carburettor air intake to advantage. As can be seen the separate louvres were fitted directly on to the original perforated intake. The louvres were a small part of RAF Mod No 622 "To improve air filter installation". The lip of the main carburettor air intake appears to be darker than the engine cowling panels. It was an alloy casting (most likely magnesium alloy) which explains the different appearance in most photos of aircraft in natural metal finish.

[15]: F/Lt Bochniak on a Mustang. This photo offers good comparison of the various styles and sizes of rivets and fasteners, including the fixings for the exhaust glare shield. The photos were probably taken in late 1946 when the Polish Spitfire Wing (Nos. 302, 308 and 317 Sqns; ex-No. 131 wing with 2nd TAF/BAFO) was also based at Hethel, and the two flight commanders in No. 303, F/Lts Mach and Budzik, were Bochniak's old friends from No. 308 Squadron.

14

15

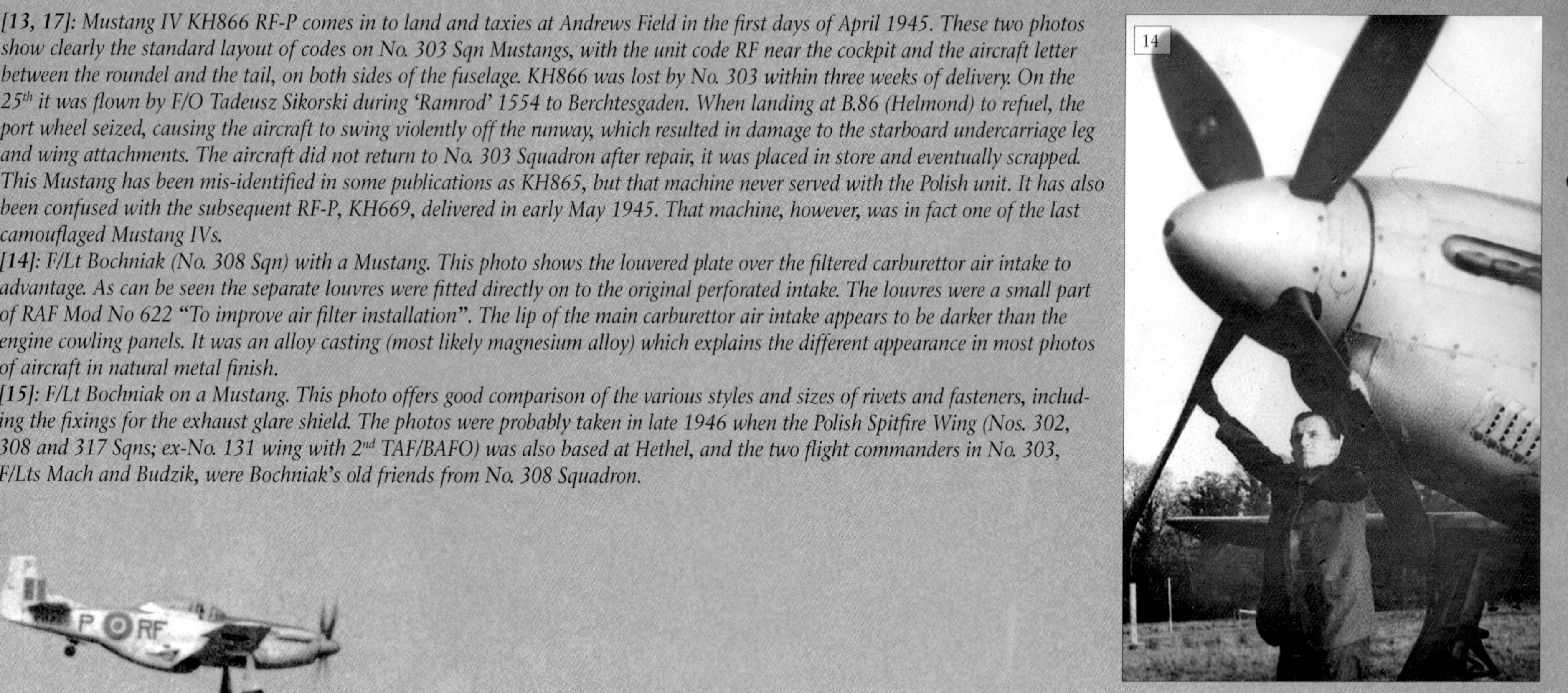

13

[16]: North American Mustang IV, KH866 RF-P, early April 1945, RAF Andrews Field.

[18]: North American Mustang IV, KH866 RF-P, early April 1945, RAF Andrews Field.

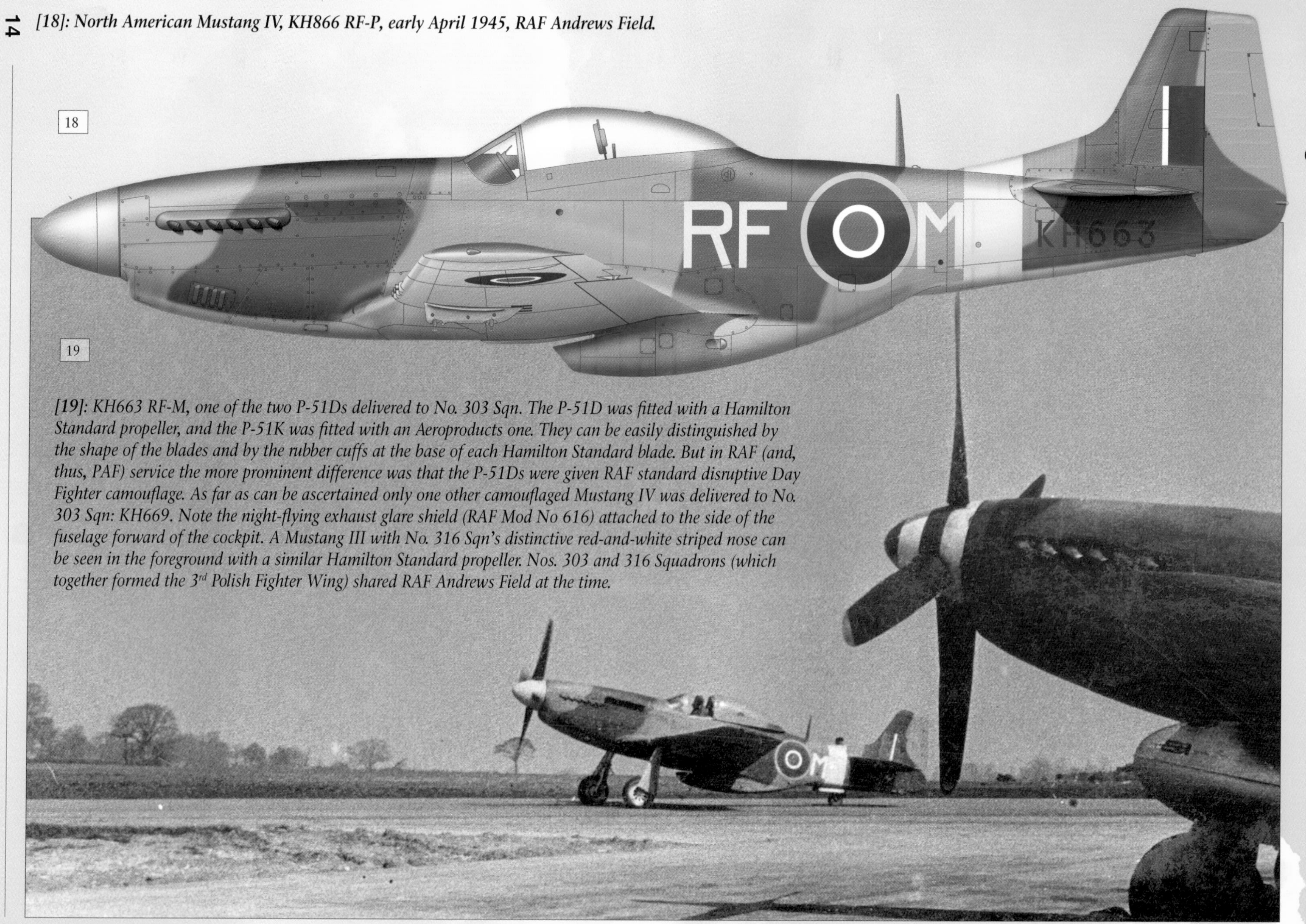

[19]: KH663 RF-M, one of the two P-51Ds delivered to No. 303 Sqn. The P-51D was fitted with a Hamilton Standard propeller, and the P-51K was fitted with an Aeroproducts one. They can be easily distinguished by the shape of the blades and by the rubber cuffs at the base of each Hamilton Standard blade. But in RAF (and, thus, PAF) service the more prominent difference was that the P-51Ds were given RAF standard disruptive Day Fighter camouflage. As far as can be ascertained only one other camouflaged Mustang IV was delivered to No. 303 Sqn: KH669. Note the night-flying exhaust glare shield (RAF Mod No 616) attached to the side of the fuselage forward of the cockpit. A Mustang III with No. 316 Sqn's distinctive red-and-white striped nose can be seen in the foreground with a similar Hamilton Standard propeller. Nos. 303 and 316 Squadrons (which together formed the 3rd Polish Fighter Wing) shared RAF Andrews Field at the time.

[20]: Top and bottom views of KH663 RF-M in the RAF day fighter camouflage: areas of Dark Green and Ocean Grey on upper surfaces, Medium Sea Grey on under surfaces. The propeller spinner and the band around the rear fuselage in Sky were RAF Fighter Command quick recognition markings.

[21–23]: Within days of delivery, still in early April 1945, KH663 RF-M has already had the anti-glare shield removed, but still lacks the Polish AF marking or the squadron badge. The aircraft was damaged on 15 September 1945 upon return from the Battle of Britain anniversary flypast over London. Whilst taxiing after landing, W/O Skrzydło in KH663 PD-M collided with F/Lt Zdanowski's KH836 PD-R, seriously damaging both Mustangs. KH663 returned to service with No. 303 two months later, re-coded PD-L (see p. 26).

[24]: North American Mustang IV, KH769 RF-Y, early April 1945, RAF Andrews Field.

[25–26]: Natural metal Mustang IV KH769 RF-Y taxies past Mustang IIIs of No. 316 Sqn. Note the anti-glare shield fitted on the side of the fuselage ahead of the cockpit and the bomb rack under the wing. The Polish markings on the nose and the squadron badge under the cockpit have yet to be applied. This Mustang had a very short career with No. 303 Sqn, being damaged (cat. AC) on 25 April. Ground mist obscured visibility on the runway and W/O Skrzydło, who was taking off as wingman to S/Ldr Drobiński (in KH836 RF-R), feared collision with his leader while unable to lift-off rapidly enough, so he landed ahead instead, overshooting the runway and crashing through the boundary hedge.

[27]: One of the important advantages of the Mustang over the Spitfire was the American fighter's heated cockpit. The pilots no longer needed extra warm clothes for high altitude flying. Sgt Marian Michalak shows standard RAF issue leather helmet with built-in earphones and the oxygen mask attached. Note that he has marked his headgear with the girl's name 'Danusia'.

[28]: F/O Zenon Krzeptowski is wearing just his service dress cap over which he has a separate set of headphones, to which the oxygen mask is attached. This device does not seem to be any of the standard RAF or USAAF headphone sets.

27

28

26

[29]: North American Mustang IV, KM220 RF-B, early April 1945, RAF Andrews Field.

[30]: Mustang IV KM220 RF-B taxiing at Andrews Field upon delivery to No. 303 Sqn, with the codes applied but no national or squadron insignia. Unlike KH769 photographed at the same spot and time (see previous page), this aircraft features no exhaust glare shield on the fuselage.

[31]: North American Mustang IV, KH855 RF-A, late April 1945, RAF Andrews Field.

[32]: Mustang IV KH855 RF-A parked at the dispersal after delivery, still with the exhaust glare shield in place on the fuselage side forward of the cockpit. Note the red L-shaped NO STEP marking on the inboard flap section. The aircraft still lacks both the Polish national marking and the squadron badge. A trolley accumulator for starting the engine can be seen near the starboard wing tip.

[33]: KH855 RF-A taxiing at Andrews Field soon after delivery, now with the exhaust glare shield removed.

[34–37]: The same Mustang IV KH855 RF-A after F/O Krok's accident on 28 April 1945. The engine cut momentarily during take-off and then picked up again, causing a violent swing to port. The pilot tried to clear a hedge ahead of him, but hit a parked tractor and crashed, seriously damaging the aircraft. Note that by this time KH855 sported both the Kościuszko badge under the cockpit and the Polish Air Force red-and-white square on the nose. At the time of the crash the Mustang carried two 62.5 Imperial gallon (75 US gallon.) jettisonable fuel tanks. The early, circular gun camera port in the wing root leading edge is well visible in the head-on shots.

[36]: Antoni Głowacki posing on the wreck (the post-accident photos of KH855 were taken with his camera). He gained fame during the Battle of Britain, when he was credited with five German aircraft destroyed in one day, the only Polish pilot to achieve that. Although he never flew Mustangs with No. 303 Sqn, he had been a distinguished member of the unit between 1941 and 1943. In 1944 he was one of the first Polish pilots to convert onto the Merlin-engined Mustang fighters during his exchange posting to the 356th Fighter Squadron of the 354th Fighter Group USAAF. At the time of this photo he commanded No. 309 Squadron on Mustang IIIs.

[38]: F/Sgt Tadeusz Rybak posing by the tail of KM186, the replacement RF-A (later PD-A), delivered in early May 1945. Note the triple aerial rods behind his head. This was part of the tail warning radar system known as Monica Mk VII in the RAF and as APS-13 in the USAAF. This equipment was fitted to Mustang IVs from KM140 onwards but at the end of August 1945 the RAF announced Mod No 710 "To remove Monica Mk VII". Clearly it was still there on KM186 when Rybak joined No. 303 Sqn in 1946. The fuselage jacking point can be seen near the bottom of the code letter, with a stencilled note above it reading 'LIFT / CAUTION / 1600 LBS'. The two white markings on the tail wheel were painted on for easier checking of tyre creep (it is unusual to see the markings on the tail wheel, they were much more common on the main wheels). The Pitot static vent can just be made out at the joint of the horizontal and left bars of the A code.

[39]: W/O Jerzy Krzysztofiński (standing) and W/O Zenon Bartkowiak in front of KM186 PD-A. The code letter 'A' can just be made out on the chock. Note the fabric patches (presumably painted with red lead/minium) on the gun ports.

[40]: Left to right: W/O Zenon Bartkowiak, W/O Jerzy Krzysztofiński, F/Sgt Tadeusz Rybak, W/O Antoni Zubiel and W/O Jan Kukuć in front of KM186 PD-A. Note the aircraft letter on the lower cowling.

[41]: The same group on the wing of the Mustang (left to right: Bartkowiak, Krzysztofiński, Kukuć, Rybak and Zubiel). The under-wing bomb rack with screw type sway braces offered a convenient place to sling the chock cord.

[42]: P/O Zygfryd Nowiński in the cockpit of a Mustang. Note the 'NO STEP' stencil below the canopy rail.

[43]: W/O Jakub Bargiełowski photographed with Mustang IV KH868 PD-E. The Polish marking, the aircraft letter on the bottom of the air intake, and the company logos, part numbers and specifications on propeller blades can be seen. The small panel between the code letter 'E' and the intake lip is marked 'REMOVE FOR GROUND HEATER DUCT'.

[44]: W/O Jakub Bargiełowski (left) and F/O Zygfryd Nowiński with Kim, the squadron mascot, on a Mustang believed to be KH868 PD-E. Note the bomb rack with its screw type sway braces, and the inboard wheel cover with the actuator jack rod. The photo also shows the yellow leading edge stripe introduced by the RAF for quick recognition.

[45]: North American Mustang IV, KH868 RF-E, April–July 1945.

[46–47]: Four pilots pose with a Mustang IV believed to be KM113 RF-F (note the F code letter marked on the chocks), with KH868 RF-E in the distance. Standing, left to right: F/O Elgin Scott RAF (a British subject born and raised in Poland, who volunteered to fly with the Poles, as his Polish was much better than his English!), unidentified, F/Lt Mieczysław Maksymowicz, F/Lt Bronisław Białecki (leaning on the blade). Of these four men only Maksymowicz flew Mustangs with No. 303 Sqn. The aircraft is fitted with 90 Imperial gallon (108 US gall.) steel combat tanks. KM113 was lost on 20 August 1945 with its pilot, W/O Alojzy Rutecki, in a collision with KM201 flown by F/Sgt Stanisław Magdziak (who was also killed).

[48]: North American Mustang IV, KM102 RF-G, April–July 1945.

[49]: Mustang IV KM102 RF-G displays the full set of standard markings as applied in No. 303 Sqn between April and July 1945. These included the Polish Air Force chequered square on the nose and the squadron badge below the cockpit. The photograph was taken by LAC Norbert Miszkowicz, an armourer of No. 6303 Servicing Echelon (the unit responsible for ground servicing of No. 303 Sqn aircraft). The aircraft was used by No. 303 Sqn for thirteen months: delivered in early April 1945, it was lost on 8 May 1946 when F/O Haczkiewicz ditched six miles off Wells-on-Sea, Norfolk following an engine failure (the pilot escaped unhurt).

[50]: North American Mustang IV, KH868 PD-E, August 1945–November 1946.

[53]: North American Mustang IV, KH663 PD-L, November 1945–November 1946.

[51–52]: Air-to-air shots of Mustang IV KH868 PD-E flying in formation with KH747 PD-F and KH663 PD-L in late 1945 or early 1946, possibly during one of the squadron moves at the time. Note that KH747 and KH868 carry 75 US gallon fuel tanks under wings, but KH663 does not. The latter is in the Day Fighter camouflage but with a replacement cockpit hood which has an unpainted frame. The Polish national marking can be seen on the nose and the squadron badge under the cockpit. Similar insignia can be made out on the side of KH868 PD-E, but there is no trace of these on KH747 PD-F. Both KH663 and KH868 were delivered to No. 303 Sqn when it re-equipped in April 1945, but KH747 came to the unit in September 1945 as a replacement machine. Note also that the dark anti-glare area on KH747 seems to reach deeper on fuselage sides than on KH868.

[54]: W/O Jakub Bargiełowski in the cockpit of a Mustang IV, possibly KH747 PD-F (note the dark anti-glare paint reaching deeper down the side than on other aircraft). The arrow near the stencilled marking 'PULL' points towards the long rectangular emergency canopy release (most likely painted red) below the windscreen.

[55]: North American Mustang IV, KH747 PD-F, August 1945–March 1946.

[56–57]: Wreckage of KH747 PD-F at Ketteringham Park after the fatal crash of W/O Konrad Sztuka on 29 March 1946. Sztuka had been the usual pilot of this Mustang.

[58]: Another taxiing shot of KM220 (compare p. 18), now with the Polish AF square on the nose and the squadron badge just discernible below the cockpit (above the innermost gun port).
[59]: Padre S/Ldr Wilhelm Stempor (right) with an unidentified civilian on the wing of KM220. Note the three part antenna for the Monica Mk VII tail-warning radar on the fin. The under-wing bomb rack with screw type sway braces was often used to sling the chock cord.

[60]: North American Mustang IV, KM220 PD-B, August 1945–November 1946.

[61–62]: Souvenir shots of KM220 showing details of the undercarriage, the landing light in the port main wheel well, the serial number in two positions on the wing under surfaces and the aircraft's original USAAF serial number (44-12343) on one propeller blade. Posing with the Mustang are No. 300 Sqn members: Sgt Marian Matejski (a pilot, holding the propeller) and W/O Edmund Miterski (a bomb aimer, leaning on the wing). On 28 June 1946 S/Ldr Jan Zumbach flew KM220 to No. 300 Sqn's base at RAF Faldingworth and probably on that occasion some members of the Polish Lancaster squadron were photographed with the Mustang.
[63]: The Aeroproducts company logo included, in large letters, 'AEROPROP' centred on a black propeller shape.

[64]: More photos of KM220 PD-B (with No. 303 Sqn pilots). W/O Jerzy Kmiecik is leaning on the propeller blade with the USAAF serial number. Note the rectangular opening for the camera gun in the port wing root.
[65]: F/Sgt Tadeusz Rybak with the same Mustang. The photo shows details of the undercarriage and the bomb carrier (with the chock cord slung).
[66]: F/Sgt Tadeusz Rybak in the cockpit of (probably) the same Mustang. Note details of the cockpit and canopy, including the long narrow latch of the sliding hood (in the framing). Such form of the latch was typical for KM-serialled Mustang IVs.

[67]: No colour photos of No. 303 Sqn badge on Mustangs are known. This is a black-and-white photo, coloured to show the probable appearance of the much simplified Kościuszko badge standardised on Mustangs.
[68]: F/Sgt Tadeusz Rybak and W/O Leszek Bisanz posing with the Mustang. Note details of the cockpit, including the gunsight, and the Kościuszko badge.
[69]: Another posed portrait of F/Sgt Tadeusz Rybak. The photo shows details of the Kościuszko badge as applied on the Mustangs. Partly obscured by the pilot's head is the spring-loaded cover of the hand hold with 'HAND / HOLD' stencilled on it.
[70]: F/Lt Andrzej Malarowski in the cockpit of the same Mustang. Note details of the windscreen framing structure.

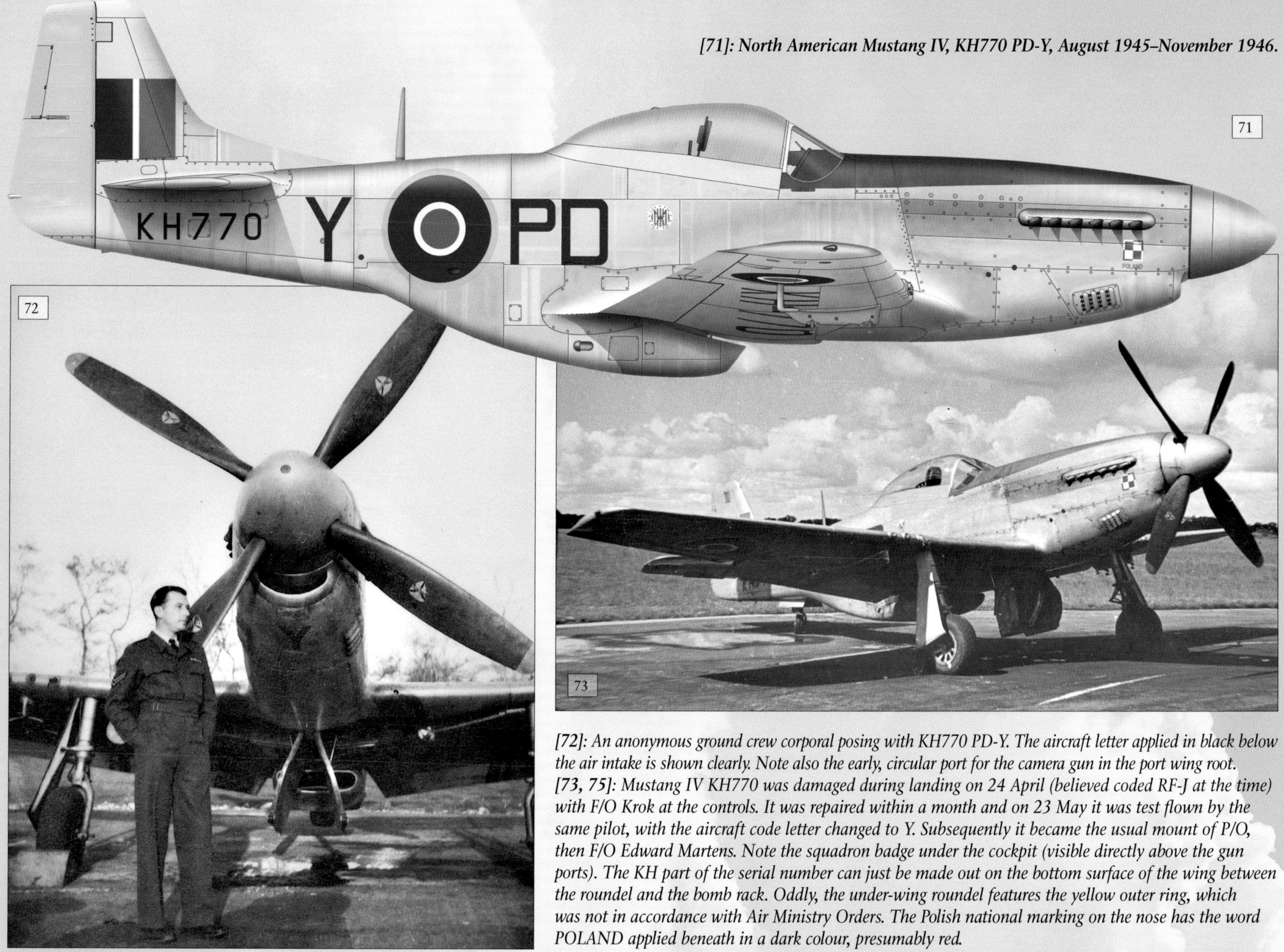

[71]: North American Mustang IV, KH770 PD-Y, August 1945–November 1946.

[72]: An anonymous ground crew corporal posing with KH770 PD-Y. The aircraft letter applied in black below the air intake is shown clearly. Note also the early, circular port for the camera gun in the port wing root.

[73, 75]: Mustang IV KH770 was damaged during landing on 24 April (believed coded RF-J at the time) with F/O Krok at the controls. It was repaired within a month and on 23 May it was test flown by the same pilot, with the aircraft code letter changed to Y. Subsequently it became the usual mount of P/O, then F/O Edward Martens. Note the squadron badge under the cockpit (visible directly above the gun ports). The KH part of the serial number can just be made out on the bottom surface of the wing between the roundel and the bomb rack. Oddly, the under-wing roundel features the yellow outer ring, which was not in accordance with Air Ministry Orders. The Polish national marking on the nose has the word POLAND applied beneath in a dark colour, presumably red.

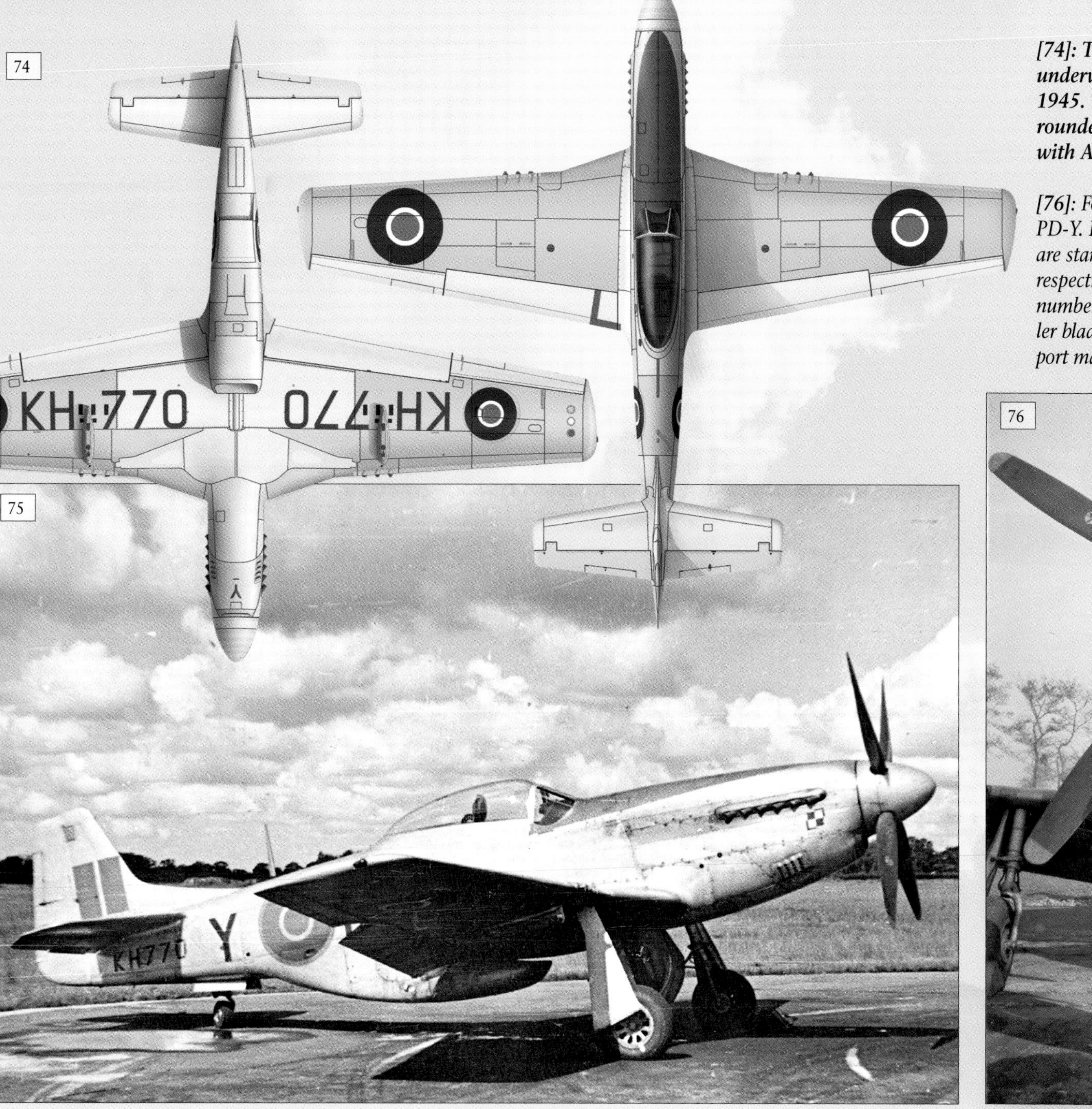

[74]: Top and bottom views of KH770 PD-Y. The underwing serial numbers were introduced in July 1945. The yellow outer ring of the under-wing roundels of this aircraft was not in accordance with Air Ministry Orders.

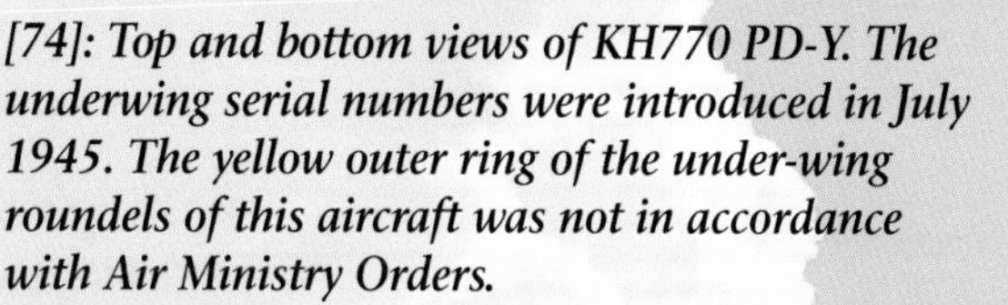

[76]: Four ground crew members posing with KH770 PD-Y. LACs Zbigniew Więckowicz and Józef Palimąka are standing on the ground, first and second left, respectively. The Aeroproducts company logo, part numbers and specifications can be seen on the propeller blades. Note the landing light extended from the port main wheel well.

[77]: Another photograph taken on the same occasion as [76]. LAC Józef Palimąka is seated near the fuselage and Zbigniew Więckowicz is standing on the ground. Interesting details of the main undercarriage can be seen, including the pale marking painted on the hub and tyre of the wheel (pointing towards the chock here) for easier checking of tyre creep. The chock has '6303SE' stencilled on its side, to identify the owners: No 6303 Servicing Echelon. Note also the small removable panel next to the elbow of LAC Więckowicz, with stencilled inscription: 'REMOVE FOR / GROUND HEATER / DUCT'.

[78]: Yet another photograph of the same group of ground crew members posing with KH770 PD-Y. LACs Józef Palimąka and Zbigniew Więckowicz are on the propeller. Note the circular port for the camera gun in the port wing root and the landing light extended from the port main wheel well.

[79]: LAC Józef Palimąka posing with KM115 PD-V in front of a hangar. The later, rectangular camera gun port in the wing root is noteworthy. The small panel between the code letter 'V' and the intake lip is also marked 'REMOVE FOR GROUND HEATER DUCT'.

77

78

79

[80]: North American Mustang IV, KM115 PD-V, August 1945–November 1946.

[81–84]: Souvenir photos of anonymous girls with an airman, using KM115 PD-V as backdrop. Despite the poor quality of these pictures, they show some interesting details, including the dorsal rail for the cockpit canopy and the tailplane fillet. The Aeroproducts logo decal on the propeller blade and the fixings for the exhaust glare shield on the side of forward fuselage are noteworthy.

[85]: A group of pilots on KM112, probably during summer 1946 at RAF Hethel. On the main wheel is W/O Jakub Bargiełowski. Seated on the fuselage are, left to right: W/O Jan Talar, F/Sgt Zbigniew Zabłocki and F/O Ryszard Górecki, and on the wing root is F/Sgt Rudolf Falkowski. The photo shows a number of noteworthy technical details, such as the under-wing bomb rack with its screw type sway braces in place, gun ports in the wing leading edge, main wheels, legs and covers, the landing light in the main wheel well, and the covered Pitot tube under the starboard wing, its long 'remove before flight' tag being blown by the wind. At far right of the photo note the aircraft's serial number applied on the undersurface of the wing. This was mistakenly painted on as a mirror image of the correct rendition! POLAND painted in red under the national insignia is badly worn and barely readable, but the square itself, as well as the squadron badge under the cockpit (behind Bargiełowski) look fresh and clear. Note also the neat yellow leading edge stripe and the pale (clean) area beneath the gun ports (probably where fabric patches have been removed).

[86]: F/Sgt Antoni Zubiel (left) and Sgt Roman Knobelsdorf in front of the same Mustang on another occasion. In addition to the details already listed in the caption above, note S/Ldr Łokuciewski's scoreboard below the windscreen (compare photos on pp. 38 & 39).

[87]: F/O Ryszard Górecki in the cockpit of KM112 PD-D before S/Ldr Łokuciewski's scoreboard was applied. Note the squadron badge shown to advantage. Interesting technical details include the main fuel tank filler under the rear end of the canopy (with stencilled instruction 'FUEL 70 / GALLONS'), to the right the stencilled instruction 'GROUND / HERE' partly visible, the hand hold above the squadron badge (with a badly worn 'HAND / HOLD' stencil), the signal pistol port (on the fuselage side) and the long narrow canopy latch (in the framing; both directly below the pilot). On top of the sliding hood a fairlead can be seen if the use of HF radio required a wire aerial to the tail.
[88]: F/O Ryszard Górecki in the cockpit of KM112 PD-D, showing details of the headrest, the cockpit canopy, its rails, and the fuselage structure underneath it. Note the pilot's initials on his headgear.
[89]: F/O Ryszard Górecki with the same Mustang. The aircraft letter on the bottom cowling is well visible.

[90]: North American Mustang IV, KM112 PD-D, February–November 1946.

93

94

95

[91]: Mustang IV KM112 PD-D was the usual mount of S/Ldr Drobiński, and then S/Ldr Łokuciewski. This photo was taken after the latter took over the aeroplane: note his scoreboard marked under the windscreen in form of eleven black crosses: eight destroyed in the upper row and three probables in the lower row (his score of eight confirmed kills included one in the Battle of France, four in the Battle of Britain and three over the continent in 1941). Other markings included the Polish national insignia on the nose and the squadron badge under the cockpit. Note the worn appearance of the fuselage roundel. The oxygen system stencil below the roundel reads 'OXYGEN / CHARGE TO / 425 lb/sq in ONLY'. The dark spot immediately forward of the aircraft letter D is the fuselage jacking point. The lighter one inside the D is the Pitot static vent. The blue ring of the wing roundel is so faded that it does not seem to differ from the natural metal finish around it. Such extensive fading can be seen on several aircraft featured in this book (and on other RAF types not shown here).

[92]: W/O Zenon Bartkowiak in the cockpit of KM112. Note detail of the victory markings in the upper row: German style crosses with white outlines.

[93]: Three ground crew members posing on KM112 PD-D (Cpl Józef Klachacz in the middle). No. 303 Sqn badge under the cockpit is shown clearly.

[94]: A group of ground crew by the side of KM112 PD-D (LAC Zbigniew Więckowicz at far left).

[95]: The same group of men in and around the cockpit. The scoreboard of S/Ldr Łokuciewski is shown to advantage. The kill marking crosses in the lower row appear somewhat thicker than those above, so probably they were given red outlines instead of white ones (as was done on other Polish fighters).

[96]: Wreckage of Mustang IV KH836 PD-S. It stalled on take off from RAF Turnhouse on 2 January 1946, probably due to propeller pitch control failure, and crashed, killing F/O Jan Schandler. This aircraft, delivered in April 1945, was initially coded RF/PD-R. Following its accident in September, KM237 was given that code, and when KH836 returned to service in October, it was re-coded PD-S. No. 303 Sqn badge is discernible on the side of the fuselage in the usual spot forward of the code letters, and the Polish AF square can just be made out on the mangled side cowling. This view shows the shape of the anti-glare finish on the upper cowling. Note also the fire extinguisher standing on the grass.

96

97

[97]: North American Mustang IV, KH836 PD-S, August 1945–January 1946.

[98]: A souvenir photo taken in the first days of February to mark the changes in command of No. 303 Squadron. Left to right: F/Lt Kazimierz Budzik (new 'A' Flight commander), S/Ldr Witold Łokuciewski (new squadron commander), S/Ldr Bolesław Drobiński (departing squadron commander), F/Lt Stanisław Zdanowski ('B' Flight commander), F/Lt Mirosław Szelestowski (departing 'A' Flight commander). Note the square-shaped gun camera port in the wing root leading edge. The Aeroproducts company logo decals, part numbers and specifications are shown clearly. The stencilling specified: BLADE SERIAL NO. xxxxx; BLADE ASSEM. A-20-156-24M and details of the pitch settings LOW ANGLE 42 IN. RAD. 22.8 and HIGH ANGLE 42 IN. RAD. 57.8.

99

[99]: Pilots and ground officers photographed on the same occasion. Seated, left to right: W/O Władysław Sznapka, F/O Borys Runc, F/O Tadeusz Haczkiewicz, F/Lt Kazimierz Budzik, S/Ldr Bolesław Drobiński, S/Ldr Witold Łokuciewski, F/Lt Stanisław Zdanowski, F/Lt Mieczysław Maksymowicz, W/O Władysław Skrzydło. Standing in the first row, left to right: F/Sgt Roman Knobelsdorf, F/Sgt Włodzimierz Gołowańczuk, F/Sgt Rudolf Falkowski, Sgt Edward Bachmatiuk, F/O Bronisław Zborowski, F/O Edward Martens, F/O Ryszard Górecki, F/Lt Tadeusz Sikorski, F/Lt Julian Jasiński, F/Sgt Tadeusz Rybak, F/Sgt Zbigniew Zabłocki, W/O Leszek Bisanz, W/O Jan Kukuć, F/O Zenon Krzeptowski, LAC Kazimierz Węgrzecki (Sqn HQ clerk who later compiled the book 'Kosynierzy Warszawscy' – 'Warsaw Scythemen', the first history of No. 303 Squadron, published in 1968). Standing in the second row: F/Sgt Antoni Zubiel, W/O Wacław Łubieński, F/Sgt Józef Janicki, W/O Zenon Bartkowiak, unidentified, F/O Julian Krok, F/O Tadeusz Broniecki.

[100]: Nos. 303 Squadron and 6303 Servicing Echelon personnel photographed at the same time. Seated, left to right: unidentified F/Sgt mechanic, F/O Julian Krok, F/O Borys Runc, F/O Tadeusz Broniecki, F/O Bronisław Zborowski, F/O Tadeusz Haczkiewicz, F/Lt Kazimierz Budzik, F/Lt Mirosław Szelestowski, S/Ldr Bolesław Drobiński, S/Ldr Witold Łokuciewski, F/Lt Stanisław Zdanowski, F/Lt Mieczysław Maksymowicz, W/O Władysław Sznapka, F/Lt Tadeusz Sikorski, W/O Jan Kukuć, W/O Wacław Łubieński, F/O Ryszard Górecki, F/Sgt Józef Janicki, W/O Leszek Bisanz, F/Sgt Włodzimierz Gołowańczuk, two unidentified. Standing in the first row, left to right: F/O Zenon Krzeptowski, four unidentified, F/Sgt Rudolf Falkowski, W/O Władysław Skrzydło, Sgt Edward Bachmatiuk, F/Sgt Zbigniew Zabłocki, F/Sgt Roman Knobelsdorf, W/O Zenon Bartkowiak, F/Sgt Antoni Zubiel, three unidentified, F/Sgt Tadeusz Rybak, unidentified, LAC Stefan Stefan Kowalski, unidentified, Sgt Stefan Suwiński, seven unidentified. Standing in the second row, left to right: three unidentified, LAC Jan Więckowicz, twelve unidentified, LAC Józef Palimąka, five unidentified, LAC Norbert Miszkowicz, all others unidentified except F/O Edward Martens far right. On the Mustangs: all unidentified except LAC Kazimierz Węgrzecki far left.

100

[101]: North American Mustang IV, KM191 PD-Z, September 1945–November 1946.

[102]: Mustang IV KM191 was delivered to the squadron in late September 1945 as a replacement for the previous PD-Z, KM201, destroyed in the crash with KM113 PD-F on 20 August. Similar to other aircraft delivered to No. 303 Sqn after July 1945, it lacked the Polish Air Force marking or the squadron badge.

[103]: Senior officers at RAF Hethel, where the 3rd Polish Wing was based (Nos. 303 and 316 Squadrons) photographed with Mustang IV KM191 PD-Z, left to right: W/Cdr Kazimierz Rutkowski (RAF Hethel Wing Leader; in army battle-dress tunic), unidentified, S/Ldr Stanisław Łapka (3rd Polish Wing HQ staff officer at Hethel), S/Ldr Witold Łokuciewski (the latter three all in civilian suits) and an unidentified army officer (wearing Rutkowski's tunic!) in the cockpit. Note the rectangular port for the camera gun in the wing root, the under-wing bomb rack with its screw type sway braces in place (the chock cord slung over), the yellow leading edge stripe with fabric patches (presumably red) on the gun ports, the main wheel legs and covers, the landing light in the main wheel well, and the badly soiled radiator fairing.

[104]: The same men with KM191 PD-Z, left to right: S/Ldr Łapka, unidentified, the army officer in Rutkowski's tunic, W/Cdr Rutkowski in army battle-dress tunic and S/Ldr Łokuciewski. Note the aircraft code letter Z marked on the chocks.

[105]: The same officers photographed with Mustang IV KM263 PD-T. Left to right: S/Ldr Witold Łokuciewski (in civilian suit), unidentified photographer, S/Ldr Stanisław Łapka, W/Cdr Kazimierz Rutkowski and unidentified army officer.
[106]: Another photo taken on the same occasion, but some changes in clothing have taken place. Standing, left to right, unidentified, W/Cdr Rutkowski (now in the army officer's tunic), S/Ldr Łapka, S/Ldr Łokuciewski (in what looks like his own battle dress tunic) and the army officer (wearing Rutkowski's dress tunic). Noteworthy items include the squadron badge in standard position below the canopy, the fuselage fuel tank filler (directly above S/Ldr Łapka), the air intake for the wing tank pressurising system (at the bottom of the fuselage near S/Ldr Łapka's leg) and the fuselage jacking point at the right edge of the photo.

[107]: S/Ldr Wilhelm Stempor, the Squadron Padre, posing in the cockpit of KM263 PD-T. Note the faded 'NO STEP' stencil below the canopy rail. This photo and [108] provide helpful views of the American N-9 gun-sight that was fitted to the P-51D/K during production. In April 1945 the RAF announced Mod No 686 "Introduction of Mk IID GGS" for the Mk IV but there is no evidence of the Gyro Gun Sight being fitted on RAF machines.

[108]: Another photo of the Squadron Padre, S/Ldr Wilhelm Stempor, with Mustang KM263 PD-T. F/Lt Janusz Franckiewicz is standing on the ground, but the F/O in the cockpit has not been identified. Note the position of the 303 Sqn badge in relation to the signal pistol firing port. Although it is sometimes claimed that the Kosciuszko badge was used to cover this opening on some Mustangs, no photo to confirm this has been found.

[109]: A poor copy of an interesting photograph, showing F/Lt Janusz Franckiewicz by the tail of KM263 PD-T. The Mustang was fitted with the Monica VII tail warning radar. The shadow on the fin flash shows the U-shaped middle rod flanked by two straight outer ones.

[110–111]: F/Lt Józef Mierzejewski posing with KM263 PD-T at the end of 1946. Mierzejewski never served with No. 303 Sqn and was probably just visiting friends at Hethel. The Aeroproducts company logo, part numbers and specifications can be seen on the propeller blades. The small panel below the intake lip was marked 'REMOVE / FOR GROUND / HEATER DUCT'. The broken line around the cockpit hood and the stencilled instruction 'BREAK WINDOW FOR / EMERGENCY RESCUE' (on the hood framing below the pilot's seat's headrest) were part of the 'escape markings' officially introduced in July 1945 (RAF Mod Nos 703 and 704), but it seems these were not applied on No. 303 Sqn Mustangs until late 1946. When applied on natural metal finish, as in this case, the stencilling was supposed to be red, but seems to be yellow here. The emergency cockpit hood release latch was also outlined in yellow (visible as a horizontal bar below the windscreen on the edge of the dark anti-glare painted area), and there is another stencilled instruction: 'PUSH / TO RELEASE / HOOD' below the accompanying push button. The yellow leading edge stripe seems quite worn at the very edge of the wing. Note the Spitfire XVI, coded L-WK, visible in the background. This was the personal mount of W/Cdr Wacław Król, who was leading No. 131 (Polish) Wing at the time of its move from occupied Germany to RAF Hethel in late 1946.

[112]: North American Mustang IV, KM263 PD-T, August 1945–October 1946.

[113]: Mustang IV KM263 PD-T, or what was left of it, awaits final scrapping. Clearly, a lot of components have been cannibalised and some are lying on the ground (including a flap, a wing trailing edge fillet and the radiator).

115

[114]: S/Ldr Witold Łokuciewski reports to G/Cpt Jerzy Bajan (head of the Polish fighter force) and W/Cdr Julian Kowalski (Polish station commander at RAF Hethel). This photo was previously captioned in publications as taken on 27 November, during the formal No. 303 Squadron farewell ceremony. However, it was in fact taken during the Squadron Day ceremony on 31 August 1946. The Mustangs in the background are, in all probability, KM191 PD-Z (visible between the officers) and KM263 PD-T (on the right).
[115]: Raising the Polish Air Force flag.
[116]: The flag is at half-mast as the Roll of Honour is about to be read.
[117]: S/Ldr Witold Łokuciewski (far right) and F/Lt Julian Jasiński (Squadron Adjutant) in the foreground, with G/Cpt Jerzy Bajan and W/Cdr Julian Kowalski during the ceremony on 31 August. F/Lt Jasiński is reading out the Roll of Honour. Note the wreath on the table behind the officers. The Mustang behind the mast is KM226 PD-G.

[118]: S/Ldr Witold Łokuciewski hands the wreath to F/O Ryszard Górecki, seated in the cockpit of KM263 PD-T, his usual aircraft. That evening Górecki in KM263 PD-T led a section of three Mustangs to drop a wreath in the English Channel, thus commemorating all pilots of the squadron lost 'in the drink' during the war. Mustang IV KM226 PD-G, delivered in May 1946, can be seen in the background. Its squadron code was positioned much further forward than on other aircraft. Note that neither aircraft display the 'escape markings'. The later style long narrow latch in the hood framing and the long narrow emergency cockpit latch below the windscreen can be seen on Górecki's aircraft.

[120]: Moments later the three Mustangs start taxiing to take off: Górecki's KM263 PD-T in the middle, with KM191 PD-Z (flown by F/Sgt Zubiel) as his starboard wingman (at far left in the shot) and KM226 PD-G (W/O Kukuć) as the port wingman. Note that only KM263 of the trio displayed the Polish AF marking on the nose.

[119 North American Mustang IV, KM226 PD-G, May–November 1946, RAF Hethel.

[121]: The PD squadron code on KM226 was applied further forward than on any other Mustang of the squadron. On most other Mustangs of No. 303 the P in the squadron code would be positioned where D was on KM226 on this side. The 'escape markings': a broken line around the cockpit hood and a stencilled instruction 'BREAK WINDOW FOR / EMERGENCY RESCUE', both in yellow, can be seen.

[122]: Mustang IVs KH754 PD-J and KM226 PD-G were the last two aircraft of the type delivered to No. 303 Sqn (in August and May 1946, respectively), and both displayed certain differences in the markings as compared to other Mustangs of the unit. The cockpit hood framing on KM226 was finished in a dark colour. This Mustang was previously used by No. 65 Sqn and the canopy frame was most likely dark blue, as inherited from that unit. Note the Pitot tube with a cover and 'remove before flight' tag under the starboard wing of KM226.

[124]: Mustang IVs KH735 PD-W, KH754 PD-J and KM226 PD-G. The PD squadron code on KH754 was positioned further forward than on most other Mustangs of No. 303, but not as far forward as on KM226. Notably, KH754 was delivered to the unit in mid-August 1946, as the last aircraft of the type.

[123]: North American Mustang IV, KM226 PD-G, May–November 1946, RAF Hethel.

[125]: North American Mustang IV, KH754 PD-J, August–November 1946, RAF Hethel.

[126]: North American Mustang IV, KH735 PD-W, August 1945–November 1946.

[127]: Mustang IV KH735 PD-W, flown by its usual pilot F/O Borys Runc, photographed from a target-towing aircraft during gunnery training at Charter Hall in March 1946. This Mustang had its code letter W outlined in yellow, a souvenir from its previous service with No. 442 Sqn RCAF, where the entire codes were outlined this way. It is possible that the yellow intake 'lip' was also retained. The dorsal identification light can just be made out on the top of the fuselage between the radio mast and the fin fillet. This fuselage light assembly was only fitted to early aircraft (up to KH750). Note the absence of the Polish national marking on the nose or the squadron badge under the cockpit. KH735 was delivered to No. 303 Squadron in August 1945 as the first Mustang after the British withdrawal of recognition of the exiled Polish Government July 1945, and was never adorned with either the PAF insignia or the squadron badge.

[128]: F/Lt Stanisław Bochniak of No. 308 Sqn in a souvenir photo with KH735 PD-W at Hethel in late 1946. This photo shows the outline on the 'W' code. Note the fuselage jacking point between the code letter and the roundel.

[129]: No. 303 Squadron pilots during gunnery training at No. 3 Armament Practice Station, RAF Charter Hall, on 8 March 1946. Seated, left to right: F/O Borys Runc, F/O Tadeusz Haczkiewicz, F/Lt Tadeusz Sikorski, F/Lt Andrzej Malarowski, S/Ldr Witold Łokuciewski, F/Lt Stanisław Zdanowski, F/Lt Mieczysław Maksymowicz, F/O Zenon Krzeptowski, W/O Józef Janicki, W/O Jan Kukuć, F/O Zygfryd Nowiński; standing, left to right: W/O Władysław Skrzydło, F/Sgt Zbigniew Zabłocki, W/O Jakub Bargiełowski, W/O Antoni Benski, F/O Włodzimierz Polaniak, W/O Leszek Bisanz, F/Sgt Roman Knobelsdorf, W/O Zenon Bartkowiak, F/O Ryszard Górecki, F/Sgt Antoni Zubiel, W/O Jerzy Krzysztofiński, F/Sgt Tadeusz Rybak, W/O Konrad Sztuka, Sgt Edward Bachmatiuk, F/Sgt Rudolf Falkowski, F/O Edward Martens, F/Lt Julian Krok, F/Sgt Włodzimierz Gołowańczuk, W/O Jan Talar; on the propeller: W/O Jerzy Kmiecik. Note the worn-out appearance of the AERO-PROP logo decals on propeller blades.

[130]: North American Mustang IV, KM237 PD-R, September 1945–November 1946.

[131]: Mustang IV KM237 PD-R was the usual mount of 'B' Flight commanders: first F/Lt Zdanowski, and then F/Lt Mach. Delivered to the unit in September 1945, it was another machine without the Polish AF insignia or squadron badge. The PD code letters were applied in a standard position.

[132]: Close-up of the nose of a Mustang IV. Note the different appearance of individual panels left in natural metal finish and the anti-glare panel on upper cowling.

[133]: 'B' Flight commander F/Lt Stanisław Zdanowski in front of his usual mount, KM237. Note the landing light extended from the main wheel well.

[134–135]: F/Lts Edward Jaworski (left) and Czesław Śnieć (at the time 'A' Flight Commanders in Nos. 308 and 302 Sqns, respectively) with KM237. These photos were probably taken in late 1946, after the Polish Spitfire Wing (ex-BAFO No. 131 Wing) arrived at Hethel. The Mustang has no Polish AF marking, nor does it carry the aircraft letter under the nose. This is yet another example of the chock cord being slung over the wing pylon sway braces. Note the uncovered Pitot tube under the starboard wing.

[136]: W/O Zenon Bartkowiak and his father Jan Bartkowiak, a WO1 with the Krechowiecki Lancers Regiment of the 2nd Polish Corps. The signal pistol port under the cockpit of this Mustang was surrounded by a particularly shaped stained patch, which helps identify it in photos. Note the rectangular opening for the camera gun in the port wing root.

[137]: An unidentified airman in the cockpit of the same Mustang. Note the other peculiarly shaped stain, on the cockpit hood framing, forward of the canopy latch.

136

137

138

139

140

[139]: P/O Edward Martens in the cockpit of the Mustang. Note the later style long narrow canopy latch in retracted position.

[138, 140]: F/Sgt Antoni Zubiel [138] and Sgt Roman Knobelsdorf [140] in the cockpit of KM237, with the canopy latch in extended position.

[141]: F/Lt Mieczysław Maksymowicz in a camouflaged Mustang IV (KH663 or KH669) with an unpainted early type cockpit hood. Note the square-shaped canopy latch (with a barely legible stencilled instruction 'PUSH / HOLD'), standard on aircraft with the serials in KH range.
[142]: W/O Konrad Sztuka in a natural metal finish Mustang IV with the same type cockpit hood.
[143]: W/O Antoni Benski photographed in what looks like the same Mustang IV, with the early type canopy. Note the signal pistol port directly below the pilot, the squadron badge and the hand hold.
[144]: W/O Józef Janicki in the cockpit of a Mustang IV. The long narrow emergency cockpit latch and the canopy unlocking button can be seen below the windscreen.

[145]: Fuel tank selector in the cockpit (a photo from a wartime pilot's manual for the Mustang IV). In a number of photos in this book chalked inscriptions 'TYLNY' ('REAR'), 'LEWY' ('PORT' or 'L.H.') and 'BOCZNY LEWY' ('PORT SIDE' or 'L.H.SIDE') can be seen on the black instrument panel cowl. Although no relevant instruction was found, these were probably to remind the pilot before flight about the correct fuel tank setting. According to the pilot's manual, the rear fuselage tank was the standard take-off option. If no fuel was carried in that tank, then the port wing tank ('MAIN TANK L.H.') had to be selected for take-off. The starboard ('R.H.') or drop ('COMBAT') tanks were never used when taking off.

146

[146]: S/Ldr Witold Łokuciewski takes the 'Kościuszko' badge off F/Lt Mach's KM237 PD-R to symbolically mark the disbandment of the squadron. The caption inscribed on the original print of this widely publicised photo reads: 'Taking the badge off a 303 SQ aeroplane / HETHEL 27 XI 46'. In fact KM237 never really carried the badge, and a plaque was used for the ceremony. It was probably this image, which caused the incorrect assumption that the 303 Squadron badge applied on Mustangs covered the signal pistol aperture below the canopy. The photo shows a number of interesting technical details and their stencilled descriptions: the fuselage fuel tank filler below the rear end of the canopy ('IMPORTANT / 35US GAL ONLY / IN THIS TANK' and 'SUITABLE FOR AROMATIC FUEL'); the grounding inlet just aft of the filler ('GROUND HERE'); the hand hold forward of the filler ('HAND / HOLD'); the flare discharger port (below and to the right of the badge held by S/Ldr Łokuciewski); the wing fuel tank filler (to the left of S/Ldr Łokuciewski's feet, no stencil there); the red, L-shaped 'NO STEP' mark on the inboard flap section; the black and white deflection angle indicator on the flap leading edge (the black segments were marked '10', '30' and '50', while the white ones were marked '20' and '40' degrees); the reinforced part of the wing fillet trailing edge section ('STEP HERE'); the oxygen bottle filler cover flap at the bottom of the roundel ('OXYGEN / FILLER'); the stencil 'COOLANT / DRAIN' can be seen at the bottom of the photo (between '303' and 'SQ' in the inscription). The small inlet (between '46' and '303') is an 'air accumulator': a ram air intake for pressurising the self-sealing wing tanks as the fuel is consumed. The canopy is somewhat mysterious as it features the square-shaped canopy latch (directly to the right of the badge held by S/Ldr Łokuciewski), usually associated with KH-serialled Mustang IVs, rather than the later one seen in previous pictures. This was probably a replacement cannibalised item as it shows the remains of some paint at the rear end, which might suggest that it was originally fitted on a camouflaged aircraft. Notably, according to the squadron Operations Record Book, neither of the camouflaged Mustangs (KH663 and KH669) flew after 13 November, while KM237 did not fly between 13 and 22 November, so there was enough time for such transfer if KM237's original canopy had to be replaced for some reason. The fairlead on top of the sliding hood (for possible fitting of an HF wire aerial to the tail), the upper portion of the pilot's seat and the framing on which it was mounted, as well as the N-9 gun sight can be seen. The 'escape markings' include a broken line around the cockpit hood, a stencilled instruction 'BREAK WINDOW FOR / EMERGENCY RESCUE' above it and another one, 'RELEASE HOOD / OTHER SIDE', directly below the badge held by S/Ldr Łokuciewski. When applied on natural metal finish these markings were supposed to be red, but it seems likely that they were, in fact, yellow (compare the dark appearance of the outer ring in the roundel).

147

[147]: S/Ldr Łokuciewski shows the badge, 'removed' from the Mustang: a symbolic farewell to the aircraft as No. 303 Squadron is disbanded at the end of 1946. 'Tolo' Łokuciewski had been a member of No. 303 Squadron when it formed in mid-1940 and fought with it during the Battle of Britain. It is worth noting that the chock cord is not slung over the pylon in this case.

148

[148]: F/Lt Eugeniusz Szaposznikow, another Battle of Britain veteran and ace of No. 303 Squadron, photographed in the cockpit of a Mustang IV with the late canopy latch. As far as can be ascertained he never flew the type. The photograph was probably taken when he attended the Squadron Day festivities on 31 August – 1 September or during the disbandment ceremony on 27 November 1946.

[149]: Mustang IVs KM186 PD-A (left) and KM237 PD-R formed the backdrop to this group photo of squadron personnel and their guests on 27 November 1946, during the formal No. 303 Squadron farewell ceremony at RAF Hethel. The last and first squadron commanders (Łokuciewski and Krasnodębski) hold the 'Kościuszko' badge that had just been 'taken off' KM237. Among those standing on the ground, left to right: sixteen unidentified, W/O Zenon Bartkowiak (first left in peaked cap), unidentified, F/O Tadeusz Broniecki (Engineering Officer), W/O Jan Kukuć, W/O Leszek Bisanz, W/O Jakub Bargiełowski, F/O Włodzimierz Polaniak, W/O Antoni Zubiel, F/Sgt Edward Bachmatiuk, F/Lt Zenon Krzeptowski, unidentified, Sgt Stefan Suwiński, W/Cdr Kazimierz Rutkowski (3rd Polish Wing Leader), F/O Edward Martens, S/Ldr Witold Łokuciewski, F/O Ryszard Górecki, W/O Władysław Sznapka, G/Cpt Zdzisław Krasnodębski, F/Lt Julian Krok, W/Cdr Robert Standford Tuck (RAF Hethel Station Commander), W/O Rudolf Falkowski, W/Cdr Julian Kowalski (Polish station commander at Hethel), W/O Władysław Skrzydło, W/O Marian Michalak, unidentified, F/Sgt Roman Knobelsdorf, S/Ldr Paweł Niemiec (commanding No. 316 Sqn), unidentified, F/Lt Andrzej Malarowski, F/Lt Longin Majewski, F/Lt Bronisław Mach, F/Lt Eugeniusz Szaposznikow, F/O Zygfryd Nowiński (behind him), F/Lt Tadeusz Sikorski, F/Lt Julian Jasiński, F/Lt Dr Zygmunt Wodecki, F/Lt Stefan Kleczkowski. In the cockpit of Mustang KM237 is F/Lt Stanisław Zdanowski and standing on the starboard wing of the same Mustang, second from left (in front of the tree) LAC Józef Palimąka. LAC Stefan Kowalski is standing in the middle of the group on the other Mustang's wing (in an overcoat).

North American Mustangs used by No. 303 Squadron
Individual aircraft data

RAF no.	USAAF no.	RAF variant*	USAAF variant	Code	Period when used in No. 303 Sqn**	Notes
AG416	—	Mk I	—		unknown	According to RAF records on charge of No. 303 Sqn from 12.04.45, but not recorded in squadron documents.
AG458	—	Mk I	—		08.04.45–17.05.45	
AL985	—	Mk I	—		07.05.45	
AM123	—	Mk I	—		02.05.45	
AM126	—	Mk I	—	5	09.04.45–15.05.45	
AM235	—	Mk I	—		08.04.45–16.04.45	
KH663	44-11255	Mk IV	P-51D-5NT	M L	09.04.45–15.09.45 07.11.45–08.11.46	15.09.45 taxiing collision with KH836, damaged (cat. AC), W/O Władysław Skrzydło OK
KH669	44-11261	Mk IV	P-51D-5NT	P	06.05.45–13.11.46	
KH735	44-11502	Mk IV	P-51K-1NT	W	10.08.45–04.11.46	
KH744	44-11511	Mk IV	P-51K-1NT	M	25.09.45–25.01.46	25.01.46 taxiing collision with KH868, destroyed, F/Lt Tadeusz Sikorski OK
KH747	44-11514	Mk IV	P-51K-1NT	F	15.09.45–29.03.46	29.03.46 take-off accident, crashed at Ketteringham Hill, Norfolk, destroyed, W/O Konrad Sztuka killed
KH754	44-11582	Mk IV	P-51K-5NT	J	14.08.46–29.11.46	
KH769	44-11597	Mk IV	P-51K-5NT	Y	09.04.45–25.04.45	25.04.45 take-off accident, damaged (cat. AC), W/O Władysław Skrzydło OK
KH770	44-11598	Mk IV	P-51K-5NT	J? Y	22.04.45–24.04.45 23.05.45–22.11.46	24.04.45 landing accident, damaged (cat. AC), F/O Julian Krok OK
KH825	44-11733	Mk IV	P-51K-5NT	C	09.04.45–13.11.45 03.04.46–26.11.46	13.11.45 landing collision with KM220, damaged (cat. A), F/L Mirosław Szelestowski OK
KH836	44-11824	Mk IV	P-51K-5NT	R S	08.04.45–15.09.45 09.10.45–02.01.46	15.09.45 taxiing collision with KH663, damaged (cat. AC), F/Lt Stanisław Zdanowski OK 02.01.46 take-off accident, crashed at Turnhouse, destroyed, F/Lt Jan Schandler killed
KH855	44-11843	Mk IV	P-51K-5NT	A	08.04.45–28.04.45	28.04.45 take-off accident, destroyed, F/O Julian Krok OK
KH866	44-11854	Mk IV	P-51K-5NT	P	10.04.45–25.04.45	25.04.45 landing accident, damaged (cat. B), F/O Tadeusz Sikorski OK
KH868	44-11856	Mk IV	P-51K-5NT	E	12.04.45–25.01.46 09.02.46–22.11.46	25.01.46 taxiing collision with KH744, damaged (cat. A), F/O Bronisław Zborowski OK
KM102	44-11955	Mk IV	P-51K-10NT	G	12.04.45–08.05.46	08.05.46 engine failed, ditched 6 miles off Wells-on-Sea, Norfolk, destroyed, P/O Tadeusz Haczkiewicz OK
KM112	44-11965	Mk IV	P-51K-10NT	D	12.04.45–29.11.46	
KM113	44-11966	Mk IV	P-51K-10NT	F	12.04.45–20.08.45	20.08.45 mid-air collision with KM201, crashed at Bromsgrove, Worcs, destroyed, W/O Alojzy Rutecki killed
KM115	44-11968	Mk IV	P-51K-10NT	V	25.04.45–08.08.45 18.10.45–29.11.46	08.08.45 taxiing collision with HB866 (306 Sqn Mustang III), damaged (cat. AC), W/O Władysław Skrzydło OK
KM186	44-12309	Mk IV	P-51K-10NT	A	04.05.45–29.11.46	
KM191	44-12314	Mk IV	P-51K-10NT	Z	24.09.45–22.11.46	
KM201	44-12324	Mk IV	P-51K-10NT	Z	20.04.45–20.08.45	20.08.45 mid-air collision with KM113, crashed at Bromsgrove, Worcs, destroyed, F/Sgt Stanisław Magdziak killed
KM209	44-12332	Mk IV	P-51K-10NT	S	10.04.45–28.09.45	28.09.45 landing accident, damaged (cat. B), F/O Jan Schandler OK
KM220	44-12343	Mk IV	P-51K-10NT	B	08.04.45–13.11.45 09.12.45–29.11.46	13.11.45 landing collision with KH825, damaged (cat. A), F/L Andrzej Malarowski OK
KM226	44-12349	Mk IV	P-51K-10NT	G	23.05.46–29.11.46	
KM237	44-12360	Mk IV	P-51K-10NT	R	27.09.45–29.11.46	
KM238	44-12361	Mk IV	P-51K-10NT	U	18.04.45–11.01.46	11.01.46 landing accident, destroyed, W/O Wacław Łubieński OK
KM239	44-12362	Mk IV	P-51K-10NT	I	18.04.45–22.11.46	
KM242	44-12365	Mk IV	P-51K-10NT	J	04.05.45–09.11.45	According to RAF records, on charge of No. 303 Sqn until April 1946, five months after its last recorded sortie.
KM263	44-12386	Mk IV	P-51K-10NT	T	13.04.45–30.10.46	
KM297	44-12420	Mk IV	P-51K-10NT	K	27.09.45–12.03.46 07.05.46–29.11.46	12.03.46 taxiing accident, damaged (cat.. A), F/Lt Julian Krok OK

* P-51K is sometimes labelled 'Mk IVA' in British publications, but this was not an official designation. Both the P-51D and P-51K were known as the Mk IV by the RAF.

** According to the earliest and latest entries in the Operations Record Book of No. 303 Squadron.

Code letter allocations

1945	Sqn code	A	B	C	D	E	F	G	I	J	K
April	RF	KH855	KM220	KH825	KM112	KH868	KM113	KM102	KM239	KH770?	
May	RF	KM186	KM220	KH825	KM112	KH868	KM113	KM102	KM239	KM242	
June	RF	KM186	KM220	KH825	KM112	KH868	KM113	KM102	KM239	KM242	
July	RF	KM186	KM220	KH825	KM112	KH868	KM113	KM102	KM239	KM242	
Aug.	PD	KM186	KM220	KH825	KM112	KH868	KM113	KM102	KM239	KM242	
Sept.	PD	KM186	KM220	KH825	KM112	KH868	KH747	KM102	KM239	KM242	KM297
Oct.	PD	KM186	KM220	KH825	KM112	KH868	KH747	KM102	KM239	KM242	KM297
Nov.	PD	KM186	KM220	KH825	KM112	KH868	KH747	KM102	KM239	KM242	KM297
Dec.	PD	KM186	KM220	KH825	KM112	KH868	KH747	KM102	KM239		KM297
1946		A	B	C	D	E	F	G	I	J	K
Jan.	PD	KM186	KM220	KH825	KM112	KH868	KH747	KM102	KM239		KM297
Feb.	PD	KM186	KM220	KH825	KM112	KH868	KH747	KM102	KM239		KM297
Mar.	PD	KM186	KM220	KH825	KM112	KH868	KH747	KM102	KM239		KM297
April	PD	KM186	KM220	KH825	KM112	KH868		KM102	KM239		KM297
May	PD	KM186	KM220	KH825	KM112	KH868		KM102 KM226	KM239		KM297
June	PD	KM186	KM220	KH825	KM112	KH868		KM226	KM239		KM297
July	PD	KM186	KM220	KH825	KM112	KH868		KM226	KM239		KM297
Aug.	PD	KM186	KM220	KH825	KM112	KH868		KM226	KM239	KH754	KM297
Sept.	PD	KM186	KM220	KH825	KM112	KH868		KM226	KM239	KH754	KM297
Oct.	PD	KM186	KM220	KH825	KM112	KH868		KM226	KM239	KH754	KM297
Nov.	PD	KM186	KM220	KH825	KM112	KH868		KM226	KM239	KH754	KM297

1945	L	M	P	R	S	T	U	V	W	Y	Z
April		KH663	KH866	KH836	KM209	KM263	KM238	KM115		KH769	KM201
May		KH663	KH669	KH836	KM209	KM263	KM238	KM115		KH770	KM201
June		KH663	KH669	KH836	KM209	KM263	KM238	KM115		KH770	KM201
July		KH663	KH669	KH836	KM209	KM263	KM238	KM115		KH770	KM201
Aug.		KH663	KH669	KH836	KM209	KM263	KM238	KM115	KH735	KH770	KM201
Sept.		KH663 KH744	KH669	KH836 KM237	KM209	KM263	KM238	KM115	KH735	KH770	KM191
Oct.		KH744	KH669	KM237	KH836	KM263	KM238	KM115	KH735	KH770	KM191
Nov.	KH663	KH744	KH669	KM237	KH836	KM263	KM238	KM115	KH735	KH770	KM191
Dec.	KH663	KH744	KH669	KM237	KH836	KM263	KM238	KM115	KH735	KH770	KM191
1946	L	M	P	R	S	T	U	V	W	Y	Z
Jan.	KH663	KH744	KH669	KM237	KH836	KM263	KM238	KM115	KH735	KH770	KM191
Feb.	KH663		KH669	KM237		KM263		KM115	KH735	KH770	KM191
Mar.	KH663		KH669	KM237		KM263		KM115	KH735	KH770	KM191
April	KH663		KH669	KM237		KM263		KM115	KH735	KH770	KM191
May	KH663		KH669	KM237		KM263		KM115	KH735	KH770	KM191
June	KH663		KH669	KM237		KM263		KM115	KH735	KH770	KM191
July	KH663		KH669	KM237		KM263		KM115	KH735	KH770	KM191
Aug.	KH663		KH669	KM237		KM263		KM115	KH735	KH770	KM191
Sept.	KH663		KH669	KM237		KM263		KM115	KH735	KH770	KM191
Oct.	KH663		KH669	KM237		KM263		KM115	KH735	KH770	KM191
Nov.	KH663		KH669	KM237				KM115	KH735	KH770	KM191

Note: H, N, O, Q and X were not used as codes on Mustangs of No. 303 Squadron.